The Great Divide

Why Liberals and Conservatives Will Never, Ever Agree

Also by William D. Gairdner

The Critical Wager (1982)
The Trouble with Canada (1990)
The War Against the Family (1992)
Constitutional Crack-Up (1994)
On Higher Ground (1996)
After Liberalism [ed.] (1998)
Canada's Founding Debates [ed.] (1999)
The Trouble with Democracy (2001)
The Book of Absolutes (2008)
Oh, Oh, Canada! (2008)
The Trouble with Canada ... Still! (2010)

The Great Divide

*Why Liberals and Conservatives
Will Never, Ever Agree*

William D. Gairdner

ENCOUNTER BOOKS
New York • London

First American edition published in 2015 by Encounter Books,
an activity of Encounter for Culture and Education, Inc.,
a nonprofit, tax-exempt corporation.
Encounter Books website address: www.encounterbooks.com

Manufactured in the United States and printed on
acid-free paper. The paper used in this publication meets
the minimum requirements of ANSI/NISO Z39.48-1992
(R 1997) (Permanence of Paper).
Interior page design and composition: BooksByBruce.com

FIRST AMERICAN EDITION

LIBRARY OF CONGRESS CATALOGING-IN-PUBLICATION DATA

Gairdner, William D. (William Douglas), 1940–
The great divide : why liberals and conservatives
will never, ever agree / by William D. Gairdner.
pages cm
Includes bibliographical references and index.
ISBN 978-1-59403-764-1 (hardcover : alk. paper) — ISBN 978-1-59403-765-8 (ebook)
1. Liberalism. 2. Conservatism. 3. Right and left (Political science) I. Title.
JC574.G34 2015
320.51 — dc23

2014039152

For my children, and grandchildren

TABLE OF CONTENTS

LIST OF TABLES

ACKNOWLEDGMENTS

Every author owes a debt to teachers, colleagues, friends, and family, to those living and those long gone. Books on a personal library shelf become like old friends, and I still find amazing and wonderful the fact that all we have to do is open them to hear voices, as if the authors were in the room. There are many important thinkers of the past and present, voices too numerous to mention, who have helped with the ideas in this book, and I thank them all for their guidance. Among family and close friends I especially thank my wife, Jean, for her incisive and helpful comments and encouragement, my children and in-laws for their forbearance, and my friends and colleagues Ian Gentles and Salim Mansur for their helpful insights. For their contributions to a list of freedoms lost under the democratic rule of the present, and general comment on economic matters, I thank Bill Robson of the C.D. Howe Institute, Peter Holle and his staff at the Frontier Centre for Public Policy, Mark Milke of the Fraser Institute, Brian Lee Crowley of the Macdonald-Laurier Institute, and Filip Palda of the École nationale d'administration publique. Lastly, I thank Roger Kimball of Encounter Books for his unhesitating confidence in my initial proposal for this book; the staff at Encounter—Sam Schneider, Lauren Miklos, and Heather Ohle—for guiding the book through to publication; and my careful editor for so many helpful corrections and comments.

INTRODUCTION

This book is written for people who are tired of living in a society in which they can't seem to defend their deeply held opinions on serious moral and political issues without stirring up a lot of scorn and outrage—people who would rather skip the emotion, dig a little deeper, and understand better the underlying differences between the liberal and conservative worldviews that seem increasingly to be separating citizens from each other.

Whether we witness it on a radio or television show, or personally at a dinner or cocktail party, the experience of the divide is always the same. Enemies are assembled on two different sides of an issue; they talk past each other as they deliver incompatible views; then they shout and overtalk each other a lot, and end up more divided than when they started. Everyone is left with a dispiriting sense that no consensus is possible or desired, because there is no longer any common moral or political language to share—just a Great Divide. Needless to say, this divide is reflected at the political level in the variously colored political maps of most nations, and in the obvious and deepening rural-urban divide that is easily sensed in most of them.

The contention of this book is that no matter what the topic, debates always take place on at least two levels—at the surface, and in the depths. There is what people believe is the cause of a problem; and somewhere else, way down below, beyond the facts as they appear, we can usually locate the real, hidden cause. Which reminds me of a lesson I learned from my horse. Before taking him for a ride he lets me lift his feet to clean them, one after the other. One day he just wouldn't give me his right foot, no matter how much I leaned into him to shift his stubborn one thousand pounds leftward. So I called the vet. "Something is wrong with his right foot. He won't let me lift it." What the vet said opened my eyes to how we so often look for answers in the wrong places, based mostly on first appearances; how we so often mistake the smoke for the fire. "There's nothing wrong with his right foot," he said. "It's the left one that's sore. He won't give you the right one because he doesn't want to put his weight on the left one." That little scenario taught me a lot: I was thinking about the foot, instead of thinking about the horse.

This book is about depths, not surfaces. The terms *liberal* and *conservative* as used here are not political party labels. Rather, they describe the two sides of a deep liberal-versus-conservative philosophical and ideological divide that is pre-political, that has been widening below the political and moral surface of ordinary life for a very long time, and that I submit is the cause of so much confusion and emotion at the surface.

The book is divided into four parts. The first provides a very brief overview of the historical mutations of liberal democracy as I see them, followed by a description of conservatism. At this early stage the reader is presented with the first of more than a dozen tables that appear throughout the book, each asking "Where do you stand?" The tables all contrast the underlying liberal-versus-conservative view of the topic under discussion, and my guess is that readers who test their personal opinions against these tables will gain a deeper insight into why they think as they do now, will assess their views in a fresh light, and will either solidify or alter them.

So this is a good place to make a personal confession. Although I was once a rather left-leaning university student, and then a professor, life experiences and a lot of subsequent thinking and reading filled my sails and took me to the conservative side of the divide. Despite this personal journey and the preferences to which it has led me, however, I have worked hard in this book to minimize, if not eliminate, my personal feelings and views, in order to articulate the stark contrasts between modern liberal and conservative viewpoints. That is not easy. It is a little like the experience of trying to play chess against yourself, knowing all along that there has to be a winner, so you do have to pick a side. Nevertheless, my hope is that after every section in this book, readers who may have been less than sure of which side should win in the internal chess battle of their own ideas will be able to say, "Now I know better where I stand, and why."

Part 2 offers a brief description of the forces that I believe are at work in all modern democracies dissolving the social and moral bonds of civil society. President John F. Kennedy's memorable admonition during his inaugural address of January 1961, "Ask not what your country can do for you, ask what you can do for your country," leaps to mind here. For once a democracy mutates, or inverts, from its original foundation in self-reliance, self-discipline, and liberty under law to an egalitarian foundation with an emphasis on rights, self-gratification, and self-expression, the die is cast. Which is to say, trouble begins once a general attitude emerges that individuals who once believed they should serve their most revered institutions and support the objects of their own civil society start to believe that those institutions and their society should be serving *them*. This is equivalent on the economic level to the stage many democracies have already reached whereby they transition from a nation of makers to a nation of takers. But the main theme of this part of the book is that democracies that mutate in this way end up creating a pincerlike pressure that dissolves their own civil societies. Egalitarian pressure from the state at the top and an individualist rights pressure from the bottom combine gradually to atomize and dissolve the social-bonding power of civil society.

Part 3 offers discussions of eight core topics on which modern liberals and conservatives are starkly divided at the deepest level. They differ over their foundational conceptions of human nature, of the role of reason in human life, of the proper role and purpose of democracy, and of the meaning of freedom. They also differ sharply on the concepts of equality and inequality; on the meaning of morality and the significance of the self; and on the role of human will in shaping human biology, and society at large. Finally, there are irreconcilable root differences in the general liberal and conservative discussions about God, the role of religion, and what these mean for our understanding of just about everything.

In part 4, discussion moves to what are arguably the three hottest social and moral issues on the democratic table—homosexuality, abortion, and euthanasia. These are watershed issues that sharply divide because they cannot be meaningfully debated without calling up the opposing liberal and conservative conceptions of freedom, human nature, democracy, equality, and so on that were laid bare in part 3.

I contend that any ideology can be shown to have a certain structure, or architecture, rather like a building. There is usually a single foundational or cornerstone argument, often defended as an article of faith, on which other, more complex arguments rest. If you can bring down or defend the cornerstone argument, the ones resting on it will fall or rise accordingly. What this book seeks to reveal is the informal structure of arguments built up on each side, so that in the end, readers will have a firmer grasp of how their own arguments—and those of their opponents—have been built, and why.

At this stage the debate gets a lot more interesting, so let us begin.

PART I

CHAPTER 1

The Background

Not so long ago it was common at a dinner party with family and friends to find ourselves drawn into discussion and debate over the political and moral topics of the day. There was usually a lot of strong feeling, praise for good arguments, some good-natured ridicule for bad ones, and of course, heated support of one's own ideas. But I cannot remember any violent personal attacks, tears, or outrage over someone else's point of view, however wacky it may have seemed, and that was because no one interpreted disagreement as offensive. Most striking of all, most people then were unafraid to state their own views, even happy to volunteer them. There wasn't the slightest hint of "political correctness" in the air. We assumed that was a moral disease of the Red Chinese, a million of whom I can remember seeing displayed on a centerfold of *Life* magazine in Tiananmen Square, all in black Communist uniforms, all waving Chairman Mao's Little Red Book fanatically in the air. The mere notion of human-rights tribunals such as we have now in most Western nations, set up by governments to "reeducate" and to control or punish thought and speech in a free country, was simply unthinkable. We were quite aware that many postwar immigrants fled from the disease of totalitarianism to the "free" world to escape that very thing. But the disease followed them.

A similar dinner party today is a very different story, almost certain to illustrate the Great Divide that is the topic of this book. The elephant in the room, as the saying goes, will almost certainly be an unspoken awareness that there are a lot of political, social, and moral issues that most are *afraid to mention*. The silence—who has not felt it?—tells everyone to keep their *true* thoughts to themselves. Share only unimportant, or even insincere, thoughts. This may be typical in the company of complete strangers, about whom we may care nothing. But to find it true among family, friends, and in our own close communities is very new and very sad, for it tells us that civil society, if not quite at an end, is comatose, that we are becoming strangers to each other. This book is one man's effort to change this situation, to help people become unafraid once again.

I hasten to add that it is not a book about politics or political parties—fickle things at the best of times. For I believe that the political history of the West (which we assume is being decided by all the party, policy, and election language with which we get bombarded) is in fact an outcome of a much deeper and less obvious ideological warfare. Volcanoes and earthquakes are a surface sign of invisible geological forces, just as shifts in the political, social, and moral worlds are surface signs of invisible ideological forces.

The Clash within Western Civilization

In his best-selling book *The Clash of Civilizations* Samuel Huntington warned us about the clashes to come *between* the West and other, incompatible civilizations. The attacks by puritanical Islamists on our deeply secularized, overly sexualized, highly materialistic culture on 9/11 and since have borne out his predictions.

This book is more concerned about a much less obvious but more pervasive war of moral and political ideals *within* Western civilization itself, because from Pittsburgh to Paris, Buenos Aires to Buffalo, Vancouver to Venice, we have been engaged in a civil war of values and principles for a very long time. At bottom it is a war between two incompatible political cultures, or *enemy ideologies*, concerning the best way to live; and I suspect that with a little effort this conflict may be found simmering beneath the surface of all civilizations, waxing or waning as historical circumstances allow.

For reasons professional historians are better equipped to explain than I, however, these two visions—today they are called liberalism and conservatism—emerged with extreme revolutionary violence in eighteenth-century Europe, and have been either simmering in peacetime or boiling over in various wars and revolutions ever since. During the 1960s, due to a growing postwar loss of confidence in the once unifying bonds of Western civilization, the tension between these warring ideologies surfaced again as a moral, political, and theological divide that has continued to separate us from each other over what used to be our dearest shared conceptions of truth. This divide is now everywhere felt (the fear on both sides to speak honestly is a sure sign of it), if not everywhere clearly understood; and it has more to do with disagreement about means than ends.

Common Ends but Different Means

The main hope of this book is that by bringing the underlying differences lurking in the silence of the Great Divide to the surface, readers will be more prepared to engage over the real differences in their philosophies of life, rather than choosing to go silent and then slipping back into the divide. Surely it is better to hear two people debating and exploring the deeper differences in their conceptions of democracy, say, or of human nature, or the role of the family in society, and how and why these necessarily give rise to a different politics, than to watch them working up personal attacks on each other or angrily shutting down the entire discussion. A rather curious fact is that both sides of the Great Divide seem often to have the same *ends* in mind, but argue frustratingly over very different notions of the best *means*. It is as if they are using different languages neither understands to explain something important to them both. Here are just a couple of examples.

Modern liberals and conservatives both agree that children need moral influence. But they cannot agree on whether it is better that the main influences be parents, family, and religion (the conservative view), or the secular state and its schools, agencies, counselors, and sex-ed programs (the liberal view). On this question I once heard a serious liberal politician argue with passion that the children of the nation do not belong to their parents or families; they belong to the nation, and they are a resource, just like our oil, or coal. Hillary Clinton mouthed this same sentiment when she said "There's no such thing as other people's children." For many liberals (so this line of thinking goes) it is the state and its professional educators and psychologists (as "change agents") who ought to lead the way in child and social development, and not parents, who are amateurs and should be licensed before being allowed to reproduce. There has been a long and continuing struggle in the West between such opposing assumptions.[1]

Or again, both sides will agree we all want less crime. But because modern liberals and conservatives have irreconcilable conceptions of human nature (as we shall see), the liberal will advocate spending more money to fix up bad public housing, while the conservative will say this is to miss the point: the real cause of crime is not the *house*, it's the *home*. It is the badly weakened moral fabric of the community and of the people living in the house that make it not a good home. Between the standard liberal and conservative conceptions of those two words—house and home—lies a yawning divide.

Many such underlying liberal/conservative disparities and divisions will be examined as I attempt to show that no matter what surface arguments someone defends, we can usually tease out their underlying philosophy of life and show how it always obliges the taking of specific moral and political positions at the surface, to prevent the underlying belief system from crumbling. Most defenders of their own arguments sense this threat intuitively, signaled by some thought such as "What did I just say? My whole case is going to collapse!"

In the example given, the liberal who insists on more public funding to repair public housing is *forced* by his own logic to adopt this "solution" because a *commitment* has already been made to the belief that, as all human beings are fundamentally good and equal by nature, whatever is wrong or bad in individuals or their communities *must* have an external cause. So it follows, as the night the day, that he will be obliged to call for better laws and more government funding (external cures for what are perceived as externally caused problems). These means-ends differences do not come about just because there is a shift in perspective, or for any other lightweight reason. They have a deep ideological root that

---

1 For a full examination of this struggle, see my book *The War Against the Family*.

is worming away beneath surface perceptions. Nothing "shifts" without underlying reasons. Let us dig a little and find them.

How and When the Great Divide Began

By the middle of the eighteenth century, in reaction to what was then perceived as the "darkness" caused by human ignorance, irrationalism, superstition, and religious warfare, there arose a rationalist movement—later called the Enlightenment—that quickly spread throughout the Western world, arguing that all customs, laws, traditions, and faith-based ways of life ought to be rejected unless they meet the test of reason, and of science. The argument was that, just as the mathematics and physics of men of science such as Galileo and Newton had been used successfully to understand and organize the material world, they also could be used to organize the political, social, and moral world. The means for human happiness can be discovered by reason; good and evil can be quantified and expressed in formulas. This was the heart of the utilitarian dream.

It was an enlightenment story, or narrative, that appeared spontaneously everywhere in Europe. But it was crafted most aggressively by French thinkers such as Voltaire, Condorcet, and Rousseau, who yearned to create something never before seen: a perfect, and perfectly rational—and therefore a perfectly happy—society. Some of them did not mind the idea of a remote caretaker God snoozing in the background of the universe. But most of them were atheists who rejected established religion, with its rigid control of spiritual life and its promise of a perfect kingdom of heaven in the afterlife, in favor of building a perfect kingdom of heaven right here on earth. In this sense, their entire project—and the modern liberal project that flows from it still—was a secular pursuit of religious bliss on earth. Thinkers such as Condorcet even speculated that the perfection of the human race through rational progress would mean that one day human life would have "no assignable limit," and that changes in the human constitution would postpone, if not eliminate, death altogether.

However, since experience could be no guide for such a venture (because no perfect society had ever existed), they relied on a collection of abstract political and philosophical concepts that had been debated in European history for a very long time. Most of them can be found today as aspects of what in this book I call *modern liberalism*, which I will show is a mutation of the classical liberalism many of us used to know and love.

Anyone who takes the trouble to become familiar with the Enlightenment program will be able to sniff it out in most of today's newscasts and editorials. From the very beginning it formed what we would today call a social-engineering program, and it resulted in such a radical revolt against the religious, moral, and political controls of the day that French society became completely unhinged. In short order, the first Western revolutionary project aiming to create a perfect world ended instead in the perfect bloodbath of the French Terror of 1793 and 1794, which took off the heads of all opponents, including those of many of the original revolutionists themselves.

This perverse and cruel outcome horrified a lot of serious thinkers in France and elsewhere who happened to love their tried-and-true way of life, customs, sacred rituals, laws, history, and traditions so very deeply that they felt compelled to take up intellectual arms to defend them. Their reaction resulted in an opposing intellectual tradition still with us today, which came to be called the Counter-Enlightenment. The most influential of these thinkers were Vico, Herder, Hume, Burke, and Maistre, men who saw the former program not as light, but as a terrible darkness; warned Europe well in advance that it would become the slaughtering nightmare that resulted; and set to work creating much of the political philosophy of life we now call *conservatism*. I do not add the word *modern* because, although it may adapt in very minor ways according to changing circumstances, true conservatism is ageless, which is part of its appeal (at least for philosophical, as distinct from party, conservatives).

I present here the first *Where Do You Stand?* table of many to come in this book, because it was in this original battleground of ideas, extending throughout Europe and the Americas, that most of the seeds of the modern liberal and conservative debate were planted. The oppositions outlined here still constitute the underlying moral and political flashpoints of Western civilization that have always—must always—result in tension and friction, and therefore in a Great Divide.

For those who fled Europe for the New World from the mid-eighteenth century onward, these moral and political tensions were

WHERE DO YOU STAND?		
On the Two Incompatible Narratives of Western Civilization		
	ENLIGHTENMENT *(Roots of Modern Liberalism)*	vs. COUNTER-ENLIGHTENMENT *(Roots of Conservatism)*
Reason	*Reason can perfect society*	*What reason can create, reason can destroy*
Rights	*Rights are natural, individual, and inherent in all human beings*	*Rights are a concrete achievement of a civilization*
Moral Foundation	*Personal choice has priority*	*The common good has priority*
Human Nature	Man is naturally benevolent and good	Man is weak, fallible, and self-interested
	Because man is good, society can be made good by man	Man is by nature neither good nor evil, but the historical record shows that when humans start forcibly engineering human societies according to their abstract plan for perfection, the results are always evil
Politics	Main goal is to perfect society	Main goal is to conserve and protect the good
	Rousseau: A legislator must be capable "of changing human nature." Education, legislation, and changes to the human environment are the tools	Schemes to perfect society destroy what is already good. Humans should not be objects of manipulation by progressives
Democracy	*Is universally good*	*Is a tool, not a good in itself*
Equality	*Inequalities and hierarchies must be ended by force of law. Inherited privilege must be ended*	*Hierarchies and inequalities are natural in a lawful and free society*
Freedom	*Individual freedom is the priority. Personal choice is paramount*	*Social freedom is the priority. The common good is paramount*
Property	*Property is the basis of inequality*	*Property is the basis of a free society*
Economics	*Wealth inequalities must be leveled*	*Leveling destroys wealth for everyone*
The State	*Is a product of human will*	*Is a product of history and venerable custom*
Society	*Is an aggregate of autonomous individuals*	*Is an organic communitarian body*

WHERE DO YOU STAND?		
On the Two Incompatible Narratives of Western Civilization		
	ENLIGHTENMENT *(Roots of Modern Liberalism)*	vs. COUNTER-ENLIGHTENMENT *(Roots of Conservatism)*
Sex, Marriage & Divorce	*These are private, individual matters*	*These matters are of paramount public concern*
Preferred Method of Organization	*Top-down unitary organization*	*Bottom-up natural evolution*
The Law	*Preference for uniform code law based on natural rights*	*Preference for an evolved common law based on natural law*
Religion	*Preference for deism or outright atheism*	*Religion is the basis of all morals*
International Vision	*One-world universalism*	*A pluralistic community of communities*
Main Thinkers	*Voltaire, Rousseau, Condorcet, Diderot, Paine*	*Vico, Herder, Maistre, Hume, Burke*

common fare, and played a large part in public debate. However, for reasons to be examined later, the United States and Canada ended up with profoundly conservative constitutions because their people on the whole were religious and conservative. Above all, the constitutions of these nations were each in their own way structured to check both the growth of oppressive government from the center and the potential for what Thomas Jefferson called "elective despotism."

Our Once Common Ground

I mentioned that the most recent sharp manifestation of the Great Divide became gaping in the mid-1960s. That was because it was a kind of "crossover" time—the point at which the dwindling influence of *community* was supplanted by the rising insistence of *modern individualism* in most of the Western democracies. Many observers suspect this was because the meaning of individualism itself had altered, from *frontier* individualism, emphasizing self-reliance and self-discipline, to *modern* individualism, emphasizing self-gratification and self-expression (the "me" generation). That is a difference worth reflecting upon.

But even in the 1960s a peek into the lives of most North Americans would have revealed the same picture—one that was about to change: lots of strident and passionate divisions over political policies, personalities, and large moral questions, but for the most part these differences were experienced by citizens who thought of themselves as committed members of *a single community*. First debate, then try to resolve differences, then count heads instead of breaking them, was the idea. It was a way of life made possible because people were still living under the influence of what we may call the *moral surplus* of the past—a once common ground of stoutly religious, moral, political, and economic convictions it had cost a great many lives to defend. I put those terms in that order because I believe morality sits on top of religion, political philosophy sits on top of morality, and economic life flows accordingly. Since World War II, however, at what seems an accelerating pace most of those beliefs have been severely tested, if not tirelessly challenged, bitterly ridiculed, or altogether turned upside down, and not by any external enemy, but by an internal one—ourselves. Here is just a glimpse of that once common ground which, as anyone can see, was a very conservative one.

The Things No One Doubted

For more than two centuries prior to crossover time, no one doubted that the very best place for any child was a secure home with a married and loving mother and father (rather than a full-time daycare center or a common-law or single-parent home—all then considered distinctly second best). No one doubted that flourishing civil societies should expect their governments to serve the common good of all, and certainly not to serve mainly the rights of individuals, as if those were prior in importance to the common good. No one doubted that the foundations of prosperity are hard work, the right to own private property, and free enterprise, and that long-term dependence on public welfare is always a shame and a scandal. No one doubted that any government that can give you everything you want must first take everything you have. No one doubted that every generation ought to pay its own way and strive to leave a surplus as inheritance for the next; and in particular, that to impose today's debts (a form of deferred taxation) on future generations of citizens unable to defend themselves against your appetites is profoundly reprehensible. Few doubted that, as finite beings living in an infinite universe that could not have created itself, there must be a providential Creator, however articulated in the various creeds; and that personal promises, public morality, and vows are simply impossible to sustain in the absence of some such overarching witness to truth. As for other matters, such as a common understanding of human nature, the central role of the family in human life, the dangers of democracy when it becomes a license for mob rule, the role of personal responsibility for oneself and one's family, the importance of upholding a rule of law rather than the rule of men, the mutually exclusive aims of human liberty and politically forced equality—on all such matters there was once a great deal of agreement, and ironically, it was this very confidence of being firmly grounded in a community of common values that produced some pretty ferociously independent minds.

E Pluribus Duum

In all democracies we still count heads to arrive at an aggregate total of disparate opinions. But in many of them there is no longer full confidence that a unified national community exists that shares common bonds and beliefs, a community in which almost everyone would wish to include themselves as "the people." Rather, what we sense increasingly is a more or less permanent tension between *two warring peoples* in the bosom of every Western nation, each vying through special-interest groups for political, legal, and moral control of policy and law—and hence for the character of the nation. A modern liberal graduate student in Germany will have almost the same set of responses to political or moral questions as a liberal grad student from New York or Copenhagen, and there will be a set of opposing responses just as predictable from their conservative-minded counterparts in each country. The homogenization of each set of opposing views, along with the bitterness, expressions of outrage, vilifications of character, refusals to engage on the unforgiving battlefield of clear ideas, and the forbidding of thought via official political correctness enforced by the laws and courts of most of these nations, has been a recent and unexpected scenario that I for one never expected to see in the free world.

A Different View of Freedom and Equality

The democracies of the Western world share mostly the same religious, legal, and cultural foundations—they are distinctly Western, and not Eastern cultures—and much of what is discussed in this book applies to them all to a greater or lesser degree. But I want to focus briefly on the United States and Canada, because they are special cases that shared a motive of origin for so many: to escape the oppressions, corruptions, and imperfections of Old Europe by crossing the Atlantic to create a better life and a better world. A brief look at what the founders of these nations were thinking will serve to show how far we have traveled since.

The first thing that comes as a bit of a surprise is that those first settlers of the New World wanted nothing to do with our modern and largely libertarian notion of freedom ("do what you want as long as you don't harm someone else"), nor with *making* everyone's condition in life more or less "equal" by tax-funded force of government. At bottom they would have considered our notion of maximum individual freedom radically deficient, because it is not grounded in the twin concepts of self-reliance and self-discipline mentioned here, and although it insists on not harming other people (which is a pretty basic thing), *it does not speak of any common good.* This they would have found an unforgivable omission.

As for making people equal by force? They would have spat on the idea. To them it was a matter of faith that all human souls, no matter how different by individual character, talent, or physical makeup, are valued equally by God. But God also gave us practical and moral freedom to choose between good and bad practical options and personal behaviors, and so each life would be a sum of free choices within constraints common to all. In this context they were real freedom lovers who believed that as long as the laws were equal for all, everyone could and should live freely, and within the bounds of moral decency be as different—or as *unequal*—as they wished, or as befell them. *The object was to make the laws, not the people, equal.* They were aware that as night follows day, forced equality means more government, *and absolute equality means absolute government.* How could it be otherwise? Accordingly, what they feared most of all was not government (they wanted a small, but strong, government)—but *arbitrary* government.

That's why there was a famous Tea Party in Boston in 1773, when American colonists, angry over an arbitrary British tax on imported tea, dumped ninety thousand pounds of it into Boston Harbor—and that's why today, due to overregulation, pervasive creeping taxation, and suffocating national debt, there are new versions of the Tea Party in our midst. There were a number of similar revolts when Canada got going.[2]

Just listen to their voices!

Here is the exasperated cry of the American Josiah Quincy, who in 1774 lamented oppressive government and arbitrary taxation in the most plaintive voice: "I speak it with grief; I speak it with anguish.... I speak it with shame; I speak it with indignation—we are slaves!" To which his compatriot, John Adams, added: "The most abject sort of slaves!" Chattel slaves had at least some hope of escape or of buying their freedom. *But from tax slavery there is no escape*—other than the painful business of leaving one's homeland forever.

And here are the words of Canada's Thomas D'Arcy McGee from 1865, fairly bursting with a proud liberty-passion: "There is not on the face of this earth a freer people than the inhabitants of these colonies." Then, in 1896, Canada's Prime Minister Sir Wilfrid Laurier proclaimed to the whole world: "Canada is free and *freedom is its nationality*." [Here and throughout this book, emphases in quoted material are mine, unless noted.] At the time—this was true until about 1912—*total* taxation (that is, local, plus state/provincial, plus federal taxation) in both the United States and Canada was around 12 percent, and only *one-third* of that total was federal.

But alas, no country in the Western world can today say "freedom is our nationality," because Tax Freedom Day (the day we have finally finished paying for all levels of government and begin working for ourselves), which was about the end of January in 1912, is now at or around the first of June in most Western democracies,[3] and in most of them a good estimate would be that *two-thirds* or more of each year's

---

2 The Papineau revolt in Quebec (then Lower Canada) and the Mackenzie rebellion in Ontario (then Upper Canada) of 1837–38 were both protesting unaccountable government.

3 Here is *total* taxation in percentages and the date of Tax Freedom Day for selected democracies. Dates can move by a few days annually according to tax increases, cuts, and yields, but hold fairly constant; the overall trend is in one direction only. The US did not reach March 31 until 1960. Figures for 2009–2010 are: US, 26.9%, April 12; Canada, 42.6%, June 6; Germany, 51.7%, July 8; France, 53.6%, July 16; UK, 40.9%, May 30; Norway, 56.7%, July 29; Israel, 47.4%, June 22. For figures for most nations see http://en.wikipedia.org/wiki/Tax_Freedom_Day.

tax harvest is paid not to local but to higher state/provincial and federal levels of government. The shift, in less than a century, has been from an emphasis on local taxation for local control to centralized taxation enabling remote control by others. And anyone would agree that if your entire income is confiscated by government, you would be a slave. What are you, then, when half your income or more is taken? I leave the answer to readers, who may at the least agree that citizens who put their heads down and work almost half of every year to pay the costs of their own government cannot pretend to value genuine freedom and self-reliance. If the figures on Tax Freedom Day tell us anything, it is this: the citizens of the Western democracies have been participating in a gradual mutation of their own political system that has all the appearances of turning them—and appallingly, their children and grandchildren—into *indentured servants of their own governments.*

The Collusion of Political Parties

Some will object that this long march into the arms of the nanny state is the people's fault, because they voted statist parties into power. But that is only a half-truth. When all parties in a nation are primarily arguing over how much *more*—never *less*—we should all be feasting from the public trough, they are in tacit collusion, at which point a citizen who yearns to escape this condition has no meaningful option. Modern democracy as a system of government is not exactly finished yet. But it is very sick, lying just outside the operating room door, a metastasizing political deformity in need of corrective surgery or euthanasia.

That is not a radical or irresponsible statement. It is just to state an obvious historical truth: all modern democratic systems that began in the fervent hope they would serve as a means for the people to control the growth of oppressive government *have been producing more of it.* Most shameful of all? The fact that *we have embraced and are practicing ourselves* a great number of the totalitarian social, economic, and moral policies that our soldiers died fighting to prevent in the two world wars of the last century. Were they here today, I don't think those who died would forgive us.

In short, although we still use the flattering term *liberal democracy* to describe our political systems, we are no longer liberal in the original sense of that word—of valuing freedom from oppressive government, and using democracy as a means to ensure that freedom. And many, such as this author, have come to believe the "democracy" part of this phrase is increasingly responsible for the decline of the West, on which more will be said as we proceed.[4]

Meanwhile, let us look back at where we started and ask how we got to where we are now. There seem to have been at least four stages in the long mutation of what began as liberal democracy.

---

4 The growth in the number of ostensibly democratic nations has been rather astonishing: By 1970 there were 40; by 1990, 75; by 1995, 115; and by 2005, 120 (of some 193 nations recognized by the United Nations). Presidents George W. Bush and Barack Obama have engaged in euphoric speechmaking about "freedom" and "democracy" and propose it as the ultimate foreign policy solution, even for nations that find democracy's foundational principles heretical. So it seems somewhat heretical and unpatriotic to suggest that democracy as practiced in the modern West may in fact be in terminal decline. From ancient times to the present, however, there has been no shortage of books critical of democratic theory and practice (including this one). Here are a few others that point a finger at modern democracy as part of the problem, rather than the solution, to contemporary ills. Craig Smith and Tom Miers argue in *Democracy and the Fall of the West* that "the concept of a 'liberal democracy' is a contradiction in terms" because it "unleashes political forces that increase the power of the state at the expense of liberty." A recent entry is F. H. Buckley's *The Once and Future King: The Rise of Crown Government in America*. Buckley compares presidential systems of government to parliamentary ones (mostly Britain's and Canada's). He offers a convincing argument that the latter type is better, but shows how both types have emerged as "Crown" governments—which is to say, as forms of kingship, or arbitrary and excessive "rule by a single person." Of interest also is James Allan's *Democracy in Decline: Steps in the Wrong Direction*, a study of five of the oldest democracies in the world: the United States, Canada, New Zealand, Australia, and the United Kingdom. The author, a committed majoritarian democrat, complains that in all these nations the practice of democracy as originally established within the constitutional framework of each has been deeply eroded by judges; by supranational organizations, laws, and treaties; and by a witches' brew of elite organizations from the realms of media, academia, NGOs, and entrenched bureaucracies.

CHAPTER 2

On Liberalism

Stage 1—Virtue Liberalism and Social Freedom

The root of the word *liberal* is the Latin noun *liber*, meaning free, unrestrained, independent. Now it so happened that most of the first settlers in North America in the early seventeenth century belonged to small, morally bonded Protestant religious communities that had been suffering persecution in Europe from which they wanted desperately to be free. So at considerable personal risk and sacrifice they migrated to the New World, with the intent of creating a better world of religious tolerance and freedom of conscience.

They were not seeking personal freedom just for themselves in the sense of having only personally chosen commitments or obligations. They would have considered such a motive selfish, unnatural, perhaps a sin, and one that contradicts the very meaning of moral and social obligation. They would have said that we need freedom not to do what we *want*, but to do what we *ought*. In other words, we need freedom to be good. Although they were definitely against oppressive big government, and so were what we would today call radical antistatists, what they really longed for was social freedom. That is a term later used by Edmund Burke, the grandfather of modern conservatism, and was for him almost an alternate name for justice, which he considered the only reliable barrier against "the dangerous dominion of will." Which is to say that what these people really wanted was *freedom to bind themselves* to their own chosen social, moral, political, and religious communities and obligations. In a nutshell, they were minimalists with respect to government, but maximalists with respect to their strong affection for the traditional family, local community, and religion; and their desire to perform their normal and natural duties was at least as strong as any desire for individual freedom (which as we saw had mostly to do with self-reliance and self-discipline). So by today's standards, they were a very conservative sort of liberal. However, this distinctive communitarian notion of freedom has been weakening for almost three centuries. We hardly ever hear anyone today insisting, in no uncertain terms, that we need to be free so that we can be good.

Stage 2—Individual and Property Liberalism

By the early eighteenth century, all over Europe (but especially in the New World) the *virtue* motive was slowly being displaced by the *individual freedom and property rights* motive, a shift that was fueled mostly by the growing influence of what we today call the classical liberal political philosophy of John Locke. Its main features were: individualism and liberty under law; the belief that individuals calculate rationally for their own advantage; the notion that civil society is an aggregate of free individuals, rather than an organic corporate entity; a system of law that enables the legal doings of this aggregate; the right to own property (including your own body); the right to free-market exchange and freedom of law-abiding expression; the idea that the people create their society and their government by contract for protection of their "natural rights," and accordingly agree to surrender some of their freedom to the authority of the sovereign for that purpose; and that the people have a right to give direct or indirect (implicit) consent to all laws under which they live or are not bound by them, and have a right of revolt in the event government breaks the contract by continued and serious abuses. The link between this Stage 2 liberalism and the Enlightenment/Counter-Enlightenment table viewed earlier is obvious.

This Lockean menu, which exalted private reason and will above normative law, was the basis of the American Declaration of Independence of July 4, 1776, which was a revolution in favor of radical liberty. Just so, the thirteen colonies were soon operating as a loose alliance of sovereign states. Indeed, many citizens in this period conceived of themselves as living in a state of nature, enjoying what they considered to be true Christian freedom. But their legislatures were soon filled by men of little experience, freedom was abused, and independence pushed too far. Seven of the states began minting their own money; some passed tariff laws against neighboring states; nine states had their own navies, which often seized the ships of other states; some states threatened war on others; in some, enraged citizens were dissolving their own legislatures and demanding the abolition of their debts; in others, the legislatures had taken all legislative, executive, and judicial powers unto themselves. Thomas Jefferson famously complained that "an elective despotism was not the government we fought for," and Alexander Hamilton wrote that the thirteen states had become "wretched nurseries of unceasing discord." Something had to be done to prevent chaos within, and war between them.

The American Constitution of 1787 was the result. It was, in effect, a revolution in favor of government (though the antifederalists of the time called it a "counterrevolution"). Among many other novelties, it checked and balanced the democratic will of the people in the existing and future states, and in this sense alone was a conservative document, with the emphasis in the phrase "United States" on *United* rather than on *States*. This was the framework for Stage 2 liberalism—a new kind of constitutionally ordered liberty—that became an example to the world, and stood America in good stead for more than a century, primarily because there was still a strong religious and moral foundation on which all were standing that prevented the individual liberty they enjoyed from descending into license, and that blocked federal government from invading the powers of the states. But there were other social and moral forces that were eroding the liberty motive.

Stage 3—Equality Liberalism

How did those original *liberty-loving* but deeply social and religious regimes mutate into the *equality-loving*, radically individualist, secular, modern liberal regimes we have now? It took only about a century and a half, but it began for a simple reason: liberty for all was not producing the perfect society of which those first liberals had been dreaming. That century and a half saw many things: the rise of science; a continent-wide rural-urban migration; a growing materialism; a corresponding steep decline in religious ideals; unprecedented levels of wealth; and along with this the emergence of systemic poverty and what looked like a permanent underclass of people who had fallen or were born into poverty, or who had simply lost their will to seize opportunities and rise by their own efforts. This engendered a new focus on equality.

At this point, sincere freedom-and-property liberals were becoming disillusioned. They saw that under a regime rooted in freedom for all, some of the people were indeed very hardworking and became rich. But some were lazy and became poor, and some were poor through no fault of their own; some were bright, some stupid, some honest, some dishonest, and so on. Time passed. The people endured two world wars, with between them a Great Depression and the rise of a lot more class envy, especially as expressed in and spread throughout the West by the European socialist and communist movements, and in a weaker but no less pervasive form by all the "progressive" liberal democracies (much as we are seeing again today with the Occupy Wall Street movement and envy of "the 1 percent"). Entire populations were now primed to abandon their original confidence in individual freedom, free markets, and personal responsibility, and for the first time to argue that social and economic success or trouble cannot all be due to *internal traits*; that a person's condition in life is also a consequence of *external causes*, and possibly of an exploitative "system." This signaled a profound modification of the entire moral bedrock of the Western world: *a slow shift in the allocation of responsibility for one's condition in life from self to others (the system).*

Meanwhile, huge increases in productivity and wealth, combined with steep increases in the income tax that this made possible, began providing Western governments with unprecedented tax harvests. By any reasonable measure there were only a handful of wealthy nations at the turn of the twentieth century, but fourfold more by midcentury. These new tax harvests in turn began fueling a massive growth of programs aiming to fix "the system," with rubrics such as Canada's Just Society, America's Great Society, and other catchy utopian labels.

For the first time in history a quasi-official argument of state was being developed to the effect that *economic and social equality are preconditions for liberty.* This boiled down to a new and—if equality must be forced by law—a logically flawed equation: *equality = liberty.* This shift was rapidly turning those original Stage 2 freedom liberals into modern liberals, or more simply, *statists.* This was inevitable, because you can't equalize people who, if they are maximally and truly free, will naturally become very different and unequal from each other, except by force of law and the enormous bureaucratic machinery required to take from some and give to others, and to implement and monitor those laws (that is, to search out and adjust inequalities in the citizenry by force). In short, the modern democracies were slowly abandoning their previous emphasis on freedom for all, under laws the same for all, to adopt the big-government banner of equality for all, under unequal laws. This shift in focus from liberty to equality was an enormous impetus to the growth of government power.

This situation continued apace through the 1970s and '80s, by which time almost every liberal democracy, each at a different rate, had completed its mutation from Stage 2 (assume a right to freedom) to Stage 3 (assume a right to equality). By now, the original motive to help only the truly needy (via the welfare state) had proceeded to the much larger "managerial-entitlement" motive ... of helping and managing just about everyone.

This was a new problem, for all the liberal democracies were embracing *a self-imposed contradiction.* Most of them were slowly becoming social democracies, more statist regimes (though the word *socialism* was still studiously avoided as a slur term for the regimes the Western nations had fought against in two world wars). But how can there be such a thing? Socialism mandates top-down authority and control to produce the desired *equality* of outcome. But a liberal democracy mandates a bottom-up *liberty* outcome whereby individuals behave independently and express their natural differences unpredictably under laws that are the same for all. Given enough time, a contradiction this deep would eventually mean complete policy paralysis and decline. There would have to be a fourth mutation.

Stage 4—The New Synthesis: Libertarian Socialism (How Social Democracy Overcame Its Own Contradiction)

The totalitarian states of the twentieth century, whether of national socialist (Nazi and Fascist) or international socialist (Communist) ambitions, were indeed aiming to control almost every aspect of life from the top down, to bring about by force of law and government what I describe further along in this book as "the triumph of the will over nature." The German Nazis called this process *Gleichschaltung*, or "bringing into line." In other words, they wanted to organize, or bring into line by force, the naturally different lives of millions of different private citizens according to a single totalizing vision of the good society. The great irony of the political history of the West is that whether as expressed by nazism, communism, or fascism, all these totalitarian movements, as the political philosopher Michael Oakeshott put it, were the "ungracious children" of modern democracy. As have all dictators since, Julius Caesar waited breathlessly for the roar of the crowd; modern democratic leaders, for the roar of the polls.

In the deepest sense, then, the World War II confrontation between the free world and the totalitarian world was in fact *a confrontation of the West with itself.* In the end, those overtly totalizing systems were largely defeated in the Western European theater. But this left all liberal democratic regimes (themselves already launched on a disturbingly similar, if slower and softer, path to state-guaranteed perfection) faced with the same ultimate question: How can we equalize, subsidize, control, and guarantee by force of law (by the will of the state) more equal conditions of life for all (as those totalitarian states were trying to do), *and still call ourselves free*? "Divide and conquer" would be the answer.

How It Was Done

The first step was the conceptual division of the democratic ideal into a *private* and a *public* realm, each with its own justifying ideology. There would be *more freedom of individual will* for all things personal and private—especially those having to do with sex and the body, such as abortion rights, easy divorce, homosexual rights, contraception rights, transgender rights, pornography rights, gay marriage, and soon euthanasia rights and more, made available to all equally in the name of freedom, many of them subsidized or free of charge. Along with this would come the astonishing imagery of virtually unlimited, uncensored sex, and all the perversities of choice, streamed into billions of homes and hotels by cable, satellite, and the Internet. *We the people have never been so free* was the intended message.

But at the same time, in most once free and minimally regulated democracies, and with astonishing speed, there would be the newly aggressive exercise of a *pervasive public will*—a new and vast public realm funded by massively increased taxation and permanent public debt, extending the tentacles of state into a myriad of formerly private properties; social, artistic, and athletic activities; and commercial operations, while positioning the state as the generous benefactor, regulator, and protector of all, equally.

The result is that the typical citizen of a modern democracy (especially political liberals, but also many political conservatives) now lives in all *private* matters like the ideal libertarian, who demands complete individual freedom with respect to things private, personal, sexual, and moral as he or she can imagine and defend as compliant with not harming others. But with respect to all things *public*, the typical citizen is similar to the socialist who reaches reflexively for government solutions and support of as many social and economic goods and services as the state has deemed it feasible to provide. What is the government going to do about this? is today the most common citizen question.

The result is that although historically libertarians and socialists have always despised each other's ideologies—each was developed specifically to oppose the other—*the two have been successfully fused* beyond the dreams of even the most ambitious social planner, into a *hybrid* system or *synthesis*[5] that is part libertarian and part socialist, with a very clear dividing barrier between the private and public domains in which each operates, the simple physical counterpart of which is ... your skin.

---

5 Hegel argued that all reality unfolds "dialectically." There is a state of affairs called a *thesis* that generates its own opposite, an *anti-thesis*. A struggle then ensues between these opposites for dominance. The struggle is resolved when a *synthesis* is worked out which becomes the new reality (and therefore a new *thesis*), and the dialectical process continues. On this model, the political longing for a maximum of individual freedom (once called classical liberalism, but now called *libertarianism* in North America and simply *liberalism* in Europe) is the *thesis*, the different forms of socialism are the *antithesis*, and libertarian socialism is the *synthesis*. My use of the term *libertarian socialism* in this book is to be distinguished from the same term used by anarchists who suffer from the utopian political fantasy that it is possible to combine socialism of any kind (beyond a fund-raising dinner) with individual freedom.

The end result is our novel regime type—*libertarian socialism*—a fusion of opposites that has become pervasive in the Western world in an astonishingly short period of time. To achieve it, the unspoken trade offered as a lure was the understanding that the people would not bemoan their diminished real political, property, and economic freedoms, nor the permeation of their lives by high taxation and minute regulation, if they were allowed more sexual and bodily freedoms and pleasures in exchange.

Libertarian socialism is now a homogenized regime type throughout the West, a new trans-ethnic, transnational form as ubiquitous as Coca-Cola and the cell phone, that by way of *erotic seduction* (offering all the private pleasures and freedoms of the flesh) and a policy *trade-off* (promising an equality of public goods and services in exchange for submission to hyper-regulation and the surrender of a bountiful tax harvest) is so conducive to the growth of bureaucratic statism that many of these regimes have already become what I would call *tripartite states*. These are states in which one-third of the people work to create wealth, one-third are employed by government at some level (when we include all full-time and part-time employees and permanent government contracts), and one-third receive significant annual income or benefits in kind from government. Once this final stage of the democratic mutation is reached, there can be no return except from eventual catastrophic decline, for in the voting booth, sooner or later, the last two segments will always gang up on the first.[6]

What Is the Future?

The implication that must be drawn is that liberal democracy did not, after all, signal "the end of history," as Francis Fukuyama famously declared in 1989. First, because history never ends unless the world ends; but also because the liberal phase of democracy had been mutating into

---

6 There is much insightful and continuing scholarship and debate in most democratic nations that forms part of a long conversation about just how Lockean or Madisonian or Tocquevillian or Rousseauean this or that modern democratic state may once have been, or is now. There is much to be learned and admired in this. But to this author at least, it seems an understatement to say that the entire conversation is made a historical curiosity, if not a nullity, by the brute fact of modern statism—a political condition none of these thinkers could have imagined, nor would have sanctioned.

libertarian socialism in Europe and the Americas at variable speeds determined by local conditions for more than a half century. Sweden, as the "third way" (neither communist nor fully capitalist), led the charge at mid-twentieth century, and was the first to transition from a profoundly conservative into a radically libertarian-socialist nation, to be followed by other Scandinavian countries, then by a procession of Continental nations, then by Canada; and in a more piecemeal way by the American federal government and many individual US states, with more to follow.

Nations may differ in the degree of libertarianism or socialism they combine according to the buffering strength or weakness of the older liberal or conservative ideologies or the strength or weakness of religion under which they have been living. But the new synthesis succeeds everywhere it has been adopted because power is addictive for those who command, and the exercise of personal will in pursuit of sexual and bodily pleasures—many of them contrary to nature—now transferred from public oversight and judgment to the private domain, is irresistible for those who obey. As Neil Postman argued in his prescient 1985 book *Amusing Ourselves to Death*, Orwell got it wrong and Huxley got it right: The "free" democratic masses would not be stupefied and regulated by totalitarian oppressors. Instead, they would surrender their most important political and economic freedoms to the state and the regulation this necessitates without a fight, in exchange for the right to pacify themselves with their own private bodily freedoms and pleasures.

The following table is a snapshot showing how Canada, for the past half century a world leader in "progressive" social change—and the canary in the mine for those Americans concerned about where the United States is heading—has incorporated the new synthesis as its official ideology, having abandoned is former liberty-based regime for a libertarian-socialist one in an astonishingly short period of time.

The foregoing has been an examination in very general terms of how the nascent liberal democracies of the Western world have mutated from their roots into libertarian-socialist regimes. With this completed, and for the sake of contrast with the mutation of liberalism I have been describing, let us now examine the nature of conservatism.

An Example of a Libertarian-Socialist Regime

This is a dramatic example from the Canadian experience, showing how over more than half a century the zone of human freedom has become reduced to, and is now centered mostly upon, the body and sexual matters; while in other areas of life once considered central to human freedom, having to do with matters such as personal medical care, private property rights, and economic rights and freedoms, freedom of thought and public expression have fallen under increased state control. A similar chart could be constructed for any modern democracy.

THE GAIN FOR SOCIALISM		
	1950	TODAY
Private Health Care & Insurance	*Legal*	*Illegal*
	Citizens free to purchase any health services or insurance advisable or desired	State monopoly on health services. Government regulation and limits on private insurance. Illegal to buy or sell private health care or insurance for government-insured services
National Language Freedom	*Legal*	*Illegal*
	Language freedom coast to coast. Bilingual services only in courts and government services	Forced bilingualism coast to coast. Affects businesses having any connection with government or government funding. All government agencies forced to offer both French and English services. The Quebec government and Canada's federal government operate pervasive language police and language surveillance systems
Private Property	*Legally Protected*	*Heavily Regulated/Unprotected*
	Lightly regulated. Deemed a historical common-law right. Private owners free to grow or harvest their own land, grow crops, and stock wildlife. Owners have rights to all the "free gifts of nature" from "heaven to hell." Abuses of private land or resources controlled by common-law legal suits	(No absolute constitutional protection of property in Canada.) Many takings-by-regulation and direct expropriation without full market compensation. Many federal, provincial, and municipal agencies and property police govern landowner uses of private property and private resources (water, trees, and wild-animal stocks). Regulatory infractions punished by government fines

THE GAIN FOR SOCIALISM		
	1950	**TODAY**
Free Speech	*Free and Legal*	*Controlled by Government*
	Except for libel, slander, etc., all classic books allowed. Free speech for third parties allowed during elections. Public discussion of all topics encouraged. If charged with libel, slander, or hate speech, truth is accepted as a defense. In general, all are free to criticize anything publicly	Human rights tribunals and thought control. Many classic books banned in schools. Third-party speech restricted at elections. Public discussion of core moral issues discouraged, and conflicts of rights generally resolved by courts, not legislatures. If charged with uttering hate speech, truth is no defense. Punishments, decided by tribunals, may include heavy fines, forced reeducation classes, and other attitude-adjustment methods formerly seen only in totalitarian states
Construction & Home Building	*Minimal Regulation*	*Maximum Regulation*
	A man could build his own home and live in it while doing so	Expensive government permits, approvals, and inspections required for all architectural, electrical, and structural work, also for government-approved toilet water volumes, fireplaces, light-bulb type, paint type, door knobs, materials used, etc.
Personal Safety	*Minimal Regulation*	*Pervasive Regulation*
	"Buyer beware" was the main rule. Private suits for damages settled problems	Strict regulation of seat-belt use, booster seats, helmet use for vehicle and sports activities. Financially and legally burdensome employee safety standards, licensing, and surveillance of workplace conditions, temperatures, air quality, site conditions, etc. Smoking banned in all restaurants, and soon in private homes and cars. Much talk of banning certain fatty and high-sucrose foods as well
Official Surveillance	*Minimal*	*Maximum*
	Unheard of by the public. Any surveillance was assumed to be only by Secret Service or FBI-type organizations (or foreign spies)	Telephone monitoring, Internet activity, RFID tracking, and cell-phone tracking are pervasive. Records are kept on many kinds of citizen and corporate activity by government. Many modern states now have privacy commissioners monitoring excessive monitoring

THE GAIN FOR SOCIALISM		
	1950	TODAY
Laws, Taxation, & Autonomy	*Minimal*	*Legal Suffocation & Loss of Autonomy*
	Taxation was minimal. A citizen could complete a tax form personally. Laws were few in number, and so a citizen was expected to know them ("ignorance of the law is no excuse"). A high sense of autonomy was felt by all. Total taxation as a percentage of GDP in this period was in the high 20% range for Canada and the US	Taxation on every aspect and action of life. Record high tax rates for peace time. The majority of citizens have to hire professionals to complete tax forms. No citizen can possibly know the many laws that now govern every activity. The result is a serious loss of autonomy, and the sense of living in a climate of pervasive surveillance by authorities, for reasons unknown. Loosely speaking, taxation as a percentage of GDP is a good indicator of the degree of statism in a nation. Total taxation as a percentage of GDP in the early 1990s was more than 50% for Canada, and is now in the 43% range. The US, at about 28% in 1960, climbed to 33% in 1990, and remained the lowest total-tax regime among the major democratic powers until the Obama presidency; by 2012, total tax as a percentage of GDP was just over 40%. The figure for Sweden for 1990 was almost 60%
Other Freedoms & Rights	*Minimal Regulation*	*Maximum Regulation*
	Can own and raise animals on private property without a license. Can cut a tree on private property or burn leaves without a permit. Can buy real estate without a heavy land transfer tax	Licenses required for many kinds of livestock. Municipal laws in many jurisdictions forbid cutting of trees or burning anything without a permit. Heavy land transfer taxes on all purchases and sales of land

THE GAIN FOR LIBERTARIANISM		
	1950	TODAY
Divorce	*Only Permitted for Cause*	*No-Fault Divorce Widely Available*
	Divorce for cause (fault) only, most commonly for domestic cruelty, desertion, or proven adultery (but also for such as addiction, nonsupport, insanity, and the like). Marriage considered a true contract requiring the consent of both spouses ("two to make it, two to break it")	Marriage no longer a true contract because it can be ended unilaterally by the choice of either party, without cause or fault attributed to either spouse. Hence, in the traditional contractual sense of binding both parties by mutual consent, marriage is no longer available ("two to make it, one to break it") except by private or religious contract or covenant
Pornography	*Illegal*	*Legal*
	Available only by criminal means	Easily available even in upscale hotels, and to very young children via TV, Internet, and the cell phone. A survey of more than 5,000 young Canadians [MediaSmarts, 2014] showed that 10% of boys in grade seven, 33% in grade eight, 50% in grade nine, and almost 66% in grades ten and eleven admitted to looking for porn online, and 40% of those did so daily
Abortion	*Illegal*	*Legal*
	Only by permission of medical committee, for rape, terminal illness of fetus, or to save the life of mother	Available on demand and tax-funded in Canada; no limit on number of abortions per woman. Only consent of mother required. Fathers have no say in the life or death of their own unborn child, but are required to pay child support until child is 18 if mother decides not to abort
Homosexuality	*Illegal*	*Legal*
	Widely shamed	Legal and celebrated
Gay Marriage	*Illegal*	*Legal*
	Considered perverted, and banned everywhere in the world. Full legal, tax, and economic benefits of marriage granted only to heterosexual couples	Gay marriage legal in Canada, and in many other democracies and a growing number of American states (33, plus the District of Columbia, as of this writing). Gay marriages and similar unions granted full legal, tax, and economic benefits of heterosexual marriages

THE GAIN FOR LIBERTARIANISM	
1950	**TODAY**
Marijuana *Illegal*	*Widely Tolerated*
Shamed, available illegally only	Still illegal. But widespread private use, punished very lightly if first offense—usually if in possession of under 30 grams [about 1 oz.]. Punishment much stricter for trafficking
Voluntary *Illegal* **Transgendering**	*Legal*
Allowed only for biological abnormalities	By choice and state-funded (Canada). In keeping with the postmodern notion that gender is as much constructed by the will as biological, Ontario citizens can change their gender on official documents with a note from a doctor or psychologist (reconstructive surgery is no longer a requirement)
Prostitution *Illegal*	*Tolerated*
Shamed as part of the criminal underworld, with an emphasis on the moral wrong of selling one's body for another's pleasure, thus converting oneself from a human subject into a commercial object. All religions disallow prostitution and provide the moral principles for judgments against it	Redefined in the public mind as *sex work*. Poll [Ipsos Reid, 2012] shows 65% support legalization of prostitution in brothels. Recently proposed laws aim to limit the violence surrounding such work and the solicitation of sex in areas frequented by minors. The harm principle has replaced moral principles. The modern emphasis is on acceptance of sex work as just another form of voluntary labor in a free market, but ignores all moral questions, seeking only to reduce social harm to minors, and personal harm to workers. Canada's Supreme Court, in throwing out the law against prostitution on December 20, 2013, specifically stated as one of its reasons that the existing laws prevented prostitutes from using "safer" fixed indoor locations (brothels), and also prevented them from using security and business measures such as hired bodyguards, drivers, managers, accountants, and receptionists

CHAPTER 3

On Conservatism

Conservative: from Latin conservator, *a keeper, preserver; and* conservare, *to protect, to guard*

The conservative philosophy of life I am going to describe presents a stiff challenge to the worldview of the modern liberal. It is a recipe, with specific tried-and-true ingredients for the good life, but it is not a speculative theory, for that would defeat conservatism itself, which has always resisted abstract, cookbook formulas, ideologies, or paper codes dictating how we are allowed to live. Rightly considered, conservatism is more like a cluster of recognizable attitudes, assumptions, customs, and traditions, a *practice* or *way of life* that serves not as a precise *map*, but rather as a *compass* pointing out a general direction. After all, how anyone gets through life always comes down to pursuing whatever they believe is worth doing, getting, fighting for, and *conserving* (the root word that is of interest here). As used in this book, the term *conservatism* describes an enduring temperament that I am convinced is essential to, and will always produce, a vital, settled, and deeply rooted community, anywhere, anytime.

Now that is a very large claim. But I think that as long as human beings live under tolerable social and political conditions, free of outright oppression, war, or threat to life and limb, their lives will always tend to be of the conservative sort (by whatever name). That is because conservatism—people living their own private lives quietly and striving to conserve what is naturally good—is the kind of life that has been experienced in all flourishing communities in history, and despite the present libertarian-socialist tenor and direction of the Western democracies, we can still easily find this sort of conservatism in most rural regions, in small villages and towns, and in pockets and neighborhoods in even the most liberal of large cities.

To this claim another, just as bold, may be added: namely, that never in human history has there ever been a permanently successful radical civilization. There have been lots of brief rebellions in history of a kind any of us might have joined in an attempt to correct a local or national grievance. And this gives us a clue: the key distinction is between *rebellion* and *revolution*. The former is a protest that aims to *restore* a cherished social or political practice that has been denied, or to *repair* a useful institution that has been corrupted. But a *revolution* is very different. It is a protest that aims to *destroy* a political or moral institution, or even an entire social system, lock, stock, and barrel, and *replace* it with something wholly new, unseen, and untried. Of course some revolutions seem well justified, such as the American one. But that event was misnamed, for it was not really a revolution at all. It was a War of Independence, or secession, a rebellion calling not for new rights, but rather for a restoration of the inherited English rights and freedoms of which the American colonists believed they had been unjustly deprived. The main point is that you may find some conservative rebels, but not a conservative revolutionary, because that is a contradiction in terms.

Some object to the claim that conservatism is a universal and historically persistent human temperament, because modern political conservatism appeared for the first time with two powerful eighteenth-century thinkers, David Hume and Edmund Burke. It is true, as previously discussed, that in reaction to Enlightenment rationalism, the political label *conservatism* came into common usage around that time. Nevertheless I maintain that the underlying predisposition called "conservatism" has been around from time immemorial.

Aristotle, to take the most important ancient example, was a philosophical conservative. He called for the priority and conservation of what is self-evidently good in nature, in human nature, in family, in law, in custom, and in social and political life. His teacher Plato, on the other hand, was the first thoroughgoing believer in a dreamland because (unless, as some believe, he was only kidding) he wanted to re-create human society anew as *something never before imagined*, along strictly totalitarian lines (though he was no egalitarian). His book *The Republic* was his paper plan for the perfect society, and a rich tyrant of the period actually asked him to implement it for the Greek city of Syracuse. But this first attempt at utopian statism failed miserably, as have all subsequent attempts. So we could say that one of the first and most impressive conservative intellectual *rebellions* in history was by Aristotle, against the *revolutionary* proposals for human perfection of his teacher Plato. Aristotle was followed by many other influential conservative thinkers in the ancient world, such as Rome's Cicero and Seneca.[7]

Subsequent examples of a very conservative way of life that thrived for more than a thousand years were the tightly knit Christian communities of the European Middle Ages that, contrary to popular belief, were in many ways far more open and free societies than what followed. Women, for example, had lots of voting, property, and inheritance rights within their own communities then; and by the Middle Ages slavery had vanished almost entirely from Europe (only to reappear and reach its distressing peak, when?—in the eighteenth-century Enlightenment, or "Age of Reason" discussed earlier). I should also mention the thirteenth-century work of Saint Thomas Aquinas, whose *Summa Theologiae* must count as one of the most rational conservative documents of all time, and one that is still a touchstone for the modern resurgence of natural law.[8]

---

7 It galls my leftist friends to learn that almost all the great literary figures in Western history have aligned resolutely with what stood for conservatism in their time. To those already mentioned, a partial list (this one prepared by Professor Virgil Nemoianu) would include Aeschylus and Aristophanes, Virgil and Horace, Dante and Chaucer, Shakespeare, Dryden, Racine and Corneille, Pope, Swift, Johnson, Goethe and Scott, Balzac, Tennyson, Baudelaire, and Dostoevsky. And that is just a start.

8 A word of caution on the political uses made of natural law is due, however, for it is a sword that can cut both ways. It is defended by many conservative thinkers as a bulwark against all arbitrary and "progressive" governments, especially against totalitarian regimes, and has been useful to conservative moral philosophers in their long struggle against moral relativism, especially as taught to young students in liberal educational establishments. On the other hand, there has been what appears to conservatives to be an arbitrary and disappointing use of "natural law" by courts to achieve the progressive goals of the state (progress from above), and by individuals fighting for their "natural rights" against traditional moral codes (progress from below). This pincer movement dissolving traditional customs and traditions is discussed in part 2. I should add that there is understandable confusion between the primarily liberal concept of *natural rights* and the more conservative concept of *natural law*. Leo Strauss explained the difference well in his 1953 book *Natural Right and History*, in which he described traditional natural law as an objective "rule and measure," a binding order prior to, and *independent* of, the human will, while the modern misuse of this term mainly describes a series of 'rights,' of subjective claims *originating* in the human will.

Conservatism famously found a public voice once again in the Restoration of the British monarchy in 1660 after Cromwell's usurping and bloody dictatorship. And as mentioned, resolutely conservative in both their intent and structure were the original constitutions of America and Canada, dead set as they were against the unchecked will of arbitrary, unrepresentative government, including "elective despotism." The only liberty they wanted was what Hume called "liberty under law." They saw more clearly than we that with the ever-present potential of the 51 percent to legitimize mob rule, *democracy has no necessary connection with liberty*. Today that seems a shocking thing to say, but only because we have been subjected to so much hype equating democracy with freedom. In fact, democracy and liberty have always been independent variables, as shown by the fact that the English people had lots of liberty long before they had any democracy, and many oppressive tyrants in history, from Nero to Hitler to Egypt's Morsi, have sailed into office on a tide of popular acclaim.

Due to this potential for oppression, the constitutions of Canada and the United States were set up to incorporate *some* democracy, on the reasoning that life is more peaceful if the laws under which citizens live have the consent of a majority of the people. But they opted for a very restrained type of "mixed" constitution that included an element of monarchy in the executive, but not too much. So worried were they about absolutism of any kind that one American Founder branded the powerful new office of the president as "the foetus of monarchy" (and given the near autocratic powers that President Barack Obama has managed to take unto himself, this was an apt warning). There was to be a role for an aristocracy of merit similar to the British House of Lords in an appointed upper house, or senate (which became elective via state legislatures in the United States in 1913), the role of which, as that aforementioned Founder, Edmund Randolph, put it, would be "to restrain, if possible, the fury of democracy." There would also be *representative* democracy—*direct* democracy was anathema—in a people's commons, or congress. And finally, they wanted a clear *separation* of powers between the executive, the legislature, and the courts, so that no one branch would become oppressive. The courts should not make the laws, any more than a legislature should try a criminal (though in seventeenth-century England, Parliament did lots of that!). In short, there were to be sufficient built-in checks and balances to block the hated arbitrariness of power, whether by power from above (the leaders), or from below (the people).

The point in speaking of these things is only to say again that *the original American and Canadian constitutions were very conservative*, because ... the people who made them were conservative by temperament, and from experience. I should add the observation that the history of the mutation of most Western democracies seems to be a gradual erosion of their original constitutional safeguards against arbitrary government and the centralizing tendencies found in all three branches of government, and at all levels of government.

The Conservative Philosophy of Life

WE ARE IMPERFECT BY NATURE. The most foundational principle of conservative philosophy is the conviction that because all human beings are fallible and imperfect by nature, *no society or government can ever be perfect*. For this reason, all utopian schemes for political, social, and moral perfection attempting to organize human life according to a theory of "progress" are unnatural, and fall automatically under suspicion. There is an old saying that "the best is the enemy of the good." This was a caution to malcontents. It means that if we destroy something that has always worked tolerably well (the good) and attempt to replace it with something we imagine will be perfect (the best), we will never reach perfection (because reality is never perfect), but in the process will have destroyed the good. Accordingly, the ordinary conservative tends to accept imperfection, in fact may love it deeply, because his feelings and affections are attached to the here and now. The liberal, in contrast, tends to be a malcontent, rarely happy with things as they are, very happy with things as he thinks they ought to be. This tendency was well described in John Stuart Mill's *Autobiography*, where he opined that "all the best and wisest of mankind" (among whom he counted himself) "are dissatisfied with human life as it is, and [their] feelings are wholly identified with its radical amendment...."

CONCRETE EXPERIENCE PREFERRED TO ABSTRACT THEORY. I have been using the phrase "philosophy of life" to imply a general attitude rather than an ideology or speculative theory, for the conservative is suspicious of speculative reason whenever used in isolation from experience, such as we find in paper charters and declarations that give voice to sweet-sounding but abstract concepts such as "the rights of man," "humanitarianism," and "natural rights." Some have described these things as a form of "legal Protestantism," because just as Protestants believe they have a direct relationship with an indwelling God, human rights, too, are said to be indwelling. But for the conservative, the problem with all such abstract concepts is that they are never self-interpreting. They are like empty pots waiting to be filled with meaning, usually meanings invented by politicized judges and interest groups. The French Declaration of the Rights of Man and of the Citizen and the constitution of the former USSR were both replete with glowing promissory terms, and both legitimized state terror. So the conservative conviction is that it is better to rely on long-trusted actual customs, traditions, and practices from a thousand years of human experience than on vague and abstract promissory concepts.

REASON NOT SUFFICIENT. Just so, there is a long-standing conservative conviction that reason is a means to an end, and not an end in itself; that "pure reason" cannot possibly produce the good life, simply because *whatever reason can create, reason can destroy.* Nothing was more "reasonable" than the argumentation of the PhDs and physicians who sat around Hitler's table reasoning that it was better to gas various classes of patients and disabled children (then Jews, intellectuals, dissidents, etc.) than to keep feeding them, because the money was needed to buy bullets for soldiers at the front. But in general, the conservative believes that we are not creatures who are very moved by reason or logic (unless using it to defend our own desires or loyalties). Rather, we are predominantly creatures of self-interest, passion, instinct, and emotion, and the restraints on these features of our being must come not only from ourselves, but from socialization via long experience, good habits and manners, customs, and prudence (doing the right thing in the right way at the right time).

LIBERTY A QUALIFIED GOOD. The fact of human imperfection impinges directly upon the question of liberty, for liberty is another double-edged sword. As Burke warned, "Liberty, when men act in bodies, is *power*" (the emphasis is Burke's). That is itself a powerful insight that beyond the establishment and defense of a cluster of natural liberties essential to moral life and a flourishing society ... watch out! When you hear people clamoring for more freedom, be sure to find out what they intend to do with it, or you may end up in their ideological (or real) gunsights. The French revolutionists slaughtered their fellow citizens with great passion in the name of liberty, as have all totalitarians since. Liberty is the most commonly asserted end for which almost any means can be justified. In short, because the liberty of some can easily be used to destroy the liberty of others, beware of the thoughtless praise of liberty, the positive use of which requires much discernment.

RESTRAINTS AS IMPORTANT AS FREEDOM. Burke drives home another conservative insight: that "the restraints on men, as well as their liberties, are to be reckoned among their rights." He meant that just as our basic practical liberties are inherited as achievements of our civilization, we also inherit the many practical restraints on our liberties, and these serve to protect us from our neighbor's unfettered will, just as they protect our neighbor from our own unfettered will. It is not contradictory to say that restraint is the guarantor of liberty.

INSTITUTIONS SHAPE INDIVIDUALS. Another foundational conservative belief is that all human beings are born unfinished, subject to a multitude of strong and conflicting biological forces, desires, and emotions, and so their flourishing depends to a very great extent on the flourishing of social and moral institutions, and not the other way around. Long-lived human institutions are the formative vehicle of our human second nature. The most important institutions are marriage and family; religion; moral customs and manners; core political, legal, social, moral, and economic forms and ideals of behavior; the rule of law; community understandings of right and wrong (and the duties and obligations that flow naturally from these); respect for property; the freedoms associated with voluntary exchange and contracts; and more. Such institutions are produced by the civilizing process over a long period of time, and "finish" our human development by providing the standards and boundaries of what Hume called "common life." However, as we will see in part 2 of this book, they can easily be rapidly and mortally weakened by radical egalitarian regimes that intentionally or unintentionally enter into a competition for citizen loyalty with their own civil societies.

LATENT FUNCTIONS. Central to the defense of institutions is the conviction that if they have endured, it is because they have *latent functions* of which we tend to be unaware, but that in large part explain their durability. In other words, in all settled societies there exists a kind of preconscious and prerational complex of institutional realities that should be disturbed as little as possible. The latent functions at work in all civilizations are the embodied wisdom of their history.

UNINTENDED CONSEQUENCES. The inevitable moral hazard of wholesale change of established institutions will usually be unintended consequences, resulting in a worse situation than what we had. Our foundational institutions are the incarnation of the best that has been said and done by our progenitors, and should be respected and conserved as the embodiment and gift of their generosity, wisdom, and sacrifice. In this sense, each and every human being is always "in the middle"—benefiting from past generations in the present, while observing obligations to future generations, who will in turn benefit from us, and so on, as long as civilization endures. The persistent emergence of unintended consequences following radical change should serve as a brake on all hasty social reform.

NO CHANGE FOR ITS OWN SAKE. The conservative recognizes that without some means of change, no society can exist for long. So he is not, as his opponents like to think, opposed to reasonable change where the benefits have been satisfactorily demonstrated. But he is opposed root and branch to radical change for its own sake. He suspects that words like "new," "change," and "hope" are a signal that the political manipulator is on the prowl, looking for more of the people's money to engineer the society of the future according to a personal vision of utopia. So long before any actual change is approved, the conservative insists that the burden of proof that the change will be beneficial is always on the innovator to demonstrate. For a decent civilization is like a spider's web, an intricate structure very difficult to create, easy to destroy. Unless the virtues of a proposal for change can be demonstrated as indubitably superior to what is customarily done, it is better to stay with the true than go with the new.

SOCIAL FREEDOM PRIOR TO INDIVIDUAL FREEDOM. Like the liberal, most conservatives will defend certain qualified individual freedoms to the death, but unlike the liberal, will insist on the general priority of social freedom. This entails the conviction that individual freedom must be evaluated not according to personal pleasure or satisfaction, but according to its contribution or damage to the common good of society. This is not far from the proposal of Kant, who argued that in deciding the morality of an action, each of us must behave as if we are moral legislators approving our choice for others similarly situated. Another way to express social freedom is to say that the rights and freedoms of all must generally be prior in importance to individual rights and freedoms, not the other way around. The conservative is especially wary that in this age of hyper-individualism, individual rights and freedoms are too often used as a battering ram to demolish community rights and freedoms. The "Golden Rule" is a conservative institution that has been with us for millennia, but even that rule assumes a prevailing and universal standard of human decency, without ever describing what that is.

"CUSTOM IS THE MOTHER OF LEGITIMACY." That is a pithy insight from the early nineteenth-century French thinker Joseph de Maistre, to the effect that in the very end, it is not abstract propositions on paper that will protect us or proffer the good life, but rather the deepest and most cherished political, social, and moral customs and standards of the people, including in the word *custom* all sound habits, manners, and prejudices (in the original sense that positive prejudices are long-accepted social or moral prejudgments that enable human societies to function smoothly). For Burke, the three Ps that guide all established societies are *prejudice*, which is a kind of preconscious knowledge we absorb from our society that gets us through life without submitting everything to the test of logic; *prescription*, which is the social and moral inheritance of the customs, traditions, and rights of all past generations; and *presumption*, or the assumptions we take for granted because all other people do—a kind of folk wisdom of the species.

SOCIETY IS AN ORGANIC, NOT A CONTRACTUAL, REALITY. For the conservative, civil society is not an abstraction. It is a real, natural, and organic product of historical experience that is prior in existence and importance to individuals. For this reason the liberal social-contract theory as spelled out by such as John Locke—the notion that civil society and government are a contractual creation of the people's will—must be considered a fantasy, a falsification of history, and illogical to boot, simply because, as Hume argued, in order for a contract creating civil society to come into being, an entire structure of civility, law, and custom protecting and policing such a contract—a functioning society—would already have to be in place. Even more damaging: when asserted as true, contract theory implicitly delegitimizes every government on earth because none are founded by contract; and if accepted, even though false, contract theory places civil society on a footing of perpetual revolution, subject always to overthrow by the fluctuating passions and popular will of the day, without gratitude or respect for the sacrifices of the past or due care for the generations to come.

THE WELFARE STATE IS AN ABERRATION. The conservative faults the welfare state and the comprehensive managerial-entitlement state that has succeeded it as a prideful aberration that willfully neglects the proper duty of government to refrain from excessive governing! For as will be explained in part 2, welfare states become powerful either intentionally or willy-nilly by entering into a deadly war for control against the authority of their own natural civil societies. They do this by progressively taking over—or substituting their own services for—a plethora of traditional forms of social authority and voluntary association, by means of legislative bullying and tax plunder.

MORALITY AND RELIGION. The conservative maintains that the human being is a religious animal, that all humans manifest a craving for the sacred in some way, formal or informal, and that even adamant secularists, in a variety of covert ways, tend to sacralize their disbelief. For the religious conservative, there is a divine principle in the universe, and God, however inscrutable, must be the author of all things. Less religious conservatives will say that religion is an essential and inexpensive form of crowd control, and that everyday secular morality survives still only because it expresses the moral surplus of a former religious morality. In any case, there is a transcendent natural moral law that is somehow written on the hearts of all. If it is true that morality sits on religion, philosophy on morality, and all economic and political life unfolds accordingly, then whenever religious belief collapses, the rest will fall in slow motion, like dominoes. The conservative will also tend to argue that an atheistic or *secular humanist* society, in which man is worshipped instead of God, is eventually doomed, because without any transcendent good as a standard, the only reference point for good or evil is human will in all its relativity, with no higher moral reality or natural law to guide or constrain. Then, as Dostoevsky's most nihilistic character warns, if God does not exist, everything is permitted.

THE FAMILY AND MARRIAGE. The conservative says that all human beings are born of a mother and begotten by a father, and so share in an eternal family triangle: a mother and a father living with their dependent children. This is the first and most basic of all societies, a social entity that survives all states and regimes, and that must be considered the bedrock of all other political and social institutions. It is also the only possible procreative unit, and so the protection and conservation of the family is de facto essential to the protection and conservation of civilization. Heterosexual marriage must therefore be socially and morally privileged over all other human relationships, and all national family policy should be aggressively pro family and pro-child, before being pro-adult or pro-individual. The conservative deplores the trend toward autonomism and the atomization of the molecules of civil society, so to speak; and all policies that implicitly or explicitly attack the family as an institution in the name of equality and individual rights are to be deplored.

DIFFERENCE AND INEQUALITY ARE NATURAL. The conservative believes that with basic freedoms under law in place and defended, there will always naturally emerge a whole range of talented, skilled, intelligent people and charismatic leaders, and so a kind of aristocracy or hierarchy of authority is natural to all human groups. The resulting social differentiation and distinction of high and even heroic character and moral worth are essential for the modeling of the young. The conservative defends this kind of natural inequality as a vibrant and certain sign of a free and flourishing society. Also defended is the conviction that the strong have an obligation to help, to teach, and to lead the weak, the less gifted, and the vulnerable, and that this responsibility is a permanent obligation of any aristocracy of merit and talent.

ENTERPRISE AND FREE MARKETS. Like the liberal, the conservative appreciates the importance of free markets under law, the constitutional right to own property, the flourishing of enterprise, protection against force, fraud, and cartels, and all related matters as central to the strength and protection of civil society, and the best means for the low to raise themselves high. But at the same time the conservative deplores the overcommercialization and money-vulgarization of everyday life. A key concern is that rampant commercialism—the turning of all things human into commodities—may, like the overgrown state, corrode the very social and moral institutions and customs that historically have restrained the worst effects of both.

COMMON LAW PREFERRED TO CODE LAW. There is a distinct and age-old conservative preference for English-derived common law, rooted in real concrete human experiences and case-law precedents, that permits us to do whatever we want except what is forbidden by the law, over a code law rooted in abstract legal concepts that permits us to do only what is permitted, decreed, or limited by the code, such as is typical in code-law jurisdictions like France and Quebec. Especially disliked in all British-derived systems is the French notion of immunity from criminal prosecution ("nonresponsibility" and "inviolability") granted to government officials for wrongdoing in the course of duty. In the British (or Westminster) system, when it comes to criminal activity, all citizens are equal before the law, and prosecutable.

A STRONG BUT LIMITED STATE. The conservative preference is for a state strong enough to protect citizens against force and fraud, defend against enemies, create and protect a framework for the enjoyment of liberty under law, handle policing and the usual national and international functions of government, but most crucially (and this aspect has been ignored by lots of "conservative" governments) to safeguard the rule of subsidiarity. This is the idea that all human action and self-governance should be completed at the lowest possible level before a higher level of authority is invoked. This means that in true conservative philosophy (if not always in conservative politics) there is a strong resistance to the ever-present encroachment of power and centralization: the tendency for larger national powers to invade and control the next lower level of government (provinces, states, regional authorities, etc.), and for that lower level in turn to invade the next lower level (cities, towns, villages, municipalities, etc.). This is only to say that in conservative philosophy there is a clear moral preference for bottom-up, local self-governance over top-down central control.

The next table is drawn from the two prior segments of this book—*On Liberalism* and *On Conservatism*—and summarizes the core ideas dividing the modern liberal from the conservative. Readers will see the considerable overlap (and some differences) with the earlier Enlightenment/ Counter-Enlightenment table, because the historical debate that began then—in what Aleksandr Solzhenitsyn, author of *The Gulag Archipelago*, described as "the disastrous deviation of the ... Enlightenment"—continues to evolve.

WHERE DO YOU STAND?		
On Modern Liberalism and Conservatism		
	MODERN LIBERAL VIEW vs.	CONSERVATIVE VIEW
Perfection	*Man is perfectible*	*Man is imperfectible*
	The basis of the liberal theory of progress, hope, and change is that human nature is malleable, and so human perfection is possible	The basis of the conservative preference for restraint and caution is that we are imperfect by nature, and so should not be subjected to unnatural schemes of forced perfection, though striving to live a good life is part of our second nature
Basis of Policy	*Theory*	*Experience*
	The reference and guide for change must be rational theory (e.g., Rousseau's *Social Contract* and Rawls's *Theory of Justice*)	The reference and guide for change must be actual experience, custom, tradition, and common-law principles. Revolutionary theories such as by Rousseau and Rawls seek to overthrow settled societies in the name of untried and fanciful theoretical constructs

WHERE DO YOU STAND?

On Modern Liberalism and Conservatism

	MODERN LIBERAL VIEW vs.	CONSERVATIVE VIEW
Reason	*Reliance on reason*	*Distrust of reason*
	Reason and social sciences are the best guides for human improvement because otherwise we must rely on failed experience and the ignorance of custom and tradition	Reason and science are the best tools for practical matters. But not in moral matters, where long experience and trusted moral codes, custom, tradition, and wisdom must rule. What reason can create, reason can destroy
Freedom	*Freedom is an absolute good*	*Freedom is a qualified good*
	The right to do whatever you want as long as you do not harm another	Freedom under law is a good; in the absence of law it is anarchy. When men act in groups, freedom is a power that must be restrained by the customs and traditions of a decent civil society
Restraint	*Restraints an impediment to freedom*	*Restraints a complement to freedom*
	Laws, customs, and public opinion that impede personal freedom as defined above should be reduced or abolished	Laws, customs, and moral codes that restrain personal behavior offer reciprocal protection to all, and make circumscribed freedom viable. The paradox is that restraint is our only guarantee of freedom
Institutions	*Always subject to replacement*	*To be protected and repaired with caution*
	All institutions should be subject to change according to the will of the people at any time as they desire. Individuals must shape their own institutions and replace them to suit their needs of the time	Social, moral, and political institutions embody the will and wisdom of all past generations and fulfill latent functions. Rash change always generates unintended negative consequences. Institutions play a key role in shaping individuals

WHERE DO YOU STAND?		
On Modern Liberalism and Conservatism		
	MODERN LIBERAL VIEW vs.	CONSERVATIVE VIEW
Individual & Social Freedom	*Individual freedom has priority* Individual rights and freedoms are prior in importance to society's needs. The focus of freedom is the present	*Social freedom has priority* Individual rights and freedoms are important, but the rights and freedoms of society must have priority. The focus of freedom is past wisdom, present use, and future consequences
Society	*Society exists by contract* Humans enter/create society by contract, and may modify or end it at will	*Society is an organic historical reality* Humans do not "enter" or "create" a society. They are born into society as a historical family with rights and freedoms, as well as duties and obligations, that are their inheritance
Morality & Religion	*These are personal choices* This is a secular age. People are free to choose any religion they want. Morality is a matter of personal choosing and is situational, and therefore relative	*Both are central to a flourishing society* Morality sits on religion, and philosophy on morality. The roots of Western civilization are Judeo-Christian, and must be protected. Total secularization spells the end of the Western way of life. Morality is always public. We cannot personally change a moral code any more than we can personally change a language
Family, Sex & Marriage	*A flexible social construct* The liberal relaxation of divorce and acceptance of all kinds of families, including homosexual marriage, is a sign of a free and decent society. All sexual behavior is legal as long as there is consent between the parties, no violence, and no minors involved	*A core human institution* The universal family is a married man and woman living with their dependent children. Procreative potential is the only justifiable motive for state support of marriage. State laws on sex should steer individuals toward procreative unions, discourage homosexuality, and design divorce laws to better protect children

WHERE DO YOU STAND?		
On Modern Liberalism and Conservatism		
	MODERN LIBERAL VIEW vs.	CONSERVATIVE VIEW
The Law	*Code law preferred*	*Common law preferred*
	Modern liberals tend to be very rights-conscious, and so prefer to justify their social and moral principles by reference to a charter, constitutional document, or code, especially if they cannot achieve their goals democratically (though both liberal and conservative political parties are guilty of this maneuver)	Conservatives prefer to ground their social and moral principles in actual human experience as embedded in common-law precedents, rather than relying on abstract code law or constitutional legerdemain. That is because no code or constitution is self-interpreting. Therefore ultimate meanings will be decided according to the subjective biases of judges pondering abstract legal concepts, rather than by actual case decisions
Equality	*Substantive equality the goal*	*Formal equality under law the goal*
	The egalitarian state must create universal social and economic national policies so that all citizens have a more equal life in substance, and not only formally under law	Forced equality and liberty are contraries, and the more we have of one, the less we will have of the other. Substantive equality is only possible by force, through policies of official discrimination. If this course is chosen, we are on the path to the total state

PART II

CHAPTER 4

The Forces at Work

History tells us that all civilizations rise energetically, sustain for a while, and then decline, for reasons peculiar to each. Why that is so is still a mystery. But if I had to single out the most important forces responsible for what looks very much like the decline of our original liberal democratic systems, I would say the first has to do with different modes of control, the second with the power relations between different levels of government, and the third with the tension between the demands of liberty and those of equality. More specifically, in the latter case, the tension between our egalitarian political philosophy and the *necessarily* antiegalitarian nature of a flourishing civil society. This last is a contradiction the modern West has yet to face.

Political life in free regimes—perhaps in all regimes—may be imagined as roughly structured into three layers, each distinguished by a specific form of control. At the very top is the *state* (for this exercise, let's ignore lower levels of government). In the middle is *civil society*, made up of countless groups such as families, clubs, churches, charities, sports teams, and so on, in astonishing variety. At the bottom are many millions of autonomous *individuals*.

Tensions arise naturally from this structure once an egalitarian imperative takes hold, because the core motive of the state is then to *level civil society* insofar as feasible by eliminating inequalities through force of law and policy. The main function of all those voluntary associations in the middle layer, however, is precisely the opposite: to *welcome and encourage the voluntary creation of inequalities* in the form of exclusive group privileges, benefits, and duties that are shared by group members only. For example, every family enjoys its own particular private privileges and obligations, as do members of congregations, corporations, sports teams, social clubs, and so on. These privileges are exclusive and forbidden to outsiders, and all thriving civil societies are a compounded matrix of such inclusive/exclusive organizations, formal and informal.

Another tension arises because, among the millions of autonomous individuals at the bottom, there are always some who may decide to claim an egalitarian right to benefits or privileges equal to those provided to members of a specific group in the middle layer of civil society—let's call this a target-equalization group that they have chosen not to join, or for which they cannot qualify for membership for some reason. Examples would be a girl who demands a change of gender-exclusion rules so she can play on a boys' soccer team, or a homosexual who demands the benefits traditionally afforded to heterosexual marriages only (more examples to come in part 3). In short, under the banner of equal rights, an individual will attack the customs and traditions that mark a group as exclusive, private, and voluntary, demanding the benefits of the group even though unwilling to abide by its membership demands. An interesting example popped up as I was composing this section. A Toronto court ruled that a student who had chosen to attend a Roman Catholic high school did not have to attend religious liturgies, retreats, or religious study programs that the school has always required of all students. This is a clear case of the war that appears to be taking place in all the Western democracies between individual freedom and the social freedom of a voluntary association to decide its own membership requirements.

Under a liberty ethos, it is the middle layer of this triple structure where most of the flourishing—and excluding—takes place in socially bonded groups. But when a liberty ethos mutates into an egalitarian one the trouble begins, because this is the layer that gets disempowered simultaneously by the leveling demands of governments above and claims to individual rights from below. At this stage of mutation the entire equalization apparatus operates like an ideological clamp, squeezing out the life, integrity, and exclusivity functions that enabled groups in the middle layer to bond and flourish in the first place. The spectacle created, right before our eyes, is of a once liberty-based liberal democracy that has mutated into an egalitarian one, striving to purge as many traces as possible of private social privilege from its precinct for the sake of ideological purity. Let us look a little closer.

Control by Power

The state is the topmost level, and the only one of the three levels granted a monopoly on *power*. The laws of state order us to behave (pay your taxes!), or not to behave (do not steal!), in thousands of precisely legislated ways. Obey, or ... it's off to jail you go. In this book the term *statism* is used to describe the totality of monopolistic power and regulatory control of the citizenry by the modern democratic state at all levels—a degree of power and depth of penetration into personal and civil life that is unprecedented in the history of free societies. The simplest indicator of the permeation of power exercised by a nation over its citizens is total taxation as a percentage of GDP, plus total debt, which must include all unfunded liabilities (because all government debt is a form of deferred taxation). We have all heard the saying that "power corrupts." But it is not true. Power is first of all an instrument. It cannot do anything on its own. Rather, it is we who misuse power to corrupt ourselves and those around us. When it comes to modern statism, however, we could say that there is no power without money, simply because very few will try to control you at their own expense. If you cut off the money, you cut off the power.

Control by Social and Moral Authority

At the middle level is civil society, which is a vast collection of private voluntary associations. All human beings are born into a variety of social groupings without their choosing, but as adults they may choose to remain, or to leave, or may freely join or decide to form any number of other voluntary associations. The key point is that none of the groups populating this middle layer has the power to coerce adult members, and so the form of control typically expressed is not power, but rather *social and moral authority*. For example, we respect our parents, our ministers, our teachers, our coaches, our boss at work, or the leader of a political group we have joined, because ... we have consented, or we admire and want to learn from them, or because we owe them felt duties and obligations, and for many other such reasons.

It is important to distinguish very sharply between power and authority when engaging in political or moral discussion, and to beware of people attempting to conflate the two, as some important and influential thinkers in our own tradition have done, such as the enormously influential libertarian John Stuart Mill. He had a deceptive habit of lumping together power and authority—especially moral authority, which he called "Public Opinion" (his caps)—as if these two forms of control were the same thing, when he knew very well they are not, and never have been.

Self-Control

At the bottom level there are autonomous *individuals* who may choose to exert an egalitarian dissolving pressure on the social solidarity, moral authority, and privileges reserved to a variety of groups in civil society, through demands that laws favoring those groups be changed to include them as individuals, or that the social and economic group privileges and rights be made available to them as individuals, even though they know very well they do not, cannot, or choose not to qualify for membership in the target group. A woman who claims a right to walk bare-chested in the street as men are allowed to do, or a man who demands the right to use a women's washroom or a women's-only golf club, are examples. This mass of citizens, as individuals, relies for control neither on power nor authority (although these obviously may, and often do, guide them), but rather on *self*-control. Their objective as autonomous self-choosing individuals on the hunt for equality is to commandeer the same social and legal privileges, benefits, and protections as provided to members of exclusive private or public groups. Individual equality is their battering ram.

It is interesting that the single best indicator of the difference between modern liberals, conservatives, and libertarians is the degree to which each tends to rely chiefly on one of these three modes of control. The first recourse of the modern liberal tends to be the powers of state; of conservatives, the authority and moral direction of civil society; and of libertarians, mostly self-control, or personal choice (the force of personal will).

Imperium in Imperio

By this Latin expression—"a power within a power"—the ancients warned us long ago that if we try to nest a lower power within a higher one, and even with the best of intentions attempt to prevent them from meddling with each other's powers by means of strictly delineated constitutional barriers, there will be constant friction between them, the outcome of which will always be that the higher, more expansive power will eventually cannibalize the powers of the lower entity in the name of unity and equality.

This has been the experience of all democratic federations, whether of the ancient Greek Delian League, the Roman Empire and its provinces, Switzerland, the United States and Canada, or (most clearly and right before our eyes today) the European Union. All power and all mutual interests seek to unify, the better to control—and to unify means to convert the Many below into the One above, a process that is carried out everywhere, and always to the detriment of the independence and self control of the lower levels. The United Nations attempts to unite the many nations of the world into one world body with various treaties and international conventions that limit national autonomy. The United States unified its many member states into one nation with a strict constitutional division of powers giving states their own enumerated rights that courts have been eroding from above ever since, ever strengthening the central government, ever weakening the lower states. The same with the European Union, which has taken over many of the powers of its separate member states by amalgamating into a single bureaucratic empire. And the same with Canada, which is an interesting case of an attempt to unite provinces by national policy dictate and fiscal bribery (national health care is the clearest example) under an original constitution that forbade this very thing.

Canadians today will say that free health care is a defining feature of their nationality. But as Canada's constitution specifically assigns health care to the provinces, and forbids the federal government to touch it, how was this made possible? By fiscal bribery. Canada's federal government simply set a universal national standard for the equal provision of "free" health care (really, it's not free; it's prepaid through the tax system), and offered to reimburse the provinces half of all their health-care expenses if they signed on to the standard. For the billions of dollars on offer, despite this breech of their constitutional rights, and after only minimal resistance, all the provinces caved in.

My point in mentioning these things is to emphasize that this unification-by-cannibalization process also takes place (as described next) between egalitarian governments and their own civil societies. When democracies were rooted in a liberty ethic, as most of them began, the fact that nations require unity did not result in a competition for loyalty between these states and their own civil societies, because their governments were conceived as night watchmen. Liberty under law. Same rules for all. Government is a referee, and must not play the game, and so on. Such states were *nonegalitarian*, minimally intrusive, and accepted as normal and desirable the thriving independence—called *social freedom* in this book—that creates the kind of intentionally *inegalitarian* social bonding and group privileging that arises naturally in all free and flourishing civil societies. The job of government was to protect social freedom, not to erode or attack it.

Once mutated into *egalitarian* regimes, however, democracies develop an immediate ideological interest in equal outcomes, and therefore in directing the lives of the people to this end. This means a change from a night-watchman ideal to *l'état dirigiste*—the directing or managerial-entitlement state. Immediately, a radical tension is created between the *concentric*, radically illiberal forces of social bonding natural to the formation of flourishing civil societies and the more powerfully *concentric* egalitarian forces of governments attempting to form all citizens into a single egalitarian state. This is generally achieved not by eliminating the exclusive privileges enjoyed by specific social groups (such as those traditionally enjoyed by married couples who meet the qualifying conditions for the benefits of marriage), but rather by declaring such privileges a right for all, equally, and by supplying the formerly exclusive benefits to them without any qualification. This equalizing move transforms an exclusive privileging *policy* into an inclusive general public *handout* that removes the taint of privilege. In this way the state transfers to itself the deep loyalties and gratitude generated by the civil social-bonding process. The gradual debilitation of the bonding and privileging power of social groups, one by one, eventually transforms the state into the most prominent benefactor of all. Now let us look more closely at how social bonding works, as it seems to be a natural and universal process.

On Social Bonding:
Why It Is Natural, and Naturally Nonegalitarian

First, let us speak a little about morality and how it is that for more than two centuries the modern Western world has been busy stripping itself of its own common moral foundation. The simplest way to imagine this process of *de-moralization* is to say that, before the extraordinary influence of Mill's "harm principle" (the notion, as one of his sharpest critics put it, that morality means we should "let every man please himself without hurting his neighbor," which Mill promoted in his somewhat confused and self-contradictory booklet *On Liberty*), the members of all civil societies in the West had always imagined themselves to exist within a kind of common moral bubble, so to speak—an intangible, invisible bubble of opinion and conviction that stretched over an entire community, or an entire country. The purpose of this bubble was to hold the common moral life of all the people together. In short, the moral code of the community was decisively a public affair, and was spoken by all as a common language.

To be fair to Mill, he never imagined his simple principle to apply other than to individuals "in the maturity of their faculties," and certainly not to "backward societies." Nonetheless, as the moral surplus of a bygone age began to diminish and Mill's principle took firmer hold, various kinds of moral relativism and situation ethics arose, and individuals began to imagine themselves as existing each within a self-created *personal* moral bubble. Morality was now to be considered mostly a matter of personal choice, and any direct harm done by a moral collision with someone else's bubble would simply be dismissed as negligible, excused, or negotiated away. Throughout this process of changing moral attitudes, very little thought was given to *indirect* harm, as when someone's immoral behavior shames and demeans a whole group, or team, or company, or has shameful consequences for the reputation of an entire community or nation. Nor was any attention paid to the possibility of future harm, where something may seem good and a harm to no one today, but may harm many tomorrow.

By the turn of the twenty-first century this moral individualism and relativism trend had gone so far in places like Canada that in the 2005 lawsuit *Regina v. Labaye*, Canada's Supreme Court directly cited the authority of Mill's little book in announcing that his harm principle should henceforth *replace* community standards of morality in Canada. This was a case in which the community complained about a swingers' sex club that had opened in their neighborhood. The court's ruling was astonishing, for in the entire long history of the Western world (as the dissenting justices in *Labaye* warned), no court had ever gone so far as to dismember by fiat the common moral bonds of its own civil society in the name of individual freedom or a simplistic harm principle—a "moral" standard that is deeply flawed simply because *it offers no shared conception of the good*. If we need a clue as to why we are breaking the bonds, we need look no further. It starts at the top.

It is probably impossible to understand conservative support for the normal antiegalitarian nature of civil society without some insight first into the fine detail of exactly how human social bonding so naturally transforms autonomous individuals into unequal social beings, and why the end result of trying to combine an officially egalitarian national political philosophy (determined to destroy the exclusionist inequalities within its own civil society) with a freedom philosophy (based solely on individual choice, without any regard to a standard of the common good) is a drastic weakening of the civil societies of the West through the loss of what many are now calling "social capital."

Of course governments are by definition parasitical on the flourishing of their own civil societies. They feed on them financially via taxation, and cannot survive without them. But because they have a monopoly on power they may, once they get out of control (as is now the case for many European democracies, and even the American one), begin to exhaust their host both morally (through the process of de-moralization I am describing) and financially (via hypercomplexity due to overregulation, debt spending, and tax exhaustion). In other words, even though it is clear (and this is a core tenet of conservatism) that a vibrant and flourishing civil society is of primary importance to the production of flourishing individuals, and hence to the very survival of the state itself, it is just as clear that this middle layer of the three-part political structure described is the one that has been directly under attack, from above by government and from below by individuals, for at least a century. Let us see why.

How Social Bonding Works

There are four stages in social bonding, sometimes formal, sometimes informal, depending on the association being created. But whether we are speaking of the Boy Scouts, a marriage, or membership in a bridge club or fraternity house, we will usually find some expression, actual or symbolic (or both), of a four-step process of *sacrifice, subordination, commitment,* and *privilege.*

Sacrifice refers to the requirement of all groups that individuals who aspire to join must voluntarily agree to place the common will of the group above personal will. From this flows loyalty to the group. The motto of well-known organizations like Rotary International is "Service Above Self." Individuals who can't make the sacrifice of self that is required will be denied admission, leave, or be forced out.

Subordination refers to the requirement that all members submit to the authority and rules of the group as an expression of group discipline. Insubordination normally triggers some internal process for dismissing, disowning, or firing, and all members carry around an internalized copy of the rules by which they feel bound, and proudly distinguish themselves from nonmembers. The important and deliberately illiberal process of social exclusion of nonmembers (who are not bound by nor expected to obey the rules) begins here. Without such social (and often a felt moral) exclusionism there can be no membership, and without membership no civil society, because there is no transformation of individual beings into social beings.

Commitment is the process whereby, the first two requirements having been met, a new member is asked formally to make a vow or a public commitment to the group. Boy Scouts, marriage partners, and club members make their commitments in words, written contracts, or deeds to the ideals, activities, and undertakings they agree to shoulder and share. No vow will mean no membership, or the rejection of membership.

Privilege is the last stage—and the red flag for all egalitarian states— whereby the group approves and bestows privileges, benefits, and protections, small or large, secret or open, on each committed member *only*. This is often accompanied by a significant ceremony or rite of passage in which the commitment or vow of loyalty is made; and by special symbols, hats, ties, rings, costume, and the like, is intended to distinguish members from nonmembers. Boy Scouts and Shriners get to wear their caps and kerchiefs, and say secret things; marital partners sign covenants, wear rings, get lawful and exclusive sexual access to each other, and become eligible for certain legal, tax, and social privileges; registered club members are expected to be loyal, carry cards, be dutiful, observe their vows, pay their dues, do required work, abide by rules, and so on.

The key point is that successful social bonding is intensely human, and intentionally exclusionist, or it cannot be successful. It is characterized by an eagerness to distinguish, that is, to *discriminate*, in a very positive sense between members and nonmembers, between those who qualify for group status and privileges by voluntarily swearing allegiance to the group and its causes, and those who don't. A vibrant civil society, we might say, is a vast organism comprised of countless such groups that organizes the conferral of positive benefits, protections, and privilege on those who voluntarily opt into its chosen social forms. By this four-step process, true civil associations seek to select from the undifferentiated and uncommitted mass of autonomous individuals only those who qualify to enter their own far more difficult and challenging forms of social unity as members, the crowning reward of which is *privilege*. It was this very tension, due to the competition for loyalty between a privileging civil society and the egalitarian state, that bothered Rousseau so much in his *Social Contract*, and it is why he insisted on the liquidation of all civil associations. His was the first theoretical justification of totalitarian democracy. Ever since, by a different road and a different dynamic, we have been heading in the same direction.

Statist Envy of Social Bonding

What all modern states of the free world are attempting, then, under what is usually called liberal democracy—a regime type that I have argued has mutated into libertarian socialism—is to hijack the deeply human desire for social bonding that is so powerfully expressed in civil society by offering state-bonding as a substitute. If you love a woman who loves another man, you try to offer a better love in hopes of transferring her love to yourself. Just so, states see the powerful love and caring generated by human social bonding at work within their own myriad civil associations. They get jealous. Without being so reckless as to weaken society irreparably, however; that is, while taking care to preserve many of its intensive labors, without which the state could not function at all, they strive to maintain the functions, but transfer the underlying emotional and social allegiances to the state through the mechanism of substitute caring. This caring is proffered in the form of equalization laws, benefits, tax privileges, subsidies, and a myriad of tax-funded services, social programs, and public institutions. When the state builds a tax-funded public fitness facility in your community, in the process putting a couple of private fitness clubs out of business (and along the way extracting tax dollars from thousands of citizens whom it knows will never use the facility), it effectively transfers the loyalty the users once felt for those private clubs to itself. In short, the aim of the state is to transfer the formerly privileging and private social-bonding powers of civil society into a single, public, state-bonding power—thereby converting a pluralist civil society (Many civil groups) into a unitary national society (One national group). Or as national leaders are often heard to say: "One national family."

For the modern liberal, individual liberty, self choosing, self-flourishing, and so on are core values within the context of an egalitarian managerial-entitlement state. For the libertarian these are core values, period, and to hell with the state. The conservative, however, typically refuses to accept the depressingly mechanical idea that society is just an aggregate—a collection of autonomous individuals, like atoms, or, as Prime Minister Margaret Thatcher once put it (in one of the few really misguided things she ever said): "There are individual men and women, and there are families.... There is no such thing as society." She said it because she always fought the idea of collectivism, which is a coercive phenomenon. But the striking feature of all flourishing civil societies is that they are nurseries of real human liberty under law that serve as real-world barriers to state coercion, precisely because they are a real organic body or entity that is indeed, and contrary to Thatcher, more than the sum of its parts.

Alas, however, what we find at the heart of all secular totalitarian regimes is that they intentionally set out to dissolve the private powers and exclusivities generated by their own civil societies. We find the same process at work now at the heart of our modern libertarian-socialist regimes, mostly because it is in the interest of newly egalitarian states to persuade the people that there is no political reality except the flattering, envy-based notion of themselves as a collection of equal individuals within a paternalistic state, rather than as members of an organic, self-directing society that thrives without any nonessential reliance on government.

That is why, ever wary of this process, the conservative argues—against both the liberal statist above and the libertarian individualist below—that civil society is not a mere fiction, or abstraction. It is manifestly far more than the simple aggregate of its individual members because its structure includes, is constituted by, real relationships that cannot be derived from autonomous individuals alone. By their very nature, these private relationships create intense loyalties and allegiances that repel interference by nonmembers, outsiders, bureaucrats, regulators, and so on. The conservative is more keenly aware than most that these inward-looking civil and moral allegiances act as powerful competition for the outward-looking allegiance that is now the organizational imperative of all libertarian-socialist regimes. That is why the conservative seeks to promote and conserve these real societal relationships and institutions, and to protect their venerable priority over the claims both of the invading hyper-regulatory egalitarian state above and of the autonomous, equality-seeking liberal individualist below. In short, the conservative defends a strong civil society and the social and moral bonding it generates as the only effective barrier between oppressive takeover from above, and dissolution from below, and therefore as the only concrete guarantee of real liberty. Individuals alone are powerless to protect a regime of liberty. Only strong civil societies can do that ... unless they surrender.

The primary social action of the modern state, then, whether overt or covert, is to individuate, the better to influence, manipulate, and incorporate. Eliminate any family basis for government services (deal with individuals only). Eliminate the old income-splitting tax return for single-earner families. Designate each citizen a taxpayer. Offer welfare to individuals, rather than to families (encourage the reliance of wayward or disobedient children on the state, rather than on their own families). Attack the qualifications for traditional heterosexual marriage as discriminatory (and then offer all the economic benefits and legal protections of marriage to "any two persons"). Set up legal systems that persistently promote individual rights and freedoms over social rights and freedoms, and so on.

At such a point, individuals gradually divorce themselves from the broader civil and moral compact of civil society, imagining themselves as no longer connected except by choice to any shared moral obligations or standards of community behavior. This is true, paradoxically—perhaps especially true—when ever larger percentages of autonomous individuals subsist in some significant measure on supports from the state, to which they increasingly owe allegiance, rather than to civil society. Mitt Romney notoriously stated that 47 percent of Americans are dependent on government, and this author has complained that the Western democracies have been mutating from nations of makers into nations of takers, and from there into tripartite states. The endgame has already been decided. Other than by some great moral and political reawakening of the people, rooted in a determined call for liberty from excessive government, for self-reliance, and independence, thus to enable civil society to flourish anew and restore itself as a barrier against state power—there is no way out.

PART III

CHAPTER 5

Themes That Divide

The purpose of this section is to show why there is a Great Divide at work in a handful of fundamental areas of thought. A wonderful professor of mine, now gone to his reward, called the key foundational point or fact on which a person relies to support an argument a "planted axiom." An axiom is a statement or proposition that is regarded as being established, accepted, or self-evidently true. It doesn't call for any further proof or material evidence, but rather is an article of faith that someone "plants" in the field of a debate as the cornerstone for the entire structure of their argument, or belief system. As mentioned earlier, the whole argument can then be conceived of as a kind of intellectual building. My professor maintained that if you can falsify your opponent's planted axiom, you will bring down the entire argument. For example, if you can falsify the labor theory of value relied upon by Karl Marx, you will bring down the whole Marxist economic theory. If you can prove that Sartre's statement "existence precedes essence" is false, you will falsify modern existentialism.[9] A Christian friend observed that Christianity rests on the foundational belief in the resurrection of Christ (and of all

---

9 Marx's planted axiom was thoroughly falsified by Eugen von Böhm-Bawerk in *Karl Marx and the Close of His System*, and Sartre's planted axiom was falsified by Étienne Gilson in *L'être et l'essence*, though neither of these devastating falsifications had much immediate effect on the ardor of believers in those two idea systems.

believers), and that if anyone ever found Christ's body, the whole belief system would collapse.

At the end of each topic in this part of the book readers will find a *Where Do You Stand?* table on the liberal-versus-conservative divide examined. A goodly number of the arguments defended on both sides are similar to planted axioms that support the structure of the argument(s) resting on them. It is not certain that the analysis of any structure of ideas for which the cornerstone has been located can go much deeper, or that trying to go deeper would do much good in terms of resolving differences, and that is because faith in a cornerstone argument can be denied or disbelieved, but not disputed. But an ongoing question is why both sides select the planted axioms they do. There will be an attempt to answer that fundamental question, too.

CHAPTER 6

On Human Nature

This topic is of utmost importance, because the starkly opposed definitions of human nature defended by the modern liberal and the conservative predetermine every other difference between them, and are fundamentally irreconcilable. The liberal view is that in the state of nature, we all are supplied at birth with some basic physical traits and instincts, but in its cultural, social, and moral aspects—and especially with respect to the workings of the mind—human nature is malleable and changeable. It is modified—and modifiable—by environment, culture, education, and socialization. In short: *human nature can be changed.* Soon we will see why, for a conservative, that is such a shocking thing to say. But it helps us understand why influential liberals from the eighteenth century forward have continued to insist that the real aim of progressivism is to change human nature. By which they mean, to change human beings as they naturally are into a new and improved kind of human being. This is the basis of the liberal revolt against nature that we will glimpse repeatedly in this book.

The conservative view is quite the opposite. All human beings are born with the same human nature, and that is what makes us humans, and not horses, or pelicans. Human nature is the same everywhere and at all times, is fixed and lawlike in its basic parameters, and is identifiable in the many social, cultural, physical, moral, and conceptual practices found in all peoples of the world.[10]

It is true that culture and socialization may add to or subtract from our human endowment to a significant degree. As mentioned earlier, the second nature that we learn from our families and society—our manners, self-restraint, moral posture, and so on—is indeed learned by all people everywhere, except by the most defective among us, precisely because we have the same underlying human nature that makes this learning possible. In this broad sense, human nature is fixed, does not change by itself, and cannot be changed by others; so attempts to change it, whether by social engineers, dictators, totalitarian states, or progressive democratic regimes, must always lead at the least to unintended consequences manifested in political and moral dislocation, confusion, and waste of resources, and at the worst to great evils. Which brings to mind the old French warning *"chassez le naturel, il revient au galop,"* which means "chase nature away, and it comes galloping back."

So it is easy to see why a struggle always develops between liberals and conservatives centered on whether what makes us human is, in its essentials, malleable and changeable or fixed and permanent. This debate often comes down to asking how much of what we are is due to *nurture* or *nature.* To which I would add a question: How much of what we are is due to personal will? But to stay with the liberal for a moment: this person is virtually forced by a faith in progress to adopt a corollary faith in human malleability, for to admit there may be permanent obstacles to progressive policy objectives due to a fixed human nature would mean the collapse of the entire progressive dream of a perfect world order. In effect, the operative logic and faith, believed if never demonstrated, is that all human beings start life the same—fresh, innocent, and as yet untouched by experience. But some become bad or poor or disadvantaged because life writes bad stuff on the blank slate of their minds. The liberal conclusion is that you can change human nature by changing social conditions.

The day I wrote this page, a headline from the *Toronto Star,* a liberal newspaper, declared: *"Poor urban planning to blame for violence,"* followed

---

10 The best anthropological work on human universals can be found in Donald Brown's *Human Universals.* The gist of his findings were central to my own treatment of this topic in *The Book of Absolutes: A Critique of Relativism and a Defence of Universals.*

by the typical conclusion to which people of this view are driven: more tax-subsidized government housing and programs are the "solution" to urban violence. This conclusion—violence is caused by bad external forces that shape human nature—is unavoidable for anyone whose planted axiom is that human nature is malleable.

The first thing the conservative finds peculiar about this belief is that such articles never try to explain why so many nonviolent people in the very same urban setting are law-abiding. There is seldom comment on this fact, because to admit such a truth would amount to blaming individuals, rather than their environment; and that single difference in approach would overturn a core liberal belief. To sum up: For the modern liberal, the locus of evil is mostly external to the person. For the conservative, it is mostly internal. These two views can never be reconciled. Hence a Great Divide.

It is hard to say where the faith that human beings are all good by nature and equally malleable (and therefore equally reformable) came from. It looks very much like a planted axiom. But a reasonable guess is that it is a simplified secular echo of the biblical idea that the first human beings were created by God equal, pure, and sinless in the Garden of Eden. The modified secular version of this story—the concealed theology—is that human beings evolved biologically with blank-slate minds, and a good or a bad social environment shapes them accordingly.

The conservative response to this belief is as follows. First, no one could possibly know what we would be like in a state of nature, prior to all social and moral influence, because no human being has ever experienced such a thing. So to imagine there was some perfect and perfectly equal original state of nature is a handy but fanciful romantic *idea*, like the idea of the Noble Savage made popular in eighteenth-century poetry and fiction. But it is not a fact of human history. The only accounts we have of such imaginary conditions are found either in mythical, fictional, or religious accounts, or, most dangerously, in the political tracts of revolutionary dreamers who want to smash everything that is, and replace it with their fantasy of an egalitarian society, their secular Eden. This destruction-for-creation voice could be heard from a member of the French National Assembly when the Jacobins were ramping up the Terror of their revolution. He cried out that everything the old generation did "must be renewed, their ideas, their laws, their customs must be changed ... words changed ... destroy everything; yes, destroy everything; then everything is to be renewed!" What was this but a secular version of the call for complete renewal found in *Corinthians:* "Then comes the end ... when He has abolished all rule and all authority and power."

When the American Revolution was taking shape, this ambition to reshape human nature and the world was given great impetus by Thomas Paine, whose widely read works spelled out the basic principles of that revolution.[11]

Paine's ideal of the best society was rooted in his notion of human beings as he imagined them to have existed in a state of nature prior to living in political society: all born free, equal, uncorrupted by the envies of wealth or private property, and not yet enslaved by the oppressions of arbitrary government. In *Common Sense* he wrote: "We have it in our power to begin the world over again." As all are equal, and therefore equally worthy, all will thrive best in an egalitarian state created on rational principles in which there will be no aristocracy, privilege of birth, or political preference. All will enjoy the greatest freedom of choice consistent with the freedom of others, and all religious humbug, superstition, and outmoded social traditions and inequalities will give way to a new society created in the light of universal human reason, which Paine considered the sole reliable guide for remaking the world afresh.

Edmund Burke defended the American Revolution because he saw it for what it was: not a revolution, but a war of independence—a restorative campaign to regain venerable English rights and freedoms. But real, radical revolution in the form of total overthrow, and replacement by wholly fanciful abstract concepts, he resisted passionately and eloquently in his *Reflections on the Revolution in France*, perhaps the finest defense of conservative political and social ideals ever written. To the aims and ideals of Paine, the French radicals, and every radical renovator since, the true conservative has answered: "No." Your program is based on untruth, on a conception of human nature and human society that is false from the ground up. We are not born free and independent, as solitary, asocial individuals who then voluntarily create a society and a government by

---

11 A lucid recent treatment of the heated ideological warfare that was carried on during the American Revolutionary period, as expressed in the seminal writings of the revolutionist Thomas Paine and the antirevolutionist Edmund Burke, can be found in Yuval Levin's *The Great Debate: Edmund Burke, Thomas Paine, and the Birth of Right and Left.*

contract. On the contrary. We are born naked and hungry, as utterly vulnerable, physically and socially dependent creatures. We are deeply social animals by nature, and beginning with our own families, we grow up in a community of complex human relations that impose obligations and duties linking us to past, present, and future generations. Each of us begins life with a very different and particular hand of nature and nurture cards to be played as well as we can—a fixed genetic endowment unique to ourselves of varied and unequal natural capacities, strengths, and weaknesses—but within the natural limitations of a general human nature that is common to all. We all have a uniquely human moral and rational capacity, but it is only a *capacity*, not a guarantee of rationality or goodness. Although our lives are in a great many respects a product of nature (identical-twin studies illustrate this) and nurture (sociology illustrates this), we are also products of our own free will. But there is not now, and never has been, any such thing as a blank-slate human mind. To the conservative, that is fallacy and fantasy. Modern studies in what is called evolutionary psychology ("Ev Psych"), for all its weaknesses and "just-so" stories, have finally ended the liberal myth of the blank slate by demonstrating that the human mind—to use a popular metaphor—does not begin life empty. Rather, it is like a Swiss Army knife: it has a large variety of innate and fixed mental modules (of which the universal human capacity for language is the most obvious).

The fact that feral children who have survived for years in the wild outside human society always grow up as savage animals without any human language or social and moral skills is a clear and brutal remind-er of another key conservative thesis: without a law-abiding, morally ordered, thriving civil society there can be no free and equal individuals worth speaking about. For it is only in the bosom of family and a flour-ishing civil society that by force of long habit (some parents will say very long, indeed!) we eventually learn to conduct ourselves in such a way as to create and incorporate with our human nature a second, social and moral nature enabling us to live with others in a common human home. In this sense only the conservative and the liberal are of one mind: a sound environment is crucial. But it is the social and moral environment of the home that the conservative considers important, not the bricks and mortar—the "housing" and the "urban planning." That is why the con-servative will give priority to the fixed attributes of our common human nature as an orientation for policy, and then to the formative concrete rights, freedoms, and restraints of civil society, and only after that to the rights and freedoms of autonomous individuals, for the last can neither come into being nor survive without the former.

The key difference between the liberal and the conservative on the question of nurture, then, is that for the latter, whether learning or teaching, we must always operate within the dictates and constraints of what is natural as found flourishing in family, religion, tradition, and culture; and should never ignore, or denaturalize, or attempt to destroy what is naturally good for the sake of an abstract plan for egalitarian perfection. For the conservative it is the height of impudence to believe that others are simply blank slates on which to write our pet scenario for reforming the whole human race, as Plato suggested in his political fantasy, *The Republic*. A great philosopher he was, but (unless he was joking) he was also an enemy of all conservative, family-based civil societies, because among many other fantasies, he said "Our men and women ... should be forbidden by law to live together in separate households, and all the women should be common to all the men; similarly, children should be held in common, and no parent should know his child, or child his parent." In short, he wanted to raise children in a totalitarian way, in mixed-gender state dormitories, as public property of the state, thus to eradicate all their private and natural biological inclinations and differences. Plato's plan rested wholly on a belief in human malleability, and in this sense his was the first social and political program devised by a Western philosopher as a totalitarian revolt against nature, and human nature. But the conservative wants none of this, and so will argue that a child needs to be raised not by any perfecting state, but by a loving mother and father under the privacy, love, and authority of the family home, according to the natural biological, social, and moral sentiments and affections of a flourishing and free human society.

The orthodox Christian view that has shaped the West for two millennia is that we are fallen and sinful by nature. The orthodox conservative view is somewhat similar, if not always so strictly Christian: we are neither radically good nor bad by nature, but rather are by nature weak, flawed, fallible, and imperfect, if not intrinsically corrupt. Paine's view, and the modern liberal one still, is sourced in a vision of human nature as it was *before* the Fall, as described in the Garden of Eden. Burke's view, and the conservative one still, is sourced in a vision of human nature as it became *after* the Fall. And I dare say that anyone in a reflective mood may agree, on the evidence of history alone, that if the horrendous slaughters of human history are any indication, the Christian and conservative views seem a lot closer to the truth. G. K. Chesterton famously opined that the doctrine of original sin is the only Christian belief that does not require any proof.

As a general response to the liberal faith in a human nature of equality, original goodness, and human perfectibility, the conservative says: Nonsense. There is no such thing. Humans are equal in general, but very different in particular. We are not born good or bad, but capable of both good and evil, and are far from perfectible. Indeed, there are all sorts of dark, disturbing, and intractable psychological and existential realities of the human condition. We are our own worst enemies, as the saying goes; we all have our devils and our angels and must decide to follow what depraves, or what ennobles. Hence the importance of that deeply embedded second nature to guide us in life, and why in so many situations the conservative tends to give priority to the formative powers of civil society over the individual. The most important consideration for the conservative is not what some social theorist believes is making people *want* to do bad things (such as to steal, or to harm or kill others) but what *prevents* them from doing such things. As Burke warned so eloquently, "Society cannot exist unless a controlling power upon will and appetite be placed somewhere; and the less of it there is within, the more there must be without. It is ordained in the eternal constitution of things, that men of intemperate minds cannot be free. Their passions forge their fetters." Fortunately, for most of us, most of the time, the most powerful of the damaging possibilities latent in human nature are filtered, embargoed, controlled, directed, calmed, or rechanneled, and shaped as workable customs, good manners, traditions, shalls and shall-nots, and religious and moral beliefs and principles gifted to us by our predecessors.

The most important political consequence of the modern liberal concept of a malleable human nature is that it legitimizes social progressivism as an ideological imperative, though historically the sequence was probably the other way around. The modern political urge to perfect human society came first, and is likely a secularization of the original Christian longing for the Kingdom of Heaven. In an age of faith, the

Christian concept of a fixed human nature that is fallen and sinful blocked the rise of a worldly progressivism; perfection is only possible in the afterlife. With the dawn of the age of secularism, however, a kingdom of heaven on earth became the goal, and a narrative of human nature as malleable had to be constructed to make that possible. Human nature must be adjusted to policy objectives. Hence the idealistic optimism and rhetoric about change and hope for which liberals are so often faulted.

In contrast, the most important consequence of the conservative equation, which also operates like an ideological imperative, is that human nature is more fixed and permanent than malleable, so neither human beings nor their institutions, societies, or governments can ever be perfected. A fixed and imperfectible human nature dictates adjusting policy to human nature, rather than the other way around. Hence the resistance to change for which conservatives are so often faulted.

The liberal sequence:

> *blank slate > malleable human nature > equality >*
> *human nature must be adjusted by policy*

and the conservative sequence:

> *fixed attributes > nonmalleable human nature >*
> *differences > policy must be adjusted to human nature*

indicate that both sides of this divide operate on the basis of mutually exclusive human-nature equations.

WHERE DO YOU STAND?		
On Human Nature		
	MODERN LIBERAL VIEW vs.	CONSERVATIVE VIEW
What We Inherit	*Basic physical traits*	*Physical, social, and moral inheritance*
	Humans are born with common basic physical capacities only. Their other traits must be taught by the right educators, and not left to ignorance or tradition	Humans are born with common physical, social, and moral capacities and instincts, which further develop in a traditional society through family, religious, and social influence, to produce their second (civil) nature. Much but not all of what we are is hardwired
Good or Bad?	*Humans are good by nature*	*Humans are not good or bad by nature*
	We are born pure and good, but can be ruined by bad socialization, poor education, and poverty. Attention must be directed to changing and improving social and material conditions to bring out the goodness in people	We are naturally sociable and moral beings. The moral law is written on the heart, but we are free to follow it or not. Humans tend to be fallible, self-interested, and prone to error in the absence of moral restraints. Material conditions do not dictate morality
Perfectible?	*Humanity is perfectible*	*Human beings are not perfectible*
	Progressivism assumes perfectibility through good government. Individuals, governments, and nations are perfectible	Progressivism often destroys what is natural and good in the name of an ideal of perfection. Individuals, governments, and nations are not perfectible
The Mind	*It's a blank slate*	*It has multiple inherited capacities*
	Our mental nature begins as an empty receptacle to receive inputs from the environment. As adults, humans are rational calculators	The mind is structured from birth by many innate and complex fixed capacities. Humans are formed more by good habits, customs, and traditions than by calculation

WHERE DO YOU STAND?		
On Human Nature		
	MODERN LIBERAL VIEW vs.	CONSERVATIVE VIEW
Human Nature & Equality	*Humans are born equal*	*All individuals are born different and unequal*
	The fact that the mind is a blank slate means human differences are learned. The bad effects of inequalities can be reversed by affirmative-action policies and income equalization	In addition to their complex capacities, every human being has a unique genetic endowment that produces natural differences in skill, intelligence, insight, and character. "Show me the child, and I will show you the adult"
Reason & Emotion	*Reason overcomes unreason*	*Humans have a dual nature*
	Progressivism and social perfection depend utterly on rational planning. The perfect society can be decided and organized by planners and governments	Human existence is marked by a dual nature, a lifelong struggle between reason and the passions. Eternal questions about human purpose in the universe create lifelong existential tensions. Reason alone is an unreliable guide to goodness
Policy	*Policy shapes human nature*	*Human nature must guide policy*
	Because human nature is malleable, good policy can create good societies. Good concepts create the right experience	Because human nature is unchangeable, policy should be fitted to human nature. Experience trumps abstract concepts

CHAPTER 7

On Reason

It is a bit shocking to hear anyone say they are suspicious of reason, for we are used to thinking it is the best way to the truth. So how could reason be a bad thing? It depends on the meaning of the word, and as it happens, there are at least four kinds or "reason" that most of us recognize.

Practical reason is thinking we rely on to make sense of everyday matters. We all know we may say "the car hit the bridge," but that it makes no sense to say "the bridge hit the car." Or we reason that John is older than Bill, because the former is the father of the latter, and a son cannot be older than his father, and so on. Liberals and conservatives do not disagree on the uses of practical reason.

Natural reason is thinking that is based on our understanding of the natural physical world, and for many, also of natural moral law (do good, avoid evil, and so on). Modern physics, mathematics, and many other sciences reveal lots of nature's profound and fixed laws, just as philosophy and theology reveal many universal understandings of the natural moral law. Liberals and conservatives mainly agree on scientific uses of reason, but tend to disagree on the existence and importance of natural moral law.

Logical modes of reasoning have to do with ideas such as the law of noncontradiction (something cannot be true and false at the same time and in the same way), with logical propositions and methods such as the syllogism, with deductive and inductive modes of analysis, and so on. This is the basis of all analytical thinking, and political differences do not usually enter into it unless logic is being used as a tool of reason to attack customs, cultural mythologies, traditions, and moral habits that have been precious to a community.

Utopian reasoning is another matter. Some have called this "dream-land" reasoning, because it is the kind that the pure rationalist, the liberal progressive, and the revolutionary all rely on to fashion their political dreamlands of the future, their kingdom of heaven on earth. We can also think of it as *fantasy* reasoning, because it springs solely from the imagination, with no basis in human experience or reality. This is the main form of reason that upsets the conservative. Its sole purpose is to use principles of practical and logical reason to undermine or overthrow what is reasonably good in the present, in the name of an imagined dream-land society of the future that has never existed before. The conservative complaint is that to destroy what exists and works tolerably well (given human imperfection) in the name of an untested dream of perfection is to play God with other people's lives. Seen from this perspective, the entire secular humanist dream can fairly be accused of an arrogant deification of Man. Insufferably arrogant, actually, and often insufferably cruel as well, for it usually leads like the iron rails of an ideological train to the gallows (because by definition, all that is not perfect becomes the enemy of the perfect, and so must be eliminated ... along with the ideologically imperfect people standing in the way).

This arrogance extends to the equation of reason with technology and modern science, too. The liberal defense of science is that it is a tech-nological extension of reason, and so must be recruited to construct the good life (which for the liberal is purely a utilitarian concept: the greatest happiness of the greatest number—a standard that, to the conservative, could apply to a herd of cattle). The pure rationalist does not believe that anything is valuable just because it exists. For this person, all that exists must pass muster at the bench of Reason in order to have value. But the conservative takes the opposite approach: that a thing exists, especially if it has existed and been loved for a very long time, suggests that a lot of wise predecessor human souls have considered it of value, and worth a vigorous defense.

The conservative complaint about the combination of reason and science is that science can tell us the *what* and the *how* of things, but never the *why* of anything. It never will, nor ever could. From this perspective, the very best science in the world is utterly dumb. And because mankind has not yet learned how to separate the goods of science (medical cures, etc.) from its evils (efficient death camps; hydrogen bombs; partial-birth abortions; its hysterical focus on doing, having, and achieving to the detriment of being; etc.), science must be kept under moral and cultural watch to protect civilization from barbarism (already here, many conservatives would say). Finally, the deepest conservative complaint about reason in the guise of science is that it has assumed the vanguard in the modern process of subjugating nature, and human nature, to human will. Indeed, as I have suggested, the story of the modern West is in many respects about the triumph of the will over nature, by force (as witnessed in all totalitarian systems for controlling, equalizing, and killing), or, as in our age of libertarian socialism, by technology (the pill, abortion, euthanasia, genetics, in vitro conceptions, transgendering, etc). This topic will be examined more closely in part 3.

The most common conception of reason for most of the history of the West has been reason-as-*meaning.* The ancients considered it obvious that we live in a cosmos ruled by universal Reason (capital R), expressed in the perpetual laws of nature that govern the creation, transformation, and corruption of all material things, all human beings, and all societies, in everlasting cycles. The universe is eternal and has always been here; history is like a wheel that keeps turning in place, *without going anywhere,* so the future can be predicted by insightful historians based on the past facts of human life. They would also have said that because human beings can understand and decipher this ordering of nature and reproduce its operations in precise mathematical symbols, theorems, and equations, we somehow share, or "participate," in the Reason of the universe.

That is why Aristotle described us as "rational animals," by which he did not mean we are always reasoning properly or logically, or in keeping with the Reason of nature as he thought we should, but that all normal humans have an innate *capacity* to do so. And so it followed, because we are also "political animals," that the goal of human life and of government ought to be human flourishing according to "right Reason" that follows nature for the common good. This very conservative guide became the foundation of the long natural-law tradition of the West.

As we saw in part 1, the rise in the prestige of reason as a tool for getting at the truth, along with successful scientific methodologies, coincided with the clamor of the European masses for more freedom from religious and political control, and for more democracy as the will of the people. Moral, religious, and social tradition and custom, they began to argue, are just as misleading as the senses, and stand in the way of human perfectibility.

At bottom, this was a sign of the slow conversion of Judeo-Christian civilization from its original basis, promising a kingdom of heaven to come, to its present basis of promising a kingdom of heaven here on earth. This is the "concealed religion," as Hume called it, under which we now live, and almost every influential social and political thinker of the past two and a half centuries—Condorcet, Voltaire, Godwin, Comte, Hegel, Marx, Bentham, Mill, Rawls, and many others—has been a lay priest of this secular religion. This is the root of modern progressivism, liberalism, and socialism, of the underlying notion that all human history is moving forward, not spiritually, but materially and politically, to an eventual state of equality and social perfection. In this modern view, history is a wheel that is not only turning, as it did in the ancient conception, but that is also *moving forward as it turns*. The influential English liberal William Godwin summed up this burning faith in rationalism this way: "There must in the nature of things be *one best form of government*, which *all intellects*, sufficiently roused from the slumber of *savage ignorance*, will be *irresistibly incited* to approve." This utterance contains all the earmarks of theological language: perfection ("one best form"), universality ("all intellects"), and faith ("irresistibly incited"). Words we hear tumbling so easily from the mouths of our politicians today, such as "hope" and "change," are just dumbed-down modern tokens for the original spiritual expectations once captured in words like "revelation" and "salvation."

This new confidence in the superiority and validity of abstract concepts in the mind over lived experience on the ground soon found its way into political writings, and spawned new kinds of constitutions, charters, and declarations aiming at a standardized political and social condition of perfection. Which is to say, they were paper mandates for the conversion of previously rule-based states into outcome-directed states. Directed, that is, by radicals who saw themselves as possessed of a superior knowledge authorizing them to create a new, more perfect and "progressive" world by means of reason and their own imaginations.

The conviction was that because man is truly malleable, and hence perfectible (a core liberal belief), all we need to do is outline rational goals clearly and distinctly in a document, and use this as a guide to the perfect society. They did just that. The French Declaration of the Rights of Man and of the Citizen of 1789 rested upon three words at the time considered the most uplifting, rational, and desirable of all: "liberty, equality, fraternity." These three words may still be found carved in stone over many French doorways and monuments. But somehow they became words that legitimized the slaughter by radicals of thousands of citizens during the Terror of the French Revolution.

Among the many horrors of this first democratic revolution aiming at a reasoned human perfection was "the revolutionary marriage." French revolutionaries rounded up many hundreds of dissenters whom they had labeled enemies of revolutionary reason, forced them at gunpoint onto a barge in the river Seine, stripped off their clothing and tied them together, face to face, stark naked, and ... sank the barge. In the name of liberty, equality, and fraternity, unspeakable atrocities of rape, torture, slaughter, and dismemberment of citizens were committed. Such were the first modern and terrifying consequences of thinking about reason and democracy as tools for human perfection. Almost every technique of killing and mass slaughter later used by national socialists (Nazis) and international socialists (Communists) was tried first by the French in their ideological defense of totalitarian democracy.

At the height of this rationalist enthusiasm—during the phase of the "de-Christianization" of France—a huge papier mâché statue of the "Goddess of Reason" was erected in Notre Dame Cathedral in place of the Christian altar, and hundreds of candle-bearing, toga-clad devotees of reason performed faux-sacramental ceremonies in her honor. One of the main themes of this book, however, is that there is a deep difference between reason as technique and wisdom as insight, and an example was the poisonous sacralization of those three revolutionary words. No one at the time was wise enough to understand that fraternity, when proposed as a consequence of the first two words, can never be achieved, because liberty and forced equality cancel each other out: as one rises, the other must fall (as discussed later in *On Equality and Inequality*). In short, the most rational formula the French revolutionaries could imagine for social perfection was in its very wording self-destructive.

Few realized then that abstract general terms by their very nature can never be self-interpreting. All high-sounding but unqualified words and concepts, in the absence of any attached experiential meaning (that is, when not limited and defined by customary meaning, examples, cases, and traditions), are just free-floating empty vessels that will eventually have to be filled with *someone's* meaning in order to be of any use in constructing the perfect society. To see how this works, imagine asking a friend: "When you go out, could you please buy me a chair?" The friend would need immediately to ask: "What *kind* of chair?" Just so, anyone seeing abstract general terms like "equality" or "freedom" in a new constitution would have to ask: "What *kind* of equality? What *kind* of freedom?" History has written in blood that the particular meanings—the qualifying adjectives and adverbs—ascribed to general abstract nouns and verbs as found in this sort of constitution are always those preferred by whichever people—revolutionaries, social engineers, radical judges, and the like—manage to capture, or are granted the legal right to supply, the missing meanings of the terms. The conclusion? Once states move from a rule-based status (here are the rules, folks; you people play the game, we'll only officiate) to an outcome-directed status (all must be steered to the outcome desired by those in charge), there is *no such thing as an innocent constitution*. When the refs without warning start kicking the ball arbitrarily into the net of their choice, oligarchy reigns.

This adoption of reason as a weapon of progressivism and its use to construct paper codes for human perfection was a revolutionary departure from conservative-style constitutions rooted in inherited tradition, precedent, and common law as derived from concrete human experience. And it seems clear that this new, abstract type of constitution, based not on how people *do* live, but instead on dreamland ideals concerning how people *ought* to live, behave, and be treated, goes hand in glove with the liberal malleability conception of human nature described earlier. Pure reason joined with science and technology soon became the go-to standard for this project. Once fired up with the prospect of social perfection, all custom and tradition, all settled moral opinion, and especially all religious belief in a higher moral law that might stand in the way of the progressive will of planners and the state became enemy ideas that reason and science were now obliged to characterize as ignorance, and so to purge and destroy.

As it happened, many of the key philosophers in the recent Western tradition who championed this belief in abstract charters as interpretable instruments of reason that could be used to convert rule-based states into outcome-directed ones were French. Descartes was the granddaddy of pure reason, and he influenced many later rationalists such as Henri de Saint-Simon and Auguste Comte, thinkers who in turn had an immense influence on the Anglo-Saxon world. For example, John Stuart Mill, whose work continues to have an inordinate influence on liberal intellectuals everywhere, was a devotee of Comte's "religion of humanity" (which Comte described as his "social physics") and a man we may consider the first true libertarian socialist.[12]

Another prominent and more recent admirer of French rationalism was Canada's former prime minister Pierre Trudeau, whose lifelong motto was "reason before passion." Those words were embroidered into a wall hanging displayed in his home all his adult life, and they were emblematic of his contempt for what he considered all irrational (not rationally organized) societies in the English mode, for the "piecemeal" (not rationally consistent) outcomes of parliamentary legislation, and for eccentric precedent-based common law (rather than uniform French-style code law) that Anglo-Saxon nations have relied upon for centuries. Nothing irks a rationalist more than to see a law in favor of something like gay marriage or abortion in one part of a nation, and a law against these same things in another. It was Voltaire, the master rationalist of all time, who mocked English common law by saying that when traveling in England, "you change the law as often as you change horses!" In this context we can understand why, to the modern liberal mind, the true conservative who not only accepts such inconsistencies and logical irregularities but—even more galling to the rationalist—may actually delight in them will always be viewed as blocking the way to a more rational world. In this vein, I always get a particular pleasure from the looks on the faces of my liberal friends who complain about the inefficiency of government.

---

12 See William D. Gairdner, "Poetry and the Mystique of the Self in John Stuart Mill: Sources of Libertarian Socialism," in *Humanitas*, Vol. XXI., Nos 1 & 2, 2008.

I say, "Be grateful. Government agencies are already everywhere in your life; just imagine how they would haunt you if they were efficient!"

So this is another Great Divide because the true conservative, who easily understands the proper uses of practical reason, rejects utterly the modern idolatry of abstract reason when used as an instrument to destroy reliable, enjoyable, and yes, even eccentric traditions. He immediately agrees with Pascal's wise observation that "the heart has reasons, which reason cannot know." Why? Because although we all have the potential for practical reason, human life and action are typically, deeply, and forever rooted in crosscurrents of conflicting emotions, passions, appetites, impulses, and odd beliefs that are kept in check only by the cultivation of a higher self, and the customary restraints of civilization—none of which will ever appear reasonable to a zealous reformer who believes that the unrestrained rational will ought to rule in all things. Pascal also observed that the problem is not reason itself, but the reluctance of fanatical reasoners to acknowledge any other form of knowledge.

So the ordinary reason beloved by everyone ("the reason I want to help you is because I care for you") must always be distinguished from the utopian reasoning favored by dreamlanders. Just as the liberal who has already committed to the malleability of human nature, and therefore has rejected all tradition and custom as guides, *must* therefore cling to reason as the instrument of choice for his planned social renovation, the conservative, who believes so much of human nature is indelible—is in fact a predictable and unchangeable nature, and therefore our compass—*must* be suspicious of reasoning relied upon to change that nature. For to subordinate the deepest springs and motives of humanity—all that is natural to the human being, and all custom, tradition, and moral authority—to a plan of some radical thinker's personal imagination—whether Thomas More's *Utopia*, John Stuart Mill's *On Liberty*, Karl Marx's *Communist Manifesto*, or Jeremy Bentham's theory of utilitarianism—is to decide the outcome of human life according to fantasy reasoning that ignores *in principle* all deep-rooted human instincts, customs, loyalties, and affections, and so is plainly doomed to failure. We can see that the planted axioms of the liberal and the conservative, with respect to reason, are incompatible.

The conservative does agree with Aristotle that the human capacity for reasoning is the central distinguishing aspect of our existence, and that there is reason at work in the universe, in nature, and human nature. He also agrees with Descartes that reason as a pure analytical skill can be detached from these larger implications and used simply as an instrument of analysis in the *physical* world of sciences, mathematics, and the like. But he insists this is not so of the *human* world in which we live directly and existentially, sensuously, passionately, in the full agony and ecstasy of our most meaningful experiences and relations. For reason considered as an instrument will generally ruin this experience. A good analogy would be the attempt to analyze a poem or a piano concerto. Such arts are unmediated experiences that touch us directly and deeply as a kind of soul food, without first going through the analytical brain. When we attempt to analyze them by breaking them into a hundred rational parts, we all too often find that the art in its original reality and power can never be put back together, and we grieve that the experience "as it first was" has been lost to us, perhaps forever. That's why, although great novelists have often written great literary criticism, great literary critics are seldom able to write great novels. By the same token, reason considered as a mere tool and applied to the analysis of myth, deep symbols, and religious sacraments, or to social and moral custom and authority, has a latent capacity to destroy utterly such practices, along with their deep cultural and moral significance. That is why Martin Luther famously referred to "the whore Reason" as the devil's handmaiden. He didn't oppose learning or intellect. His problem was the arrogance of autonomous reason, which assumes that reason alone possesses the key to truth. The English poet William Wordsworth also took aim at the damage done to the richness of human experience when it is analyzed by mere reason when he wrote, "Our meddling intellect Mis-shapes the beauteous forms of things: We murder to dissect." Well, he meant we have to murder the richness of human experience in order to serve it up in dead analytical parts.

The teaching of the ancients was that reason should be used to help citizens pursue the common good, rather than as a weapon to attack and dissolve their ideals and practices, many of which, though loved and revered as wise and workable, would never be considered logical. Accordingly, philosophers who taught the young the tricks of logic in order to attack their own society would be ostracized or, like Socrates, condemned to death. Who has not heard their own children protest that something they have been told to do is not reasonable? "But why? But why?" comes the persistent demand. Typically, the parent enters into a lengthy dissertation on reasons the child is too young to comprehend, and finally, exasperated by the whining and blank looks received, says "There is no reason. It's just the way we have always done things in this family, because it works. So get on with it!"

So in sum, and in stark contrast to the liberal, the conservative will argue that *detached reason* as a mere technique is neither good nor bad. Its utility depends on what it is used for, or against. Another way to say this is that reason is like fire. You can use it for something good like cooking your dinner or warming your hands, or for something evil like burning down your neighbor's home. G. K. Chesterton put the modern instrumental conception of reason in a memorable frame when he said that a crazy person is someone who has lost everything *except* their reason. Now that was a head-scratching thing to say, and it doesn't make sense until we realize that what he meant was that a sociopath, for example, may still know the *instrumental* value of reason, such as 2 + 2 = 4, or he may know enough not to walk in front of a speeding car. Indeed, such a person often has a very calculating mind and knows all the tricks of reason better than most, which is why he can deceive so well. But he has lost all his *habitus*, or second nature, the crucial complex of self-restraint, shared moral sense, respect for truth, compassion, and good manners, and uses reason to dismiss those very things.

Here is a repugnant example of how the misuse of strict logic can lead us astray morally. A grown son, inebriated by logical concepts, tells his father he wants to have sex with his grandmother. The father is shocked and mortified. "What? How dare you say such a thing?" To which the son replies: "It's only logical and fair: you had sex with my mother, so I want to have sex with yours." This son has lost everything *except* the ability to make a logical equation that serves his personal will. It is the seduction of the logic of equality that enables his attack on custom, morality, and natural biology. If you think logic is the superior value, you will side with the son; or you will admit it is not superior, and side with the traditional wisdom and teaching of the father.

Another example of the misuse of reason was given in a definition of the logical syllogism by Ambrose Bierce in his *Devil's Dictionary*:

Major Premise: Sixty men can do a piece of work sixty times as
quickly as one man.

Minor Premise: One man can dig a posthole in sixty seconds;
therefore—

Conclusion: Sixty men can dig a posthole in one second.

What I am leading up to is that for a conservative, while the capacity
to reason is potentially a great and unique human tool, it is only half the
story. For as mentioned, human beings suffer from a disabling dualism.
Even though we are indeed reasoning animals, we are also forever bur-
dened with an inner spiritual, moral, and intellectual warfare between
passion and reason that cannot be escaped. Which is only to say that
what we must beware is not reason, but wrong reason—reason unchecked
by self-restraint, by a standard of good, and by a sense of the higher self
to which we ought to aspire. We are, as Pascal emphasized, creatures
so shot through with contradiction and ambivalence that mere logic is
helpless to grasp our true nature. In his *Pensées* he wrote, "What kind of
freak is man! What a novelty he is, how absurd he is, how chaotic and
what a mass of contradictions—and yet what a prodigy! He is judge of
all things, yet a feeble worm. He is a repository of truth, and yet sinks
into such doubt and error. He is the glory and the scum of the universe."

WHERE DO YOU STAND?		
On Reason		
	MODERN LIBERAL VIEW vs.	CONSERVATIVE VIEW
Kinds of Reason	*Pure reason is one and absolute*	*There are many kinds of reason*
	Reason and science are the most logical and reliable instruments for social perfection and for changing human nature. Social and moral customs must be changed or eliminated if they contradict logic	Practical reason is good for practical things and for sciences. But speculative reason can destroy the social and moral good, which can be good without being logical. There are many forms of knowing: intuitive, imaginative, customary, religious, cultural. To believe that a desiccated logic is superior to the inspired penetration of insight is a form of gross egotism, for insight is "wisdom above reflection"

WHERE DO YOU STAND?		
On Reason		
	MODERN LIBERAL VIEW	vs.	CONSERVATIVE VIEW
Quality of Reason	*Reason is good in itself*	*Reason is neutral*
	Reason used logically will always point to the best scientific, moral, and political solutions. What is not clearly and immediately reasonable should be dismissed	Reason is a tool, and that is why we must distinguish its good from its bad uses. The good is a value independent of reason. It may be discovered by reason; it cannot be created by reason alone
Rational Charters	*Constitutions must be rational*	*Constitutions are not self-interpreting*
	Rational concepts, correctly worded, serve as guides to progress. A constitution must be constructed by means of clear and universal abstract concepts that apply equally to all human beings. Politics should always be adjusted to reason	Abstract words in charters, etc., must be interpreted by someone, and so as words cannot be relied upon to preserve the good. The constitutions of the French Revolution and the Soviet Union, for example, were noble-sounding documents used to justify atrocities. A constitution is a construction of history, ancestry, ethnic habit, particular culture, religion, national character, and mores; it is not an a priori construction of abstract concepts, an invention of the moment aiming for a social condition never before seen. Politics should always be adjusted to human nature rather than to reason
Reason & Tradition	*Reason before tradition or custom*	*Reason is irrelevant to tradition and custom*
	Reliance on reason is the only enlightened standard for deciding policy. All customs and traditions rooted in emotion, religion, or folk ways must be replaced with rational policies	Techniques of reason work well for analytical matters, facts, and causes for what is visible and measureable, but not so well for things less apparent or visible, such as cultural systems, faiths, and tradition, most of which have deep subconscious roots

WHERE DO YOU STAND?		
On Reason		
	MODERN LIBERAL VIEW VS.	CONSERVATIVE VIEW
Reason & Morality	*Morality must be reasoned* Individuals and children can learn and practice morality by means of reason. No moral injunction should have authority unless it can be justified by reason and is consciously chosen by a rational person. Right actions, if not chosen according to a rational rule of right conduct, are not moral	*Rationalism can dissolve morality* Reason applied as a test of morality leads to skepticism, and then to nihilism. Human kindness and benevolence are justified by love and sympathy, not by reason. The modern rationalist is an enemy of authority unless that authority meets the test of reason. But no society can possibly cohere for long if every citizen must on every occasion approve all moral and social authority according to a personal standard of reason
Reason & Planning	*The best system will be rational* Rational planning produces rational societies anywhere it is applied. There can only be one best solution for a problem, no matter where it occurs, because reason is universal (anti-local)	*Reason can create totalitarian systems* Reason has too often been used to defend rational totalitarian systems. The main logical device relied upon is that the end (a perfect and rational society) justifies the means (force and violence). There should be local solutions to local problems (localism)
Reason & Human Nature	*Humans are rational animals* Rational social engineering must be used to change human nature. When the causes of irrationalism are eventually removed for good, natural reason will reign, because truth is universal, and so must govern all things. Reason points the way to human well-being for all	*Humans have a rational capacity only* Reason is a human capacity only. Its use must be directed to the good and restrained from the bad by our second (civil) nature, which is learned from family, religion, and community. The modern worship of reason is like a new Puritanism seeking dominion in the name of personal will. Such a society ends in the worship of economic utility, hedonism, and moral relativism

WHERE DO YOU STAND?			
On Reason			
	MODERN LIBERAL VIEW	vs.	CONSERVATIVE VIEW
Some Key Words Compared	Intellect	vs.	Insight
	Measurement	vs.	Penetration
	Analysis	vs.	Intuition
	Prose	vs.	Poetry
	Clarity	vs.	Vitality
	Deduction	vs.	Imagination
	Proof	vs.	Belief
Reason & Part/ Whole Reality	*Analysis of parts equals the whole*		*The whole is more than the sum of parts*
	Progress is only possible by the breakdown of wholes into analyzable parts to which solutions are then applied. Reason is a technique of analysis *external* to the object analyzed. The logical reasoner is speaking from outside the object of thought, as an *observer*		Reason works well for analyzing objects, but seldom for subjective beings. Human societies generate emergent properties and relations that are more than the sum of the parts. They sustain themselves through an *internal* knowledge and belief that is destroyed when broken into its constituent parts. Valued customs, morals, and traditions are a kind of blind and *intuitive* reasoning that can be destroyed by logical reasoning. The intuitive reasoner is speaking from inside the object of thought, as a vital *participant*

CHAPTER 8

On Democracy

The word *democracy* is formed from two Greek words—*demos* (the common people) and *kratos* (power)—and so means "people power." But in ancient Athens, where it all began, it meant only the power of adult male citizens who had completed their military service, and not females, or slaves of either sex, or foreigners. Only about 15 to 20 percent of the adult population was considered "the people," so this was not a democracy in the sense of the word as used today. It was more like a government directed by a minority of privileged males, made possible only by the existence of pervasive slavery (which alone gave "the people" the leisure to participate fully in democracy).

This designated group gathered regularly on the Pnyx hill in Athens, in assemblies of up to six thousand, to debate, drink, and vote. In our day we believe that in a democracy, the people ought to initiate the laws and send them *up* to their government to execute. But that was not always the case in Athens, where the Council, a body like a senate, would not only set a strict agenda for every meeting of the people's Assembly, limiting what could be discussed, but in many cases would pass *down* laws or decrees for approval or rejection, with no debate allowed. Another interesting feature of the Greek system was that any citizen could propose a law. But as a protection against radicalism, anyone who proposed a law that was afterward shown to have harmed the Athenian people could be tried and punished severely. Estimates are that only about half the laws passed were proposed by citizens in the Assembly. Demosthenes praised the Lokrians of central Greece because they did not change a law for two hundred years. Lokrians had a habit of placing a rope around the neck of the proposer of a new law; if it was voted down, the rope would go up. That stopped most political dreamlanders in their tracks.

If you ever go to the Pnyx (the taxi drivers pronounce it *puh-neeka*), don't miss the opportunity to have your own Periclean moment by standing on the same rock slab on which the great orators of Greece held forth. After a hard rain, it is still possible to find lots of 2,500-year-old clay shards from ancient Greek drinking cups mixed in with the freshly overturned earth.

Although medieval and Renaissance societies and religious groups and towns since ancient times have practiced various forms of qualified democracy, each in its own way, our modern democracy began as an unexpected child of the sixteenth-century Protestant Reformation, and had little to do with the ancient Greek model. Because of the invention of the printing press, the Bible had become increasingly available to ordinary people, who were finally able to access the word of God straight from scripture, without need of church intermediaries. Believers were getting the truth directly or indirectly from God himself. It did not take long for a widespread Protestant self-sacralization to take hold—the conviction of many evangelicals that to feel the divine spark within meant the believer is sacred, too. It did not take long for that feeling to spread to the notion that "the will of the people is the will of God" (*Vox populi vox Dei*).

Nor did it take long for Protestants to discover that, although they were unified in protest against the slackness and corruptions of the church, they were not united as to how to interpret the word of God. So they ended up protesting against each other, as well. The unexpected consequence was a multiplication of sects, each claiming its own absolute higher truth, and this in turn produced a more general religious individualism and political toleration (believe what you want, but leave my belief alone).

At roughly the same point in history secularism and scientism were on the rise throughout Europe, and so eventually what began as a call for the right of *spiritual* individualism became a call for a right of *political* individualism as well—which is to say, for a right of democratic self-expression. This mixture of personal religious and political conviction characterized the entire course of the English Civil Wars of 1642–1651. This was also the time of the first settling of what would become the United States and Canada, and the political truth that interested most of the colonists of those two nations may be viewed as the combination of a *culture* and a *method*.

The *cultural* aspect, which was distilled from the early stages of liberalism described in part 1, became what we retroactively call classical liberalism. It was mainly devoted to features that classical liberals still support, such as self-reliance and freedom from arbitrary government, so-called natural rights (still today deemed to be intrinsic, like the word of God), consent of the governed, and so on. But it was also rooted in a number of ideals we would today call conservative, or liberal conservative, such as the equal value of all persons before God and the law (these early liberals, as we saw, vigorously rejected the modern liberal idea that governments ought to make people equal in the outcomes of their lives); the concept of individuals as free and responsible moral agents responsible for the outcomes of their own lives; a demand that governments stay out of private religious life; and so on. Most of these ideals as modern secular principles are easily sourced in the core values of the Christian religion, all were ideals the founders of the New World wanted to conserve, and they were important in European life long before the methods of modern democracy got worked out.

The *method* aspect related to the development of various democratic systems that were attempted, modified, and preserved over the centuries in order to manage the legal allocation of the power of some over others. In the United States this system ended up as a unique federal republican system. In Canada it ended up as a unique federal constitutional monarchy combined with a Westminster parliamentary system. Meanwhile, every European nation evolved its own particular method, from similar cultural roots, for including a democratic element in government.

A key point is that although the original (and, as I say, rather conservative) liberal culture of the West and the democratic method are now joined, if not cemented in everyone's mind, the culture was practiced, enjoyed, and deeply rooted long before the democratic method took hold. And in terms of the effect of the method on the culture, the result, as I have suggested at many places in this book, has not been very good. Indeed, many are surprised to learn that the citizens of the Western democracies today, in terms of levels of total taxation and the regulation of commercial and private life and property, have far fewer political, economic, and property freedoms than our ancestors had prior to the onset of democracy.

There is only one exception to this fact of our history (as explained in part 1), and that has to do with the extraordinary expansion of our bodily and sexual freedoms, of which we now have far more. As argued in this book, this was the tacit trade-off or deal with the people that all modern democratic regimes settled upon as a means to rationalize the internal contradiction of modern democracy: the fact that liberty and forced equality cannot be sustained in a single democratic system without a splitting of the political domain into a private and a public body.

Anyone who bothers to look back from our own freedom and democracy-boosting age will be surprised to learn that for most of history, democracy has had a very bad name. Among the things that bothered our more conservative ancestors were certain bald facts, among them the concern that there are essential truths in the universe by which all should strive to live that cannot be discovered or decided by a popular vote, no matter how large. Another concern was that in a democracy, equality gradually tends to displace liberty, even though everyone knows that other than before God and the law, there is no equality of any kind among people or things (see *On Equality and Inequality*). Even worse, democracy as a tally of the majority opinion equates what is right with numbers, the masses, power, and brute force. But it does not in any way whatsoever indicate the right or the good in itself. A further confusion is that it pretends to rest on a theory of consent to the laws by the people, who are thereby said to rule themselves. But how is that really possible? Are individuals to be bound only by laws they like, and not by laws they dislike? Even if we argue that there is indirect, implied, or tacit consent of the people, there is never unanimity. So either many of the people (sometimes less than half, if there is a minority government) must submit unwillingly to laws to which they have never consented, or they must coerce themselves to obey, which is not only impossible, but the farthest thing from consent. No political scientist, left or right, denies that in all political systems public ignorance seems to be the rule, and that the most troubling truth for a democracy is that the vote of a fool will always cancel the vote of a wise person.

For these reasons and more, the story of democracy has not always been encouraging. Educated Europeans and the leaders of the British colonies in North America were well aware of the theory of *anacyclosis* made famous by the ancient historian Polybius, according to which political systems seem destined to evolve from anarchy to monarchy, monarchy to tyranny, tyranny to aristocracy, aristocracy to oligarchy, and oligarchy to democracy, which then degenerates to mob rule and back to anarchy, and around again in a cycle. Their main concern was that when the idea that "the voice of the people is the voice of God" becomes deeply implanted, it can ignite a spontaneous and dangerous antiauthoritarian mood.

A bizarre case of such democracy mania occurred during the English Civil Wars when the egalitarian-minded soldiers in Cromwell's army demanded that the generals take their orders ... from the troops! What? One modern historian correctly described this as "the world turned upside down." Another interesting case was raised just prior to the American Revolution, when aggrieved colonists who were demanding freedom from arbitrary government argued they had a set of real and *inherited* English rights rooted in the ancient Anglo-Saxon constitution that long preceded democracy, rights that could not be altered by, nor submitted to, the democratic will of the British Parliament. They were attempting to resist the tyrannies of their own democratically elected British Parliament by appealing plaintively for help from the king of England, on the grounds that they were subjects of the king, and *not* of "the people."

Almost the moment the colonists became independent, however, "democracy" became their rallying cry, as mobs in various of the newly minted thirteen states immediately began voting to abolish their appointed senates, which they deemed impediments to the will of the people. Farmers shouting "usury!" demanded the abolition of personal debts. Some of the thirteen states began minting their own money; others raised armies and navies in preparation for war on each other. Many voted to abolish not only their senates, but also their elected legislatures, preferring to live isolated within their villages as town-hall democracies.

The bitterest European case of democratic theory run fanatically amok was the complete overthrow (rather than gradual reform) of an entire established society and political system during the French Revolution. This was the first full-fledged case of totalitarian democracy, during which the whole world watched the glorious "Rights of Man and of the Citizen" rise, and then fall, under the blade of *la guillotine.*

Only half a century later, while shaping their Constitution Act of 1867, the Canadians, still conscious of the French democratic implosion, found themselves looking directly south at their American neighbors, who were engaged in one of the worst fratricides of all time in the name of republican democracy. The Canadians were determined not to make the same mistakes. If an element of democracy was to be allowed, "the people" would need protection ... *from themselves!* Among other measures, this was to be ensured by a constitution barring excessive central government intrusion into specified local matters—a provision gradually eroded, and then abruptly reversed, with the advent of Canada's Charter of Rights and Freedoms of 1982, which specifically opened the way to a regime change in the direction of libertarian socialism.

A more recent (if much tamer) example of the theory of radical democracy being used to protect the people against their own democratically elected government was the efforts of the Reform Party of Canada in the 1990s. Almost all the members of that party were socially and fiscally *very* conservative, many of rural and Christian stock, and so, we might think, would not normally choose a radical democratic strategy. But they were so frustrated and disgusted by decades of wasteful government spending and by libertine social and moral policy innovations that they opted for direct democracy as the only tool available to restore what had been lost. Like those first American colonists, they were seeking to restore Canada's traditional unwritten constitution, which they considered to have been betrayed by their Parliament and judges.

Switzerland is an example of an entire nation that is deeply conservative, and yet has for more than a century and a half managed to remain so by using the tools of radical democracy—recall, the referendum, and citizen initiatives—to block radical policies and ensure local citizen control of taxation and law. America's current Tea Party movement is a similar town-hall initiative urging the use of radical democratic tools to stop a galloping US regime change initiated by President Obama in the direction of more statism. These methods of democratic radicalism can work well to preserve a conservative culture and repel big government as long as the majority cling to their original values of self-reliance and self-discipline. But once the nation mutates into a tripartite state (wherein the majority of the people is a combination of those who work for government and those dependent on it), the culture will shift to a statist mind-set, and then *democracy will create big government as rapidly as any totalitarian system*—if without the bloodshed.

Although the foregoing cases suggest that democracy has had a very bumpy ride in the history of the West, nothing in that history has prepared us for the possibility that democracy would mutate into a system that would *systematically undermine itself.* How has this happened?

The older *corporate* democracies (most Western nations until about the middle of the twentieth century) steered themselves by way of shared and enduring principles that were respected as a unifying common good. In part I, "The Things No One Doubted" gave a sense of this unity. But an *aggregate* democracy is very different. It is steered (if this can be called steering) more by the blind outcome of individual wills in a vote. This may be described as a "hyper-democracy" because it imagines sovereignty to be vested in the separate wills of autonomous individuals—millions of them. But if a pie is cut in a thousand pieces, where is the pie? And if the *demos*, or people, are individuated, or atomized into millions of separate individuals who have little to do with each other—where are "the people"? Surely there is a difference between a mass of individuals who tacitly agree that the common ideals and relations between them constitute their corporate unity (making them a people) and an aggregate, a collection of disparate individuals each of whom believes that the ultimate sovereignty lies not in any relations between them, but in each autonomous individual alone.

In our tradition, as previously explored, John Locke and John Stuart Mill have been the chief theorists of individual rights and freedoms (though Mill ended up as a confessed socialist), and David Hume and Edmund Burke the most influential defenders of what I have called social rights and freedoms. For the former two gentlemen (and for modern libertarians who carry their torch), individual rights and freedoms are generally held prior in importance to social rights and freedoms. For Hume and Burke, however, while fundamental individual freedoms are highly valued, the emphasis is reversed. The inherited customs, rights, and traditions constituting what Hume called "common life," and what Burke and most conservatives would describe as a voluntarily sustained and flourishing civil society—which they saw as the most effective buffer to protect individuals from arbitrary state power—are considered to have a real substance or existence that is more than the sum of its parts. The difference to be illuminated here may be captured in the contrast between a ship wandering aimlessly at sea because the passengers are only interested in living their own lives and a ship on which all have a shared idea of where and how they ought to go, and arrange to steer the ship accordingly. The latter requires at least tacit agreement as to common ends. The gist of this book is that this is precisely what we no longer have.

The danger to people living under the hyper-democratic or individual-sovereignty ideal is powerfully summed up (to continue the maritime metaphor) in the story about passengers lost at sea in a crowded lifeboat. They hear a worrisome grinding sound, and soon discover one of the passengers drilling a hole in the floor of the boat. "Are you crazy? What are you doing?" they cry. "We will all drown!" To which the fellow answers: "Don't panic. There's nothing to worry about. I am only drilling a hole under my own seat." For a conservative, this sums up the social and moral significance of the lifeboat we call civil society, and stands as a sustained argument against the liberal-individualist atomization of society.

The foregoing has been a little historical scene-setting. But without wishing to appear too cynical, there is a general truth about all democratic systems that holds everywhere—namely, that politicians of all stripes will advocate for "more democracy" to get what they want if they believe the policy they prefer has popular support. But if they calculate that a vote will go against them, they will as strenuously avoid the democratic system, opting instead to influence their favored media, to call on powerful bureaucrats and lobbyists for support, to influence and infiltrate the education system by blocking or favoring certain textbooks and teacher hirings, to beg for government grants, to initiate court cases if (and only if) judges of their leaning are on the bench, and, well, to do just about anything but ask the people their opinion; in other words, democracy is a whore for hire, and not a spouse.

What follows is a brief sketch of some opposing liberal and conservative points of view with respect to what a democracy is supposed to be and to do. The first and perhaps most striking difference has to do with time. The modern liberal focus tends to be on democratic self-expression now, in the present. Democratically speaking, the modern liberal lives in a kind of eternal present that trumps other tenses of time, past and future, thus authorizing a near-sacred right to trump all other wills: those of past democrats as incarnated in today's laws and institutions (many of which are deemed defective simply because they are old); and the will of all future generations, which, it is assumed, will look after themselves democratically. In short, the purity of democratic will in the present, free from all unwanted past or present authority and future obligation, is the most stirring sense of democratic freedom for the liberal.

The conservative attitude is generally opposed, on the grounds that a democracy that sees itself predominantly as an expression of the will of the moment suffers from short-sighted egotism, because it ignores both the wisdom, sacrifice, and civilizing gifts of past generations and the obligation we have to sacrifice for future generations yet to be born. In effect, while the liberal sees each democratic citizen as obligated to express his or her will of the moment, the first complaint of the conservative is that there may often be a difference between the will of the people and what is in their best interest in the long term. In a democracy, wise statesmen elected by the people should be expected to see this difference, and in some cases to *protect the people from their own will.* That was originally to be the role of an appointed senate in which statesmen concerned about the next generation were beyond the reach of politics.

Unlike the liberal, then, who imagines each of us to be living in an eternal now, the conservative imagines each citizen as a link in a historical chain of *full democratic obligation,* past, present, and future. And there is more. The conservative understanding raises the all-important question as to the nature of the Common Good we ought to be conserving—the reliable principles and common interests by which the people ought to steer their ship. For as mentioned, principles of the common good cannot be found by reference to democracy alone, because *there is nothing in the term "democracy" that signifies or demands the good.* Now that is a statement that shocks most people. But as mentioned previously, it is simply the case that in its root sense, democracy has never been more than *a method for deciding the distribution of power*—that is, for counting heads instead of breaking them (even though lots of heads have been broken in the name of democracy).

The conservative will argue that, whether or not it has a democratic system, it is only the felt obligation of a culture to pursue the good and the well-being of future generations that can make a people heroically devoted to purposes beyond themselves—or not, as the case may be. We are not heroic, because we preserve only our own present lives, or create a high standard of living to enjoy as a present pleasure in a kind of democratic gluttony. For, absent any real devotion of those alive today to the next generation, "the people" surely live in a system of "doctrinaire selfishness," as this condition has been described. The most obvious sign of it in the twentieth-century democracies of the West is the omnipresence, with few exceptions, of massive national debt; it bears repeating that *all government debt is deferred taxation* that is being downloaded onto the backs of the children of the future, who are not here to defend themselves against our democratically produced gluttony.

This leads us to the liberal/conservative difference with respect to some explicit goals of democracy. Under our present regimes we could say that for the liberal, the main goal is no longer just personal liberty (the libertarian part), but also equality of outcomes and the elimination of differences in privilege (the socialist part). Meanwhile, the conservative argues yes, let's have personal liberty under law, but let us give priority to the social rights and freedoms of all (else what can a democracy mean?), and therein may all human differences flourish, because these differences are the truest signs of liberty at work.

Yet another opposition has to do with the implied purpose of democratic life, which for the modern liberal is personal freedom and happiness, to be obtained by living freely under one's own chosen contracts. Whereas for the conservative, who of course also wants to be happy, the challenge is not so much how to be as free as possible (for freedom without restraints is anarchy), but rather the question of how one lives as a good person. Such an answer has to do not just with personal freedom and choice making, but also with assuming the burden of our natural, inherited, and freely chosen obligations and duties.

This latter matter brings us face to face with the difference between the liberal and conservative notions of morality. For the liberal, morality is generally viewed as relative and situational—a thing to be decided personally, preferably by a clear rule of conduct (discussed in *On Morality and the Self* in part 3). But for the conservative, this is an echo of the old existentialist idea that human beings construct their own human essence through the sum of their choices. It was an idea many of us fell for at least once. But it does not make any sense, because we are born as human beings, not as horses or pigs, and the "essence" of a human being as we saw in *On Human Nature* is, well, just another name for human nature. So for the conservative, while we indeed become moral through our choices, we also behave morally because of our learned second nature, *whether or not we consciously choose* such behavior. This is a major distinction, because for the liberal, moral behavior must be freely chosen. But for the conservative, what is morally right must be done, whether freely or unfreely (unconsciously) chosen. That is why conservatives value the three Ps discussed earlier (prejudice, prescription, presumption) so highly. But whether actively or passively chosen, all morality unfolds in the framework of a transcendent universal standard of natural moral law which serves us not as a strict map, but as a general compass, and except perhaps for the most dire situations, is not relative in the least.

And this brings us to the question of the priority of rights in a democracy. For the modern liberal, rights are often said to trump duties and obligations. The conservative tends to reverse this priority. It is a question of emphasis. Accordingly, the liberal democrat will tend to place great importance on the individual, considered as the basic political as well as social unit; and so, because there is a planted axiom that all people are the same underneath, and the disadvantages between them can be rectified by correcting the evils of society, politics in a democracy should be guided by the goal of individual flourishing. In contrast, for the conservative, the individual may indeed be the basic political unit, but the family is the basic social unit; and so, duties and obligations easily trump most, if not all, individual rights (especially a lot of the newly invented ones). In short, in a democracy, the flourishing of civil society ought to have priority of importance, because that is how and why individuals flourish. In the conservative vision, goodness begins with correcting the self, rather than by correcting society at large. If everyone followed this procedure most social problems would evaporate. This brings to mind a little jingle found in Irving Babbitt's wonderful book *Democracy and Leadership*, which he saw in an Ohio newspaper and on which he wrote, "The author of this doggerel is nearer to the wisdom of the ages than some of our college presidents"—

> *And so I hold it is not treason*
> *To advance a simple reason*
> *For the sorry lack of progress we decry.*
> *It is this: Instead of working*
> *On himself, each man is shirking*
> *And trying to reform some other guy.*

To summarize: a central argument of this book is that for a long time, but especially since the middle of the last century, the Western democracies have been mutating into regimes ever more deeply rooted in the supposed egalitarian rights of autonomous individuals, and this trend has fed the citizenry into the hands of the state ("first individuate, the better to manipulate"), resulting in a hyper-democratic people who, in order to resolve the contradictory aims of freedom and equality, have been easily split into a private and a public body to produce libertarian socialism.

A regime such as this that produces a maximum of individual bodily and sexual liberty and a maximum of statism at the same time is a type never before seen in all human history, a novel form that has been corroding the vitality of the original moral and civil culture that brought liberal democracy into being in the first place. In the end, it bespeaks the cry of the individual will to be free from all unwilled authority or restraint, both the restraints and moral authority of a shared common life and culture and, most radically, even the natural restraints of one's own human nature and biology.

The following table is a comparison of the main liberal-versus-conservative meanings of democracy that may be perceived today. These differences have become so stark that fruitful discussions about democracy around the dinner table or in the public square have become almost impossible. The two sides are talking past each other, as the table shows. Nevertheless, my faint hope is that such a comparison might at least make us a little more alert to the different meanings intended when the word is used, and that this in turn will spur more genuine discussion about these two irreconcilable visions of democracy. The first person to whom I showed these comparisons was an English gentleman. After studying it a little, he shook his head, and said: "Everything on the right side of the page is what I was taught at home. Everything on the left side is what I was taught in college—it was aimed at undoing everything I learned at home."

WHERE DO YOU STAND?

On Democracy

This table is not about theoretical differences over democracy. Rather, it reflects general opposing attitudes concerning what it means to live in a modern democratic regime. A number of these items have little to do with democracy as a system, and more to do with common misunderstandings and confusions equating liberalism and democracy.

	MODERN LIBERAL VIEW	vs.	CONSERVATIVE VIEW
Definition	*The will of the people, now*		*The will of those past, present, and yet to be born*
Purpose	*Make the lives of people equal (eliminate differences)*		*Provide liberty under law (natural differences expected)*
Goal of Democratic Life	*Personal freedom and happiness*		*To live as a good person*
Democracy and Will	*Will of the people is best for them*		*Will of the people may not be best*
	The people's will always reflects their best interests		It is the job of wise leadership to make distinctions, and if necessary, to protect the people from majority rule
Freedom & Democracy	*Personal freedom and choice first*		*Social freedom and natural obligations*
	Freedom and equality are democracy's main values. Freedom is doing whatever you want without harming another		Though often found together, democracy and freedom are independent values. Freedom is not a good in itself. It is like fire, and can be useful, but when out of control can create havoc

WHERE DO YOU STAND?		
On Democracy		
	MODERN LIBERAL VIEW VS.	CONSERVATIVE VIEW
Basis of Democratic Life	*Living under chosen contracts*	*Living under the compact of civil society*
		(which precedes us, and will continue after us)
Rights	*Rights are primary*	*Obligations and duties are primary*
	Rights are abstract, universal, and inherent in all humans	Rights are secondary, concrete, and particular to each cultural tradition. They are not abstract entities with some kind of spiritual internal existence or status
Political/Social Unit	*The individual is the social and political unit*	*Family is the primary social unit. The individual is the primary political unit*
The Good	*Is achieved by correcting society*	*Is achieved mostly by correcting the self*
Politics	*Guided by individual flourishing*	*Guided by the flourishing of civil society, which in turn enables the flourishing of individuals*
Role of State	*Establish equal national benefits for all*	*Establish equal rules for all*
	The state is referee and team captain	Referee the game, but do not play it

CHAPTER 9

On Freedom

Before exposing the liberal-versus-conservative divide on this topic, I want to lay out some of the most common meanings of the word *freedom*, a word that since ancient times has been as much used as misused, and which is probably the most blood-stained word in our vocabulary. Like so many others, I have a reflex affection for this word, even the occasional surge of passion. Nevertheless, whenever asked to explain what it means, I pause. Most people today answer, "It means doing what you want," to which they reflexively add: "as long as you don't hurt someone else." This common response speaks of an age—our own—that sees self-expression and personal satisfaction as the key to freedom and authenticity. This has not always been the case. Throughout history various cultures and civilizations have had vastly different concepts of freedom, and even within our own tradition the meaning has changed a lot.

The Greek sense of freedom differed from the Roman, though for both of them the most basic and important meaning was *not being a slave*. That is, not being subject to the arbitrary will of another. This is probably the most universal meaning of all times and places, and in the more recent history of the West—especially in the United States, where colonists had the unusual opportunity of initiating a government from scratch, freedom meant *not being subject to the arbitrary will of government* (although they didn't mind owning slaves).

Looking back, it is clear that the earliest Christian ideal of freedom differed radically from the pagan one; freedom in the Renaissance, in turn, meant release from the supposed darkness of religion and a return to the humanism of the classical past. By the eighteenth century freedom meant living by the light of reason. In the Romantic period that followed, from the mid-eighteenth century to about 1830, people increasingly revolted against cold and restrictive reason, as popular poets like William Wordsworth defined poetic insight as "emotion recollected in tranquility," hailing a new freedom of natural feeling and self-expression.

By the middle of the nineteenth century, classical liberals (as distinct from their modern liberal brethren, who are statists) were extending the romantic emphasis on personal freedom deep into political life, now defining freedom as a radical individualism, free from unwanted authority, especially the nonessential authority of the state.

And finally, after a period of building welfare-state democracies in the West to ensure adequate care of the poor and needy, our most recent ideal of freedom is a rather paradoxical one. We want a radical combination of personal rights and freedoms, but *also* a broad range of goods and services provided to all by the state. I have described this historically novel combination of enemy opposites as libertarian socialism, under which citizens have all the personal, bodily, and especially sexual freedoms imaginable, while their former political, economic, social, and expressive freedoms are increasingly either eliminated altogether or heavily regulated by the state, its courts, and tribunals.

The foregoing suggests that the definition of freedom is not a simple one, and that a better approach might be to try a working classification of the different *kinds* of freedom. To my mind there are at least six of these, as explained presently. But first, there is an all-important distinction to be made between the terms *freedom* and *liberty*, as these two are often used interchangeably.

The distinction that seems to make sense is that the word *liberty* should be used to refer to freedom in its physical context, and not to other kinds of freedom. A man in jail, for example, has almost zero liberty, but retains all his freedom in the sense that he has not lost the ability to choose among myriad options, attitudes, and values. He can sleep, count the miles while pacing the floor, or write poetry. He can also decide to lie to the warden to protect a fellow criminal, or to tell the truth.

Most people, it seems, busily use their freedom to restrict their liberty in all sorts of ways. For example, selling oneself into slavery for a few years for money used to be common in the ancient world. Sometimes whole towns sold themselves as slaves to a neighboring city in exchange for military protection. And there have always been people who have chosen to become hermits or monks, voluntarily restricting their liberty in the hope of finding spiritual freedom. Less dramatically, most of modern life for everyone is freely spent getting tangled up in all sorts of ways that reduce liberty. Mortgages, bank loans, contracts, leases, business deals, and family and personal promises and obligations are mostly how we use our freedom to restrict our liberty. Indeed, a bit of reflection will reveal that most human beings most of the time build a lockstep kind of life for themselves ... and then complain that they would like to be more free. With this distinction hopefully clarified, let us consider the six kinds of freedom.

FREEDOM OF MIND. The first and most basic type of freedom is embodied by the chap in jail. He has all his freedom of mind, but no liberty. All mature human beings remain free in the most important sense that they are forever and at every conscious moment freely choosing beings, and every life is a delicate tapestry of millions of such personal choices, for better or worse. We cannot escape this kind of freedom even if we try, for we must then freely choose among means of escape, and so on. From this perspective we are indeed condemned to be free, for even choosing *not* to choose is a choice. Freedom of mind is of the greatest personal intimacy and secretiveness, lies at the core of our being, and is unknowable by others. It also distinguishes us (as far as we know) from the animal kingdom, and from each other, and is the basis on which we are able to become moral persons. That is why some people call this moral freedom. But it is not in itself moral. Rather, it is the unique capacity we have to become moral, immoral, or amoral, according to how, in using our freedom of mind, we construct a worldview.

FREEDOM OF SELF. Most of the world's freedom talk as found in the great religions and philosophical movements has had to do with freedom from ourselves, in the sense of learning how to escape the ever-present danger of becoming enslaved to our bodily passions, or victims of our own ignorance. For the ancients, self-freedom had to do with the practice of self-control, restraint, and balance to achieve the admired master-slave relationship of soul over body that they were certain is essential for the good life. In modern times, this ideal has largely been turned upside down, with expression of strong feelings of our "true self" elevated to the role of master. The goal of this kind of freedom is therefore often expressed as the need to "find myself," where the self is conceived as a kind of surrogate soul (although no one ever seems to ask how we would know whether the self seeking, or the self sought, is the "true" self). This inversion of the traditional relation of mind over feeling has, according to many, produced what our forebears would have called a disorder of the soul. But whatever the outcome, few moderns ever escape a lifelong dialogue with themselves on this kind of freedom.

EXTERNAL FREEDOM (SOMETIMES CALLED "FREEDOM FROM…"). This refers to the normal and common freedoms expected in daily life in the West, and in most countries throughout history; for all human beings tend to resist oppression, slavery, and suffocating authority imposed on them by others. For this reason it is sometimes described as freedom *from*, because it implies immunity from undue authority, especially the authority of arbitrary government. This is also sometimes called *negative* freedom, and we can think of it as meaning the freedom to do anything *not forbidden* by the laws (in contrast to a totalitarian system, which allows you to do only what is *permitted* by the laws). Many in the Western tradition consider this, in combination with *political* freedom (explained next), to be the most important kind of freedom. Citizens of the Western world had lots of this kind of freedom (especially in England) long before democracy came along, and classical liberal constitutionalism was its political expression. This political form is still much praised by isolated university professors and such, but over time it has mutated into equality liberalism in the manner described in part 1, and from there, since the post–World War II era, into the libertarian socialism we have today.

POLITICAL FREEDOM (SOMETIMES CALLED "FREEDOM TO…"). Try to imagine a world in which you are ruled by a tyrant who lets you do what you want on Monday, but not on Tuesday, and so on, unpredictably. You would likely conclude that whatever your external freedoms may be, they are too unpredictable to be of any use. Political freedom has to do with establishing certain predictable and actionable *rights* (whether we act on them or not) and the *limits* to government power that enable the practice of those rights. The most common political freedoms are the qualified right to speak freely (but you can't yell "fire" in a crowd, or slander or libel others), to associate with people of your choice, to own property and to buy and sell it freely, to worship, to leave and reenter your country, to be tried by a jury of your peers, to vote in elections (if you live in a democracy), and so on. When these rights exist we can say we have freedom *to do* these things (though to speak truthfully, we are only free to do them if they are permitted; that is, if we can do them without getting jailed, or killed). They comprise the normal rights associated with a free society (which may or may not be a democratic one). For example, ancient Athens had many of these freedoms for male citizens, but not for slaves, women, or foreigners. England had all these rights fully two centuries before it became democratic. The former Soviet Union promised all these things to citizens on paper, but did not allow them in practice, because the main sense of freedom expected there was collective freedom.

COLLECTIVE OR HIGHER FREEDOM (SOMETIMES CALLED "FREEDOM FOR..."). Many commentators on freedom take the view that the external and political freedoms explained previously are just formal concepts that mean nothing to the poor and disadvantaged, and often amount to a recipe for a chaotic liberal society for the rest, an uncivil nightmare of clashing wills in assemblies of the people and, under capitalism, of disconnected citizens chasing bucks to see who can die with the most toys. So what is really needed is a *higher* freedom based on a unified collective will of the people to achieve the common good. This is sometimes labeled freedom *for*, because it is based on an ideology of collective unity that prescribes distinct social and moral values and objectives *for* all. For example, under this ideal the state alone is allowed to control the production and supply of many basic citizen goods and services, thus giving citizens freedom from want (in exchange for most of their income being taxed away). Believers in this sort of collective freedom continue to argue that the classical liberal idea of protecting citizens from their own government is not logical, if the government is the embodiment of their will in the first place. This type of collective freedom got its first modern formulation in Rousseau's *Social Contract*, and was put into practice in the disastrous totalitarian experiments of the past two centuries—namely, in the French Revolution, and then the Communist, Nazi, and Fascist regimes of Europe. It is the deadly enemy of the sort of individual political freedom found under liberal constitutionalism.

SPIRITUAL FREEDOM. In its purest form, this type of freedom comes from striving for a complete identification with the person of God (or with God's will, or with all creation) to arrive at a condition of soul that transcends the confusion and disharmony of the physical self and the material world. This spiritual yearning has been expressed by mystics from all religious traditions, and also by many with no particular religious affiliation. When taken to an extreme, some seekers after this kind of freedom—I am thinking now of the many kinds of Gnosticism, ancient and modern, in the Western tradition—have taken a number of opposing routes. Some engage in a kind of libertinism of the flesh on the ground that, because the material body is contemptible and of no importance whatsoever, it may be used, abused, and enjoyed until spent. Others take the ascetic route, denying the body altogether on the ground that worldly desires, pleasures, and especially longings prevent achievement of a complete spiritual freedom.

Now that we have discussed the most common definitions of freedom, let us look at the some of the differences between the modern liberal and the conservative with respect to this word.

Surely the most basic difference is that the modern liberal argues that liberty and equality can be promoted together by government to produce fraternity, as the French revolutionary slogan went. But the conservative wholly disagrees. Equality in the eyes of God and of justice has always been true (or ought to be). But when people are left alone to develop in life as they wish and are able, there is no equality to be found. Beyond our common human nature, there are mostly differences. If we are talking about equal justice, there is no dispute. But there can be no inherent right, as radical egalitarians and communists like to claim, to an equal dividend for some taken from the efforts and merits of others. For all free human beings will be different, and the different cards in a pack cannot be made the same just by shuffling them repeatedly.

Another key liberal-versus-conservative difference is between *abstract* and *concrete* freedom. The liberal tends to praise freedom in the abstract, as a concept, a natural and universal right applicable in all times and places. The conservative disagrees. Freedoms of very particular concrete and actionable kinds—such as the medieval, English-derived guarantee against unlawful detention or imprisonment (the act of habeas corpus), which is still on the books today—are concrete achievements of particular and often heroic citizens, in particular civilizations, embodied in law, each in their own way. So for the conservative there is no such thing as freedom in the abstract; there is no "freedom of humanity." There are only concrete actionable freedoms (freedoms that can be enforced on the basis of precedent)—real English, French, and Polish freedoms, and so on.

When pushed, the conservative would also likely say that freedom is not natural at all; that a people has to be ready for a regime of freedom, ready in the sense of already enjoying the habits of self-control, discipline, civility, honesty, and trust that will make a home for freedom instead of a hellhole. Nations and peoples follow the same pattern as children: they must grow into the capacity to deal with freedom. Freedom necessitates control, else it cannot survive; and the possibility for any person or society to become or remain free has to do with the ratio of inner versus outer control at work.

In this respect, history informs us pretty bluntly that only very small portions of humanity have ever been free in the modern liberal sense of that term, and that most human beings crave security far more than they crave freedom. The perverse genius of our libertarian-socialist regime is that it gives people the freedom they crave most—their own bodily and sexual freedoms—while holding them in a kind of tax and regulatory servility with respect to so many forms of freedom they once considered sacrosanct. Name one, you say? That's easy: the citizens of all the modern democracies have in a mere half century suffered the virtual elimination of their ancient right to speak their minds in public freely (subject only to the normal and ancient bar of libel and slander). In the very recent past we pitied people in the totalitarian nations, such as the USSR, North Korea, Cuba, and Communist Eastern Europe, as brain-washed. Now we call it political correctness. The punishments are softer, but the mind-set and the fear of censure in our own regimes is the same.

The powerful and telling insight given us by Burke that really puts the idea of abstract freedom as a supposedly unqualified good into perspective bears repeating. He said that "liberty, when men act in bodies, is *power*." Despite being a longtime freedom lover like so many, I have not been able to think of freedom in the same way since reading that statement. Burke was basically warning that freedom is never innocent, that groups of people can easily combine for or against anything in the name of freedom. That is possible because, just like reason and democracy, and except for very obvious conditions of outright oppression or slavery, *freedom is a neutral concept that is not naturally attached to any particular value.* In other words, to hold the word *freedom* sacred without any qualification is tantamount to intellectual laziness. That is the reason for the traditional conservative fear of the freedom–democracy linkage, one that can so easily be, and has so often been, turned against the good, and even against concrete freedom itself. There were lots of examples of this in ancient times, the most memorable being a democratic vote of ancient Greek citizens to end democracy itself. Two examples in recent times of how democracy conceived as freedom can backfire are the free elections of the terrorist Hamas organization in Palestine and of the fanatical Muslim Brotherhood in Egypt (soon to fall in a military coup in a story that is far from ended).

A charming example of freedom thriving under autocratic rule was described by the philosophy professor Walter Stace of Princeton University, who worked as a student in what used to be the British colony of Ceylon. The British, he noted, were never under the illusion—as were, and are, the French to this day—that politics is a science, having known it for centuries to be something closer to a very high art. Accordingly, above the door to the colonial office of administration was a sign that read: "There's no reason for it. It's just our policy." Many who had gone there to complain simply chuckled and went back home. Stace remarked with admiration that the British gave their subject people no political freedom at all, but all the civil and economic freedoms anyone could ever want—of thought, speech, assembly, work, the press, religion—and even the right to harsh public criticism of their British governors. He concluded that the citizens of Ceylon in the early twentieth century "had less to fear from speaking their minds under that autocratic government than is the case in the democratic United States of today," and he wrote that in 1936!

A further and key liberal-versus-conservative difference is the distinction between individual freedom and social freedom, as previously mentioned. For the liberal, what matters most is individual freedom. If all individuals are maximally free, civil society will be maximally free, is the operative equation. What the conservative seeks, however, is not raw individual freedom—doctrinaire selfishness—but the freedom of all in the context of a viable and effective social freedom that enables civil society to carry out its social and moral functions of teaching, restraining, and permitting certain behaviors. The social and moral authority of a voluntary civil society (remember, we are talking about the exertion of authority, and not of state power), whether as parental authority, moral shaming, religious sanction or praise, leadership and direction from superiors, and so on, is what constitutes the binding power of society, and it must often exert priority over individual freedom, with which it will—and ought to—come into conflict. The conservative laments that the social-freedom functions of civil society have been dissolving rapidly in modern times in the way explained in part 2: they are dissolved from above by the egalitarian action of governments jealous of citizen loyalty to their own civil society, and from below by attacks from persons and groups in the name of individual freedom and rights.

Finally, and not least, the conservative rejects the modern—especially the romantic—liberal notion of natural freedom as something that has been enjoyed in a state of nature and in the absence of restraining law. For the conservative, it is only the restraint of custom and tradition, and especially of law, that makes freedom viable in the first place. The venerable maxim "liberty under law" must be the guide, and not unqualified liberty in itself (for there is no such thing). For the conservative, it is order that guarantees freedom.

WHERE DO YOU STAND?		
On Freedom		
	MODERN LIBERAL VIEW vs.	CONSERVATIVE VIEW
Freedom & Equality	*A maximum of both is possible*	*Freedom and equality cancel each other*
	The state can ensure maximum freedom to all in personal and bodily matters, and through tax and affirmative-action policy can provide maximum equality of public goods and services	There must be equal justice for all, but no equal dividend of the merits and efforts of others. Progressive tax and affirmative-action policies are both discriminatory. A maximally equal society will always be minimally free, and vice-versa
A Concept, or Concrete?	*Freedom is a conceptual ideal*	*Freedom is a concrete achievement only*
	The ideal of personal freedom is universal and timeless, and the freedom of humanity is an international goal	Abstract freedom exists only as an idea. There are only real freedoms as concrete achievements of particular civilizations, usually won by heroic individuals and protected by vigilant societies. There is no "freedom of humanity." There are only free (or unfree) English citizens, Americans, Canadians, and so on
Condition of Freedom	*Freedom is natural to all*	*Freedom is not natural, it is acquired*
	Everyone is born free but is everywhere restrained by bad laws and institutions, which must be eliminated and replaced with more enlightened policies	Freedom is essential to moral, social, and economic development. But it is not natural. People crave security more than freedom, and freedom will cause only chaos in a culture unprepared by sound customs and traditions, manner, trust, and legal safeguards to protect free people from each other
Freedom & the Good	*Freedom is a good in itself*	*Freedom can be good or evil*
	Individual freedom is the goal, and freedom in itself is a sacred concept	Freedom, when men act for the good, is highly desirable; but when men act in groups it is transformed into power, not freedom, and it can be used for good or evil causes

WHERE DO YOU STAND?		
On Freedom		
	MODERN LIBERAL VIEW	vs.	CONSERVATIVE VIEW
Freedom & Society	*Only individuals can be free*	*Social freedom must be protected*
	Only individuals can be free; societies are just collections of individuals, and this means a society is just an abstraction, and does not exist	Civil society is a real corporate body comprised of real, concrete human relations, and is not in the least an abstraction. Social freedom (the freedom of civil society to carry out its social and moral functions of teaching, restraining, and permitting certain behaviors) must often exert priority over individual freedoms
Freedom & Order	*Freedom stands alone*	*Freedom without order is chaos*
	Freedom can be defined and promoted to the world as an independent ideal	Freedom has no value or existence without order in the form of law, tradition, morality, custom, and many other constraining devices of civilization. These are the only things that protect freedom

CHAPTER 10

On Equality and Inequality

In this egalitarian age, if you dare to mention to someone that *inequality* might be a good thing, you will get a very strange look, because they assume exactly the reverse: it's *equality* that is good. But why? This has not always been so. The ancient Greeks had reason to fear the dangers to freedom posed by fanatical egalitarians. They drove this lesson home with the myth of Procrustes, the wicked son of Poseidon, who had the word *isotes* (equality) carved on his belt. He had one guest bed, and was fanatical about ensuring that all his visitors would fit in it. So when they showed up, he would either stretch them painfully on a rack if they were too short, or cut off their feet if they were too tall. The simple lesson of the myth, taught but never learned through the intervening centuries since, is that at the least, forced equality produces distortions of natural life, and at its fanatical worst, a lot of pain and blood. In our time it means that a political system aiming for complete equality of outcome cannot succeed without violence, whether deadly physical violence such as the equality-motivated killings, tortures, and death camps we witnessed in the twentieth century or the softer sort of psychological, legislative, and moral violence to freedom now quite typical in democratic regimes. Where did the modern idea of equality come from?

The American Declaration of Independence famously rested on the belief that "all men are created equal," so perhaps that is a good place to start this discussion. As it happened, from the first colonists who settled the Plymouth Colony in 1620 in search of their New Jerusalem to those who supported the declaration of intent to form a new nation a century and a half later, all were eager to avoid the inherited social biases of aristocracy, privilege, and birth that make lives unequal. They were keen to replace the old regimes of status with a new regime of merit. We are all of equal value in God's eyes, so everyone should have the same chances, which means we should arrange things so that everyone *starts* the race of life evenly. But no one imagined for a moment that without a lot of force they could ever be arranged so that everyone would *finish* evenly.

That the force of government should be used to equalize life for everyone is a very recent egalitarian conceit that began with the Stage 3 liberalism discussed in part 1—the radical shift from the classical liberal ideal of liberty under law to the modern egalitarian ideal of forced equality under law. It is worth repeating that the roots of this vision of equality are found in the story of the Garden of Eden, where the first humans lived in equality and harmony—a kind of gentle communism prior to the invention of private property and the envy created by "mine and thine." Which is to say, before falling into the post-Eden condition of human strife, envy, and war that resulted from disobedience to God. This is the basis of what is called the *secularization thesis*, the idea that our modern egalitarian democracies are at bottom secular projects aiming to restore human society to an Edenic condition here on earth, instead of in heaven. The philosopher David Hume recognized this tendency in the eighteenth century, and called it "concealed religion." The liberal assumption—the planted axiom—at its heart is the faith that as all are the same by nature, all should have an equally good life. The differences between us are mostly due to our condition in life and to our environment. This set of beliefs, which operates like an equation, forms one side of the modern divide over equality.

The conservative view—an opposing axiom—is rooted in assumptions to the contrary. It conceives of human beings as they became *after* the Fall: weak, fallible, self-interested, subject to the full force of seductive human passions, and prone to internecine jealousy, strife, envy, and war. The evidence for the truth of this view is the record of human history, which is so appalling that no final perfection of human society on earth is imaginable. We may be morally free to be good or bad, and there is always the possibility of self-correction, forgiveness, and charity to others. But the permanent human condition is weakness and imperfection, and this explains why conservatives are instinctively antiegalitarian and wary of progressive theories that, when tested against the experience of actual (as distinct from idealized) human beings, end up producing so many unintended consequences. To the conservative, the liberal operates on a false and misleading conception of human nature that functions as a kind of vital lie, because it relies on abstract generalities and hope for change rooted in a faith in the innate and equal goodness and perfectibility of all. The conservative, in contrast, relies on concrete human particulars and differences, and a conviction that the best predictor of future behavior is probably past behavior.

Of course, we all know that at a certain level of abstraction, things are equal. To say a human being is a rational animal is true for all (though we may be tempted to exempt a relative or two, or any number of politicians). But for the conservative, life is not about theories of social justice, progress, or equality. Life is pretty good just as it is, and it happens to unfold by way of an enormous range of *freely expressed* natural aptitudes, skills, and differences arising from unpredictable expressions of individual talent and effort (or the lack of same). So in contrast to the modern liberal, the conservative is most uncomfortable with programs that seek to forcibly equalize or change the social conditions of very different people; to penalize the strong, or to compensate the weak, the dull-witted, the lazy, or the wasteful to achieve what the liberal calls equality, which is something never seen in nature. If the word means that the law applies to all equally, the conservative will say that is fair and just. But if it means adjusting outcomes by force for some at the expense of others, he will call that plainly discriminatory and unfair.

In reply, the modern liberal will argue that the dice have already been loaded by the force of a systemically discriminatory society that biases outcomes in favor of some over others, so the game of life needs to be readjusted through affirmative action, and so on. The liberal wants equality of *outcome*, now. The conservative wants equality of law and of *opportunity*, only and always, and to let people freely determine their own outcomes. I was in a debate some years ago against a radical feminist who argued passionately for the use of government force to equalize an unfair society. So I asked her: "If you could arrange society by force so that it was finally fair and equal in the way you desire; if you once and for all got the perfectly equal society you have always wanted, would you then stop all the interventions, discriminations, and legislative use of force? Would you then leave all those equal citizens alone to live as freely and naturally as they might wish, and let the cards fall where they may?" She was stymied, and became speechless. She suddenly realized that a free and natural society will likely always result in inequalities, and so the coercive laws and intrusive policing of the lives of others that she freely admitted to supporting, but had always reasoned would only be temporary, would never come to an end.

Equality or Equity?

This points to a key liberal/conservative divide over the meanings of *equality* and *equity* that I think underscores the difference in the liberal and conservative approaches to fairness. The difference between these two words is that equality has to do with the *equal division* of things like money, food, votes, and government services. But equity has to do with *what is deserved* in the circumstances (sometimes called *just deserts*). For example, a father may want to leave all his children an equal share of his wealth (equality reigns), but if he discovers one of his children has cheated the family, he may decide to leave that child nothing (equity reigns). In political terms, it seems that much of the difference between the modern liberal and conservative temperaments has to do with the mutually incompatible principles of equal division and just deserts. In almost every case, the liberal will seek to eliminate equitable distinctions between potential beneficiaries of a policy, in order to extend benefits equally to all; while the conservative will downplay equality, seeking instead to reinforce the distinctions and equity at which the policy originally aimed. As we saw in the case of marriage, the liberal will try to loosen definitions and extend marital benefits equally to all, while dismissing all but the most basic qualifying conditions; whereas the conservative will strive to limit benefits to those who fully qualify. Liberal governments are notorious for encouraging people to take welfare (giving them fish) and for overlooking welfare fraud, while conservative governments are as notorious for restricting welfare (people must learn to fish) and for policing fraud. In broader national or international terms of political economy, the modern liberal and conservative will again take opposing sides. The former will support political and economic equality (via statism, centralization, egalitarianism, libertarian socialism, etc.), while the latter will support political and economic equity (via free-market societies, decentralization, liberty under law, risk and reward, natural individual inequalities, and so on).

The conclusion to which we are driven is that the conservative principle of equity allows inequalities and hierarchies to evolve as natural social and economic consequences of a free society, while the liberal principle of forced equality creates inequities and policy discriminations of state that favor some at the expense of others. As the basis for a just society, the opposing principles of equality and equity cannot coexist unless their domains are separated into equality as the basis for all applications of law, and equity for all judgments of performance. Attempts to conflate these two principles makes a population cynical about both. Cynical about equality because the equalizing laws of government, which are clearly a form of official discrimination (nothing "reverse" about this trend), can only be subjective (selecting one group as a target for official discrimination, favoring another group as beneficiary), and so may be enforced against anyone without warning. And cynical about equity because affirmative-action policies result in a tokenism so widespread that no one knows for sure who has properly qualified for their title, their pay, or their station in life, and who has not.

Equality Has Replaced Equity and Hierarchy

It seems that over the course of the past two or three centuries there has been a relentless effort that has been growing in intensity in all the Western democracies to replace the time-honored *moral* principle of equity with the *political* principle of equality. Which is to say that there has been a slow but steady leveling tendency aimed at eradicating the natural differences between human beings and their social and biological circumstances, such that equalization has replaced just deserts, sameness has replaced difference, a demand for equality has replaced a demand for equity.

Accordingly, whether speaking of the radical levelers of the seventeenth century or the millions of their secular brethren of the last century, what all egalitarian ideologues have in common is a profound anger at the conservative principle of natural hierarchy. The modern liberal carries the leveler torch, and everywhere it is upheld we see an automatic attack on hierarchy in the name of equality. Natural differences in mental ability and on IQ tests are dismissed as culture or race bias; for things like military or police training, natural physical differences in strength between men and women are ignored or adjusted; schools shy away from traditional moral rankings of character and courage in favor of nonjudgmental feel-good concepts of self-esteem; governments enforce pay-equity schemes in an attempt to equate the value of very different kinds of male and female work so they can legislatively raise female incomes to levels that cannot be commanded in the free market; natural sex differences are leveled via teachings on androgyny and the notion that gender is not natural, but socially constructed; little girls are given tanks and trucks and boys are given dolls in an effort to iron out natural gender preferences in toys; and so on. The common theme is a war against nature in the name of equality.

The conservative says, why? Why must everything be forced into an egalitarian mold? From childhood onward we participate in hierarchies of all kinds—of moral behavior, of authority and leadership, of skill and talent, of artistic ability and work ethic, of courage and steadfastness, of social respect and status, and much more. And in a situation where there are no hierarchies, we immediately set about creating them. Organizationally speaking, the conservative understands that no human group can move in a particular direction without some form of authority, and that all authority entails leadership and a hierarchy of command and obedience (and therefore difference and inequality). The hierarchical reality is found in all armies, all universities and schools, all corporations, and all political systems, and is a natural feature of human life. For the conservative, to level such hierarchies by force of law or policy is to attack the natural and organic body politic. Just as an ordinary human body cannot function without its interrelated but unequal parts, from the simple to the complex, human society cannot function without citizens and institutions of varying and unequal but complementary function and complexity.

Equality or Freedom?

This brings us to the connection between equality and freedom. For the modern liberal, *those who are not equal cannot be free*. But for the conservative, equality (in the sense of being made the same) and freedom are opposing principles in any political regime. They operate like a teeter-totter. As one goes up, the other must go down. It is impossible to have the most of both. Accordingly, the conservative finds especially poisonous and deeply immoral the idea of dumbing down the bright by falsely praising the dull-witted, of eliminating or driving underground into the recesses of private opinion all the apt and accurate words that describe our obvious failings, while permitting only words of praise even for what is clearly not praiseworthy; or, through taxation and policy, trying to raise the weak by weakening the strong. For the conservative, there is no such thing as a truly egalitarian society, except perhaps inside a prison (not counting the guards). And worst of all, history teaches that whenever levelers gain sufficient power (and tax dollars), they always form into a class of social planners of various kinds who cluster into media, universities, and government agencies in an attempt to turn the whole of society into a kind of egalitarian policy prison they are convinced is good for the people—while reaping a harvest of above-market special privileges, pay, and pensions for themselves as they do so. Surely one of the deepest ironies of modern debate over political philosophy is that it is the liberal, progressive, and egalitarian factions of modernity (by whatever name), rather than the conservative factions, who strive so passionately to create a final, perfect, just, and unchanging society. In this sense, they are the only pure conservatives.

Equality and Democracy

When it comes to the connection between equality and democracy we find yet another key divide between the liberal and the conservative. On one side is the liberal belief that as all humans are basically good, more votes are better than fewer. Let us have *a rule by equals* resulting in a collective wisdom. This has been the underlying constant of the liberal push for "one man, one vote" all over the developed world, even extending, in many countries such as Canada, to equal voting rights for certain classes of prisoners. The logic seems to be that because their crimes were due to bad social circumstances, they can eventually be rehabilitated (returned to their condition of original goodness), and the respect that comes with the privilege of voting is part of their rehab.

The conservative view is opposed. Although democracy is a holy word now and has swept over the developed world like a wave, its popularity does not necessarily make it always a good thing, nor less dangerous if unchecked. As we saw in *On Democracy*, the conservative is cautious about the democratic principle of rule by equals for many reasons. When democracy was equated with classical liberalism and the ideal of liberty under law it was less to be feared. But once mutated into an egalitarian juggernaut, there arose many concerns. Among these are the truth of the hierarchical principle discussed here: human beings are unequal in terms of talent, intelligence, wisdom, and experience, and tend to lead with their emotions rather than with reasoned thought. So a democracy unrestrained by principles teaching ordered liberty, decency, and restraint is bound to descend into a mood of public envy, self-indulgence, and a general feeding at the public trough. Far from a democracy of equal voters resulting in a collective wisdom, we are far more likely to see a collective cancellation of the votes of the wise and the good by the votes of the foolish and self-interested, leaving a residue of the mediocre to rule. As for allowing prisoners to vote? The conservative cannot understand why anyone would allow those who enjoy *breaking* the laws to *create* them. For all these reasons, and without mistaking education for wisdom, the conservative prefers *rule by unequals*—by a cultured, morally astute elite of the wise and the experienced, instead of by the equally mediocre. These are the kinds of elites a good political system ought to search out. But as it happens, political systems of different types tend to attract specific personalities, and the type attracted in a democratic system is the popularity-hungry individual much more concerned about the next election than the next generation. This is a systemic reason to be wary of the connection between equality and democracy.

Finally, when faulted for elitism, the conservative replies: On the contrary. Everyone is an elitist. That is normal. We all want the best physician for our brain surgery, the best mechanics to fix our car, and the best teachers for our children. Elitism is the general preference in every walk of life … except in the case of democracy. It is not the desire for the best that ought to be questioned, but the democratic satisfaction with mediocrity.

Equality, Economic Life, and the 1 Percent

Neither is the conservative surprised that the same freedom that allows an open and free expression of unequal talents, intelligences, and work effort gives rise to social and economic inequalities. Rather, he is delighted to see a highly variegated and fluid society pregnant with economic potential and possibility, and welcomes the inequality this always generates. For inequality is the most obvious sign that there is a lot of real freedom and mobility in the system. As long as we all are governed under the same rule of law (rather than an arbitrary rule of men), and decency and charitable instincts are encouraged everywhere (especially at home and in local communities, where we have a duty to care for the weak and for those who, despite their own best efforts, fall between the cracks), *the inequality that is always generated by freedom* will eventually provide economic opportunities according to effort and talent for all who are willing and able to work hard. So: far better a free and mobile society wherein naturally different citizens have opportunities to risk and rise or to fall, perhaps to rise again by their own free hand, than a rigid and static society of "equals" deprived of their real freedom to move up or down—and in which the one and only visible permanent upper class is comprised of all the privileged, tax-funded politicians and bureaucrats arranging equality for the rest of us. It is surely a paradox of our time that the modern liberal progressive states that so pride themselves on change, hope, equality, and social justice have as their single fixed and rigid objective the most conservative regime of all: *an equal world that never changes*, in which all citizens are the same in every matter on which state policy can touch, stuck as equals in the same monochromatic social and economic class forever, which is to say, *equally unfree* to break out and express their own unique and unequal talents and dreams, each in their own way.

So now let us look more closely at so-called income inequality. The modern liberal position on this question (unlike the classical liberal position: as long as all are free under the same laws, fend for yourself!) is again put in the form of a moral equation that the conservative will say is based on lazy-minded assumptions. It states that when it comes to income, *a more equal society is a more just society*. Indeed, the energy behind every progressive taxation program in history, and the main theme underlying the entire communist enterprise—"from each according to his ability, to each according to his need"—has been inspired by the moral conviction that it is unfair that some should be rich while others are poor.

The conservative replies: Although a free society may indeed produce inequality of outcome for all the reasons mentioned, that is fair because all live under the same laws, and no one has been coerced. Rather, it is our liberal, progressive taxation regimes that are profoundly discriminatory and unfair to millions of people. Instead of taking the same percentage of income tax from everyone equally (which one should expect from an egalitarian society), the tax rates are graduated to "soak the rich." In short, the very state that stakes its reputation on equality practices the most widespread inequality of all. What is this but a modern liberal version of the communist slogan just cited?

The conservative pleads that free societies produce an inequality of blessings because they are free, while egalitarian states produce an equality of mediocrity because they are not. When asked why the USSR failed, the Communist workers answered: "Because they pretended to pay us, and we pretended to work." To avoid ending up with this sort of sham society and hobbled economy, the conservative argues that what is wanted is a maximum of ordered liberty, which indeed will always produce a natural inequality; but as long as there is also a maximum of economic mobility, the talented, entrepreneurial, and hard-working will do well, while the lazy or incompetent will not. This combination of liberty, inequality, and high mobility is defended by the conservative because it generates an exciting economic churning phenomenon visible to everyone, in which people imagine that through a combination of hard work, risk taking, luck, and creative imagination, they too might be lifted up some day. It is the reality of the log-cabin-to-corner-office dream—the equality of possibility—that lends the whole system a pervasive inequality tolerance. Frequent examples of individuals rising or falling in the churn are crucial to the optimism and peace of free and unequal societies.

This is why many free countries track economic mobility. How much mobility is there? A lot, both downward and upward. Readers can find information on this for the United States by researching the Economic

Mobility Project, which seeks to discover "the ability to climb up or fall down the economic ladder within a lifetime or across generations." Scholars at many institutes, including the Brookings Institution and Stanford University, have published separate critiques of the findings. In Canada, a recent, massive Statistics Canada study showed that 6 percent of sons whose fathers were in the lowest tenth of the population in terms of income eventually made it to the top tenth, and almost 9 percent of sons of the richest fathers ended up in the lowest tenth. That's a long way to travel, in either direction.

We can feel happy for those who climb, and sorry for those who fall, but happiest of all that no one forced them to rise or fall. So the conservative reaction is: "Three cheers for freedom, mobility, and inequality." Oprah Winfrey, Wayne Gretzky, and Bill Gates did not steal their fortunes. They were given to them voluntarily in little bits by millions of people willing to pay for what was offered. There was no hardship for the buyers, and no coercion by the sellers. Most of the buyers very likely continued with their modest incomes, while happily making these sellers multimillionaires. This rubs the liberal the wrong way, while the conservative asks: Where is the injustice?

In an effort to end the inequality of a progressive income tax, Robert Hall and Alvin Rabushka of the Hoover Institution have developed a flat-tax model that looks like the fairest and most equal of all systems because everyone pays the same percentage of whatever they earn, and can fill out their own tax return on the back of a postcard. With no loopholes or corporate goodies or government incentives, the flat tax actually generates *more* tax revenue than a progressive tax system. If that is the case, the conservative asks, then why do we tolerate the injustice of a progressive tax system? The answer seems to be that we do so because of the optics: envy and pity trump fairness and justice. As modern democracies age they grow more complex due to overregulation, growth of government, and unstoppable national debt as a proportion of GDP. So taxes must rise.

In order to deflect public anger and forestall tax revolts, governments learned long ago that an emotional, envy-based "tax the rich" foil calms the masses. But proportionally speaking, "the rich" are a very small percentage of any nation. A 2005 Canadian study by the Fraser Institute used a cutoff income of $80,000 to define citizens as rich, then calculated that if *all* the income from the 7.4 percent of Canadian taxpayers who earned more than that amount was confiscated and redistributed to all *taxpayers*, every taxpayer would receive $2,582. However, if instead the confiscated income was distributed to each and every *citizen*, the one-time amount received would likely be about half of that, and the rich would be wiped out. So much for the fruits of envy.

As it turns out, income inequalities are largely a reflection of the earnings life cycle, in which young, inexperienced workers earn much lower salaries than older, experienced workers, with a whole range in between. In other words, even for people with identical life histories, education, and training, if you peek at income at any particular point in a life you will see large inequalities in their earnings history. Differences in work ethic, likeability, organizational skills, ability to control emotions, comfort with risk taking, the presence or absence of social skills, leadership, and so on are also reflected in income differences. And there are more jobs today requiring higher education, and fewer requiring lower; proportionally, there are more part-time workers than in the past, and many more single-earner households mostly run by low-earning moms. All of these factors produce differences in income that ought to be described as natural, rather than as inequalities.

But of what exactly does the calculation of income inequality consist, and how reliable is it? The liberal tends to focus only on income earned, and cries poor if it stagnates, or unfair if the gap between high and low earners increases. The conservative looks at the difference between *income* (dollars reported as income on tax returns), and *net wealth* (what you are worth if everything you own after settling all debts is converted to cash). Why? Because many people, such as senior citizens, arrange their personal affairs to report low income (I certainly do), even when their net worth continues to rise due to the increased value of their investments and their homes. A further skewing of income inequality is due to the fact that millions of people insist on being paid in cash (ever done that?), or they report no income at all because they benefit from barter exchanges, cash gifts, inheritance, foreign income, unreported child support, or cash from black-market activities that in most countries add up to many billions of dollars. Most estimates show that the underground economy in most democracies is somewhere in the range of 15 percent of GDP, and by any reckoning such a massive amount of hidden income is going to produce a very high reported inequality on a nation's tax returns, especially if most of this cheating is found in the lower income groups where there are more taxpayers.

Notwithstanding how hard economists and statisticians work to give us a clear picture of income inequality, underreporting, tax avoidance, and the underground economy are such large factors that income data alone as a measure of social justice is simply misleading. As Canadian economist Chris Sarlo asks, what is "too much inequality"? He cites Nobel economist Kenneth Arrow, who in 1997 said, "I find inequality to be in and of itself objectionable," by which he surely meant immoral. And this seems to be the standard liberal view.

The conservative sees this differently: as long as liberty under law is preserved and the charitable sentiments of civil society are always encouraged, inequality is not a problem unless it results from force, fraud, or inequitable laws that bar access to job opportunities. Then, as economist Greg Mankiw put it: "As long as the process determining the distribution of income is just, the resulting distribution is fair, no matter how unequal."[13]

In short, modern liberals will tend to say that inequality is unjust in principle because they have their eye on the fairness of the outcome, rather than on the fairness of the process. Conservatives differ radically and irreconcilably because they care more for liberty under law than for equality, *and liberty under law will always produce inequality*, simply because the more free people are, the more the outcomes of their lives will naturally differ. What it comes down to is whether inequality is institutionally created by a discriminatory system, and ought to be adjusted by force of law, or whether inequality is natural for all the reasons given, and is therefore one of the best signs of a truly free and fair society.

I offer a personal comment on the 1 percent debate: income inequality doesn't matter. What matters is real (not relative) poverty. People who worry about inequality either belong to a culture of jealousy and class hatred or they are confusing inequality with poverty. Poverty—children hungry and in rags—is easy to understand, and to do something about.

---

13 The quotes by Arrow and Mankiw and many of the details and arguments on income inequality presented here, which I hope I have reflected accurately, are taken from Chris Sarlo, *The Economic Well-Being of Canadians: Is There a Growing Gap?*

But inequality, as we have seen, is relative and ambiguous. Muammar al-Qaddafi was a filthy-rich man who made his money by terrorizing the Libyan people. But Bill Gates made his money by giving people what they wanted. That is why to complain about the 1 percent is pointless when it is free people who made them that way. In terms of eliminating real poverty, a nation's standard of living is what matters, not individual differences in income. Relative poverty can never be eliminated, precisely because it is relative. Sarlo cites a 2009 Statistics Canada survey showing that among the 20 percent of Canada's population with the lowest incomes, around half owned a car, a cell phone, or a personal computer, and had an Internet connection at home; three-quarters had either cable or satellite television. Most people suffering real poverty would consider these people fortunate and well off.

It seems clear that given the right conditions, where people are committed to hard work, where there is no war, where rights to private property exist, and there is economic freedom under a rule of law preventing force and fraud, the standard of living will always rise. How much and how fast? Dividing the number 70 by the average annual rate of growth yields the doubling rate of a nation's wealth in years. For example, a steady rate of 2 percent growth in GDP will mean a doubling of wealth in 35 years; 3 percent will mean 23.3 years; and so on. A war on the wealthy is likely to foil this optimistic picture, and things will end poorly for everyone for the reason given by the Nobel Prize–winning economist Milton Friedman, who offered the paradox that the only way to redistribute wealth equally, once and for all, is by destroying the incentives to create it in the first place.

WHERE DO YOU STAND?		
On Equality and Inequality		
	MODERN LIBERAL VIEW vs.	CONSERVATIVE VIEW
Equality & Freedom	*Equality trumps freedom*	*Freedom and equality are opposites*
	Policies and laws are needed to correct socioeconomic inequalities. People cannot be free if unequal	Freedom and equality of outcomes are opposing principles. As one goes up, the other must go down. People are naturally different. A free society will result in natural inequalities that reflect those differences
Equality & Justice	*An equal society is a just society*	*Forced equality requires injustice*
	Inequality is unjust in itself, and must not be tolerated	What is naturally unequal can only be made equal by force against some to benefit others
Equality & Human Nature	*All are equal by nature*	*All are equal as well as unequal by nature*
	All human beings are created equal. Inequalities arise from unequal social and economic circumstances, and these can be corrected with the right policies and affirmative action	It is true that all are created equal in the eyes of God, and must be treated equally in law. But we are all different in terms of our physical and mental abilities, skills, and ambitions, and so social and economic outcomes will be necessarily unequal in a free society. Only police states can forcibly "equalize" society
Equality & Discrimination	*Free societies discriminate*	*Equality policies discriminate*
	In societies that begin free, different interest groups, races, cultures, and genders create barriers and inequalities that privilege some and disadvantage others through no fault of their own, and so society must be constantly readjusted by force to keep it fair and equal for all	Much of the liberal complaint is true. Nevertheless, societies must choose an ethical foundation that enables the greatest number to freely flourish. But the most egalitarian states also discriminate, via inequalities that spring more from political privileges in a police-state culture than from freedom to express natural differences, or from free markets. So the choice is: Do we want to live in a free society that discriminates, but offers countless escape routes from the inequalities and disadvantages that arise, or in an unfree society that legislates permanent counterdiscriminations?

WHERE DO YOU STAND?		
On Equality and Inequality		
MODERN LIBERAL VIEW	vs.	CONSERVATIVE VIEW
Equality & Equity	*Equality must be the focus* Because all are created equal, differences in social and economic outcomes must be mostly due to social and economic conditions. Therefore coercive corrective policies must be applied to return everyone as close as possible to a condition of fairness and equality	*Equity must be the focus* Closed and unfree egalitarian societies must be rooted in an ethic of equality—in what is equal for all, deserving or not. But free and open societies have to root themselves in an ethic of equity—what is deserved in terms of work effort, talent, character, and so on. The principles of equality and equity cannot coexist successfully unless their domains are separated: equality the rule for all law; equity the rule for all performance
Equality & Hierarchy	*Privileges produce hierarchies* Most hierarchies are functions of privilege and power, and they demean people at the bottom of the ranking. Rankings of authority, social privilege, moral worth, gender, and work should be de-emphasized in favor of group and collective activities where all are valued equally. Open classrooms, open offices, removal of gender distinctions, and ungraded, equally valued group activities are better than rankings	*Hierarchies are natural and necessary* All human activity requires some kind of ranking of authority or talent or leadership to proceed, whether in the family, social, or business organization; politics; or the military. Command and obedience are an eternal reality of all human functions. The various unequal parts of the body politic naturally work together, each fulfilling its particular function, from top to bottom

WHERE DO YOU STAND?		
On Equality and Inequality		
	MODERN LIBERAL VIEW vs.	CONSERVATIVE VIEW
Equality & Democracy	*Democracy means equality*	*Democracy as equality equals mediocrity*
	One man, one vote is the ideal of modern democracy. All citizens must have an equal voice	The vote of the fool cancels the vote of the wise man, and the result is mediocrity. Democracy should be arranged to find the wise and the experienced. We are all elitists who demand the best in the services and goods that we buy. This should apply to the method of choosing political leaders, too
Economic Inequality	*Income inequality is intolerable*	*Income inequality is inevitable*
	A society cannot be just if there is great inequality in incomes between rich and poor. Government must tax the rich more heavily and redistribute to the poor to equalize incomes	In a free society that is highly mobile, incomes will vary greatly over the lifetime of individuals, and therefore of society at large. In free societies individuals get what they want (goods and services) by giving sellers what they want (money). Governments promote the idea of soaking the rich as a sop to the vast middle class, which is where all the real money is

CHAPTER 11

On Morality and the Self

The single most important moral question in the entire premodern period centered on how people are to achieve moral excellence as described in religion, philosophy, the law, and heroic legends of culture. In general, the call was for integrity of character, and this did not mean merely abstaining from harm to others. That was taken for granted. Rather, it meant the exertion of personal and communal effort to achieve the good. The big moral question until very recently was, how ought we to live as a people?, with the emphasis on *we*, not *me*. There was general agreement that those who try to substitute the latter for the former are guilty of trying to turn the natural world upside down. To run afoul of the communal standard of the good was to feel a deep shame and personal unworthiness.

Shame and unworthiness! Do we hear such confessions today? On the contrary. We are more likely to hear about how to pump up our "self-esteem." But not so long ago even a schoolboy would have said this is a twisted ideal, because esteem is something we earn from others through estimable actions; it cannot originate in ourselves except as self-congratulation. The ultimate question has never before been how, as individuals, we are to evaluate moral principles, but rather, because the great moral principles precede our existence and reflect a moral tradition and consensus of the community: In what ways can I uphold those principles, and how will I be judged in their light?

This question has all but disappeared in recent times. We are far more likely to witness individuals adjusting their moral principles to suit their personal circumstances or point of view, or judging the moral views of their own community negatively, rather than feeling judged by them. In the infamously relativist 1960s, "situational ethics" was all the rage in the schools, and by the '80s, "moral values education" (or "values clarification") was widely taught by morals educators. The underlying thesis was that in order for moral principles to be legitimate (morally binding), you had to reason your way to them yourself.[14]

Many educators have backed away from that approach since the turn of this century, but the effects have lingered. Hume would have described values clarification as a "moral inversion," whereby we judge the moral laws, instead of being judged by them. Conservatives got very angry about this trend, charging that values clarification education, then and now, undermines a moral community. For a moral principle that has worked well over the ages ought to be followed, whether or not we have personally managed to reason it out for ourselves. As previously stated in *On Reason*, stand-alone reason is not always a guide to the good. It tends to produce rationalizations of personal desires, rather than any good for others. For those interested in pursuing this topic, my book *The War Against the Family* has some biting critiques of values clarification as used in schools. If you decide to read it, better be sitting down!

For a conservative, the word *values* reeks of relativism, and therefore of a contemptible egotism—the belief that nothing is good or bad unless an individual values it as such. This has been the tendency of modern morality, which centers less on the community and more on individual

---

14 In *Taking Religion Seriously Across the Curriculum*, Warren Nord and Charles Haynes describe how morals education in schools recently has been moving away from this individualist and relativist model and back to a more communitarian one, which is to say, from the modern liberal model back to a traditional one. They write: "For the past several decades values clarification programs have been widely used in public schools. In this approach, teachers help students 'clarify' their values by having them reflect on moral dilemmas and think through the consequences of the options open to them, choosing that action that maximizes their deepest values. It is unjustifiable for a teacher to 'impose' his or her values on students; this would be an act of oppression that denies the individuality and autonomy of students. Values are ultimately personal; indeed, the implicit message is that there are no right or wrong values."

will—a theme that keeps popping up in this book. Although the conservative is certainly not looking for a rigid drop down menu of moral solutions that will eliminate personal engagement in moral questions, he does seek something rather like a *compass* pointing to overarching principles and standards that ought to be incorporated as a guide in the navigation of life. For you cannot know south unless you know north, nor good unless you know evil; and basic universal moral standards such as "might does not make right," "honor your vows and contracts," "do not murder," and so on are naturally known—by instinct? By human nature? Or "written in their hearts," as Saint Paul so memorably wrote?—whatever. But such universal moral principles are either known intuitively and expressed symbolically or in religion and ritual by all moral communities, or they are discovered by natural instinct or through reflection and insight by people the world over, whether or not articulated in abstract reasoning. As pre-reflective principles, these norms precede all charters, paper constitutions, and temporary human laws, now and for all eternity. We have all heard of, seen, or read about courageous people who without hesitation put their own lives in danger to save or help total strangers, whether in a house fire, a robbery, or a drowning. Some amazed interviewer always asks: "Why did you do that? You could have died!" A short silence follows. Then we hear, as reliably as our own breathing: "I had no choice. I just did what anyone else would have done. *It was the right thing to do. I couldn't help myself.*"

The Self: Like a Glass House, or an Onion?

There are two opposing understandings of the self that underlie modern times, and we may think of them in the contrasting images of a glass house and an onion. The first image tends to be favored by those of a conservative persuasion, and the second by the modern liberal.

The first imagines each human soul entering the world unfinished at birth and enclosed in an imaginary structure made of hundreds of panes of opaque glass, beyond which are the central truths of life and the universe, perceptible only as faint shadows beyond the glass panes. The truth of life is *external* to ourselves, something we hope to incorporate through wisdom and right living. As we mature, we discover that every time we achieve an insight through moral exertion or some other kind of soul work, one of those panes of glass shatters, allowing a more full and free glimpse of the universe outside ourselves. Everyone has experienced such moments of profound insight, when suddenly the scales fall from our eyes as something formerly confusing and misunderstood becomes luminously clear. The goal of life is to break as many of those glass panes as possible before the end, when all will be luminous, the self at peace with truth.

The onion image is quite the opposite, and reflects the modern liberal belief that because so much of getting through life is a matter of relative values and personal choices, the truth of most things must be *internal*. Hence the job is to peel back enough layers of the false outer self—a construct made up of the authority laid down by society, religion, family, tradition, and so on, to find the true inner self deep within. The search is for the one and only *authentic* self with which the seeker can identify at last, content and "happy with who I am," as the saying goes. It is rather bothersome to conservatives that while it is common to hear people say such things as "I am searching for my self," we never hear discussion of the question, How are we to know which is the true self—the one searching, or the one sought? And what if the self we call true is in fact a deceiver, and the seeking self a dupe? This liberal conception of self is irksome to the conservative because the sole reference for the search and discovery of the authentic inner self is the person seeking. So it seems like a self-fulfilling prophecy, an exercise in narcissism. This idea of the *true me*, trapped by and struggling to escape the surrounding falseness and inauthenticity of the material, social, and moral world, is deeply rooted in the West, and for many observers is but a secularized version of the unsaved soul struggling to emerge in the light of salvation—in this case a salvation conferred upon the self by oneself.

In political terms this liberal image of the self, hyper-individualist and self-sacralizing as it appears to be, serves as a kind of public warrant for the dignity of democracy, and is in turn the source of the sacralization of the people in a one-man, one-vote democracy. The vote is sacred because the authentic self—the surrogate soul—is sacred. A powerful example of this modern tendency for democratic self-sacralization rang out in the New World long ago in Walt Whitman's euphoric essay *Democratic Vistas*, in which he spoke of "perfect individualism," of the "fusing" of all free citizens in democratic unity, and even of something he called a "cosmic" democracy! But the tip-off to this feverish selfism came when he defined democracy as *"freedom from all laws or bonds except those of one's own being."* This self-love of a free and democratic Walt had already been on display with the opening words in his 1855 poetry collection *Leaves of Grass*: "One's-self I sing, a simple separate person," and in the poem "Song of Myself," which begins: "I celebrate myself, and sing myself / And what I assume, you shall assume / For every atom belonging to me as good belongs to you." His was a kind of groupie radicalism. For Walt, the Self is sovereign in the moral realm—there is no higher law; just as in modern democratic theory, personal choice is sovereign, and therefore the aggregate of authentic selves and voices is sovereign. In this view, truth is no longer transcendent, outside the glass house; it is internal, must be searched for, and released from the prison of ignorance (conservative tradition, custom, morality, and so on) by which it has been confined. Ultimate democratic truth is the result of a head count after all the little onions have been peeled.

It is surely this peeling activity, this act of self-coincidence with a newly discovered authentic self that in turn has produced the rights climate of our time, which is to say, the sense that personal rights are prior in importance to obligation, duty, custom, and convention (all of which are deemed to block access to the true self within). We can see this trend if we track the trajectory of what may be called "the descent of sovereignty" over time. First there was the unchallenged sovereignty of God; then the sovereignty of kings who claimed they got their right and duty to rule from God; then we got sovereignty of the people.

But the descent of sovereignty did not stop. The modern democratic conception of the common good as embodied in the people has not been entirely abandoned, but, as explained in part 2, is under persistent attack in the name of autonomous individual rights. In other words, modern democratic ideology seems to end—and I do think this may be its end point—by attacking the very concept of a free civil society (the people) as a sovereign organism having an importance prior to and greater than that of individuals. It is likely that we will not be able to restore the old notion of a free civil society to its proper role as custodian of the common good until we return to a more realistic and modest concept of the self, and of our obligations.

Especially since the 1960s there has been a growing trend for the liberal masses in the Western democracies to embrace the unprecedented idea of the *privatization* of morality—the notion that morality is primarily a personal and private, rather than a public, matter. This needs to be challenged. For while it may be true that, when only two people are involved, there are simply two private wills—and therefore probably a dispute and a negotiation—this changes when three or more are gathered together. For then there is immediate potential for the substitution of force for morality—two against one. So even if just for self-defense, a principle of justice must be sought aiming at the best result for all, thereby giving rise to a public moral language or code that cannot be altered privately or arbitrarily by the individual choice of anyone, any more than a rule of grammar can be altered by individual choice. This is one of the reasons a conservative will always insist that morality is inescapably a *public* matter, privately exercised, that inevitably reflects directly or indirectly upon the whole community. Just as the rules of a human language regulate public speech so that all may understand each other, the rules of a human moral code are shared and "spoken" by way of normative human behaviors so that all may understand right or wrong motives and actions. Private languages are only spoken by crazy people, just as private moralities are followed only by people in revolt against their own moral community, or by criminals and sociopaths.

Can There Be Practical Morality on the Moon?

We can test the claim that the practice of morality is always a public matter with a thought experiment. Try to imagine a solitary human being situated alone somewhere, forever out of reach of all other human beings: abandoned on the moon, say, with no hope of rescue. Let's also imagine that this fellow is an atheist (so no one can object that he is not really alone because he is keeping moral company with God). Can we then say that *anything* this utterly solitary individual might do is either moral or immoral? Can such words have any practical meaning in a world empty of others? Surely there can be no morality if there is no one with or against whom our isolated fellow can act or speak morally, to whom he can lie or tell the truth, or from whom he can steal (for private property would have no meaning, either); or whom he can hurt or kill, or harm or help "morally," whose character he could besmirch, or who could do such things to him. The point is that we can have moral thoughts anywhere. But in the absence of a moral community, morality has no practical meaning or effect. Which is to say that, in order to have practical meaning, morality is always public, and never private.

The Flow of Morality

Liberals do not deny that the people have some common moral views. But on this they usually have two things to say. First, that public morality is generally behind the times or old-fashioned, and ought to be adjusted to modern life; and second, that public morality should be and ought to be the result of individual reasoning (which will add up to a sum of citizen moral opinion, producing a kind of bottom-up moral aggregate). The belief is that when individual values change, public morality should adapt, mostly by dropping moral and legal constraints on all private matters having to do sex and the body (thus producing the libertarian socialism of modernity). Favoring the assumption that morality flows from individuals upward to civil society, and not the other way around, many liberals consider themselves to be in the vanguard of enlightened social change and progress. Traditional moral concerns about internal sexual, bodily, and spiritual matters have been removed via privatization from the modern liberal's public playbook, and all residual moral concern transferred to external public matters such as global warming, recycling, income equality, and so on.

The conservative view is exactly the reverse. It is obviously true that some once useful customs and manners lose their purpose and change over time. But general moral principles are not determined by individuals, and they are not merely customs. They preexist all of us in the form of those aforementioned moral absolutes, such as "do good, and avoid evil"; "do not steal, lie, or murder"; "honor contracts and vows"; "might does not make right"; and so on. These are commands of our universal human nature and of natural law, and are grasped by all normal people through experience, by intuition, and by right reason, and they flow downward to individuals in the form of social, moral, and behavioral sanctions and interdictions as a moral language understood by all normal people, who must learn to speak it properly in order to coexist in society. Lying, cheating, stealing, raping, murdering, slavery, and so forth are not bad because individuals reason about them and agree they are bad. They are bad in themselves, always have been, and always will be.

This topic looms as another canyon in the Great Divide. Does society nurture and conserve a common moral language that is handed down to individuals, as conservatives believe? Or, as liberals are prone to think, do individuals decide the terms of their own personal and private moral language and then hand these up to society? Another way to imagine this difference is by way of a family metaphor: the conservative believes the parents (civil society) preexist the children (maturing individuals), and parents have an obligation to instruct children in moral behavior, not the other way around, just as teachers instruct students, and not the reverse.

Can What Is Good for You Be Bad for Me?

We often hear the liberal reply to what we consider a factual statement with "It may be true for you, but it's not true for me" (with no thought given to the fact that it is impossible for a fact to be true and false at the same time). Just as often, the liberal will use the most common three words in the modern discussion of morality when he insists he is *outraged* by the *judgment* of those who dare to *impose* their moral views on others. It is precisely such words that are the most obvious tokens of the modern trend to moral individualism (which parallels the trend to hyper-democracy, as discussed previously). In effect, the modern liberal is engaging in an initiative of moral quarantine, or segregation. He does not deny morality (for the modern liberal, above all, is self-conceived as a moral renovator), but he equates its meaning more with personal and private will rather than with public will. That is why the modern liberal will always try to predefine a personally chosen behavior as good solely on the ground that it does no harm to another. Here is an example of this moral code from a visitor to my website in January of 2014 (though this fellow does not mention harming others).

> True freedom for me is the option to choose, speak, or do anything that is within my natural ability that I want, without interference from anyone or any power or law, with the only limitation being that the exercise of that freedom does not inhibit or interfere with anyone else's

right to exercise the same. I measure the correctness of one's actions and the legitimacy of any law or regulation by this standard. I refuse to recognize any coercion that does not pass this standard.

There is much revealing confusion in this essentially anti-moral statement. This young man wholly equates freedom with personal desire and will. If he feels like throwing his food on the floor, and doesn't mind others doing the same, that is the kind of world his freedom will produce. All human conduct is to be dictated by feeling (what "I want"), in a world without any *ought*, in which all law originates in self.

The conservative responds that there are many things that individuals deem good for themselves and harmless to others that in fact are directly or indirectly harmful to society as a whole. What? The very notion seems heretical to the liberal. But is it? Consider, for example, the young man who loves to drink beer and watch pornography on a Saturday night. He is alone. No one else is directly harmed. When upbraided for this choice, he responds that it's personal, a private habit, "What's your problem? Why are you judging me?" You remind him that all pornography depicts sexual activity between paid strangers who can only be objects for each other; and that instead of participating in the normal world of authentically subjective male-female relationships, learning about courtship, or his future role as husband and father, he is instead enjoying a deeply inauthentic relationship with himself that entails mock subjectivity and mock sex, the enormous income from which spawns a huge international porn market, legal and illegal, that reaches into every aspect of modern society and drags into its maw a host of outlaw activities including child pornography, bestiality, violent and kinky sex, criminal behavior, drug use, and countless other unsavory social consequences that indeed fall upon us all.

Physicists and especially climate scientists will claim that when a butterfly flaps its wings in Hong Kong, it can contribute to making a hurricane in Florida. Everything affects everything: this is called "the butterfly effect." And it is curious that most of the same people who are adamant that their personal moral decisions are private, affect only themselves, and harm no one will staunchly defend the butterfly effect when, say, a single capitalist outsources production, or income inequality increases. Or consider the example of the female soldier who deems it a good thing to engage in active military combat (as I write, the US government has just lifted its ban on women in combat). The conservative responds: She may indeed love it, but so what? Consider the venerable, if presently weakened, conviction that all civilizations have a vested survival interest in protecting women and children from undue risk of death ("women and children first!"). An objection may be: But isn't that also true for men? Yes, but less so than for women. To speak only of the procreative truth, men are more expendable. Only women carry and nurture the next generation from their own bodies (including the next generation of soldiers). To test this claim, try to imagine sending *only* women into battle, in the same way that we have sent *only* men into battle for most of human history. About fifty million male combatants were killed in all the wars of the twentieth century alone. That was bad enough; but to lose the same number of women would have been a far greater debit to civilization, simply because a healthy man can father a great number of children in sixty years or so, whereas a woman is limited to the small number of children she can produce and raise in less than half that time. Reproductively speaking, to send a male soldier into battle risks a certain debit to civilization, but to send a female into battle presents a much greater risk and debit because she has a higher reproductive value. So just in terms of the survival of civilization, it seems a rather self-destructive thing for a nation to promote.

But I have left the guy watching pornography back on the couch. I will just add that there is something very wrong with a society that considers it acceptable for strong young men to sit around drinking beer and enjoying their porn on a Saturday night while women soldiers are overseas with assault rifles risking their lives to ensure that those men can enjoy themselves in peace. And to stick with the military vein, I doubt anyone would say that a soldier sent to defend us who runs from the enemy, though without having directly harmed any one of us, is morally unimpeachable. He has endangered his fellow soldiers (male or female) and the security of his nation, and shamed his people. This calls to mind the story of the Greek soldier in the war with Sparta who showed up at his family's door with a knife in his back—whereupon his mother slapped him for cowardice.

These brief examples illustrate the conservative point that a collection or aggregate of disconnected individuals, each with a private moral agenda and who merely agree not to coerce or harm each other, *cannot possibly constitute a thriving society*, no matter how attractive or morally convenient to themselves their freedom of personal choice might at first appear. For the moment we stop asking ourselves how our behavior adds to or subtracts from the common good of others and to the thriving and survival of our entire civilization, common life is at an end.

On the matter of the reasonableness of morality, the conservative warns that logic, propositions, and practical reasoning have only a minor role to play in the discernment of truth. For as mentioned (see *On Reason*), reason is a tool that can be used to help or to harm. And the plain facts of human history are sufficient to inform us that without some grounding in a permanent higher standard or source of truth, moral views created by reason are easily destroyed by reason; and the common life of society, absent underlying moral principles and practices, is soon reduced to a contest, first of irreconcilable reasons, then of opposing political powers. As Ulysses (in Shakespeare's play *Troilus and Cressida*) so memorably put it: "Then every thing includes itself in power, power into will, will into appetite; and appetite, an universal wolf, so doubly seconded with will and power, must make perforce an universal prey, and last eat up himself!" Eat up himself! What a profound warning. That is what Lord Acton meant when he wrote, "Power tends to corrupt, and absolute power corrupts absolutely." Though of course it is not power that corrupts. Power, like reason, is just a tool—it is by our bad use of power that we corrupt ourselves and others.

On Morality as a Simple Rule

Despite such eternal truths, many liberal intellectuals have in recent centuries attempted desperately to substitute their own rationalized systems and theories for what they consider the illegitimacy and ignorance of custom, cultural tradition, religious faith, and other long-upheld ways of life, as if to say that human moral behavior is simply blind unless it follows an intellectually justifiable logic or rule. In other words, they have strived to move the justifications for moral behavior from the *prerational* felt certainties and insights of religion and custom of the whole community to *rational* formulas that individuals can apply for themselves through a test of logic. This trend is surely due to the rise of science.

There is a single law of gravity, an ultimate speed of light, and a single and constant mass of the electron, and so on. So why not a single law of morality? We can see the appeal: instead of feeling morally judged by society for reasons that can seem obscure, or that are beyond personal control ("It's just the way we do it"), let us have a clear and simple rule so everyone in the whole world can easily figure out how to be good. Such a rule would empower individuals morally by converting them into judges in their own case, thereby enabling an escape from the (conservative) moral impositions of society and religion. Perfect rule. Perfect logic. Perfect world, is the thinking.

But what am I saying? For thousands of years the Golden Rule has served us well, hasn't it? It is found in every religious and ethical tradition in history, either in a positive or negative form. The positive one says, "Do unto others as you would have them do unto you." The negative one says, "Do *not do* unto others as you would have them not do unto you." Either way, this is a *rule of reciprocity* that has been universally respected for a very long time. The problem with it is that if you happen to be a member of the Mafia and think violent crime is the best way for anyone to get what they want, or a sociopath who thinks everyone should deceive the way you do, the rule breaks down, because it has nothing to say about the best standards of conduct for civilization as a whole. In other words, the Golden Rule can be used to justify any behavior you happen to talk yourself into believing is good for everyone, even if it is not. So, in some frustration, many thinkers have tried to come up with better moral rules. What are some examples?

The hugely influential German thinker Immanuel Kant tried to create a drop-down menu of moral rules (which he called "maxims") that he thought would serve all people for all time. The most important of these is the *categorical imperative*: "Act only according to that maxim whereby you can, at the same time, will that it should become a universal law." It is a version of the Golden Rule, except that it generalizes reciprocity to all humanity, instead of limiting it to immediate "others," and changes it from an *action* (*do* unto others), to a moral *law* (*legitimizing* your actions for all). The problem with this notion is that it only works for those who already uphold a standard of good behavior that they would like to see universalized. It doesn't work for people unable to reason clearly, or for criminals, cheaters, adulterers, drunks, con men, sociopaths, the predominantly selfish, and, well, for those most in need of some absolute moral standard and constraint that does not originate in themselves or their behavior—as Kant, the patron saint of all modern liberals, thought it should.

To clarify, the main difference in this aspect of the liberal-versus-conservative divide is the question: Will morality work best as a system of self-generated rational maxims because people are good by nature (as liberals tend to believe), and so they will want to rely on such maxims? Or will morality work best as a system of eternal and transcendent moral dictates of natural moral and religious law that command us to behave well (because we are flawed and less than perfect), whether we have jus tified this to ourselves rationally or not? In the end, Kant's rule-making effort failed to catch on (except among liberal intellectuals) because of the obvious fact that most people make their moral choices emotionally, and with their whole being, rather than as analytical philosophers.

The conservative view is that the objective of all true civilizations worth the name has been to ensure that in our whole being, we are wholesome beings. But the process of inculcation is only possible if a civilization cultivates a common moral language that provides citizens with the deep satisfaction of meeting complex moral challenges by means of the nuanced moral language they have learned to speak reflexively, without any unnecessary thought. Morality without thinking? The mere thought of *that* horrifies the liberal moralist, just as the pure liberal ideal—the notion that every man is the legislator of his own moral-ity—horrifies the conservative. And that ideal (it first reared its head in existential theories after World War II) has all but saturated Western civilization. In its radical form, the solution to the problem of how as radically free beings we are to know the good without guidance from an inherited moral standard goes something like this, as voiced by Jean Paul Sartre: "In choosing myself, I choose man." This was a version of Kant's rule that also said nothing about the good. So how are we to know the good in order to choose it? Sartre's answer is: "We always choose the good" because we are not ever able to choose the bad. *To choose is at the same moment to affirm that what we choose is good,* and "nothing can be good for us without being good for all." To the conservative this seems the weakest of arguments, because it basically asserts that everyone can print their own moral money, so to speak, without worrying whether anyone else will accept it. But it would be hard to find a statement that more clearly voices the liberal belief that *the act of choice validates the action chosen*. But I have gotten ahead of myself, so let us back up a little.

After Kant, along came the English philosopher Jeremy Bentham. He was a utilitarian thinker so frustrated by the political disasters and moral dilemmas of his time that he invented a quantitative, or *mathematical*, rule of morality. His maxim was, "It is the greatest happiness of the greatest number that is the measure of right and wrong." Human actions should be evaluated only by their consequences in producing either pain or pleasure (happiness). This rule was to operate according to his "felicific [happiness] calculus," which he invented as a formula for deciding in advance the moral desirability of any situation. We might have expected that, in an age of growing materialism and democracy that counts heads, someone would eventually try to identify the good with a head count, without concern for the presence or absence of intrinsic goodness of human action, or motives for action other than happiness. Bentham's calculus was a big hit for a while, until its weakness was exposed by other thinkers such as the young John Stuart Mill.

Mill was a child prodigy, and also a prodigy of naïveté in moral matters. He worshipped at Bentham's knee, edited much of his work for him, and said he considered utilitarianism to be like "a religion." But it ended up depressing him seriously for two years, until, in a stroke of insight that arose from his newfound emotional attraction to the romantic poetry of William Wordsworth, he realized that happiness cannot be about *quantities*; it can only be about *qualities*. In the recantation of utilitarianism that followed, he wrote that "it is better to be a human being dissatisfied than a pig satisfied; better to be Socrates dissatisfied than a fool satisfied." It was not long before others began to think of Bentham's rule as a "swine morality."

Mill proceeded to invent his own "very simple principle," now called his harm principle, which has been mentioned often in this book; translated, it states that you can do whatever you want as long as you do not harm someone else. This was an Enlightenment notion of individual freedom that had been influential during the French Revolution, and was becoming widespread by Mill's time. As one element of moral life it is indeed a sound principle. We should not harm others. But Mill's formulation seemed to give it a dignified philosophical status as the only necessary moral principle. As such, it amounts to a radically self-centered and historically unprecedented idea of morality because it says nothing whatsoever about the good. It offers nothing at which people *ought* to aim in their own behavior except a negative: do no harm. I have so frequently taken aim at Mill's principle because it has canonical status today as *the single most common principle of liberty and morality in the Western world.* In this writer's opinion it has had a devastatingly corrosive effect on the common bonds of civil society everywhere it is believed.

How and why did Mill adopt this rule? Perhaps his well-documented affair with Mrs. Harriet Taylor—a sick man's wife—whom he adored, and then married after her husband died, sheds some insight. He justified this immorality (which he refused to recognize as such) on the grounds that, because her husband was at first not aware of very much, no harm was done (see Mill's *Autobiography* for the partial story). Could his "one very simple principle" have grown out of his need to justify his own immoral behavior, such that instead of changing his behavior, he argued for a change in the moral law to suit himself? If so, this is a pretty slippery basis for the philosophy of a whole people, and whether or not this was the case, in practice Mill's principle—popular as it has been beyond anything he could have imagined—is the most deforming of all possible moral ideals. First because, as mentioned, it says nothing about the good; and second, because it dismisses the importance and authority of the social and moral bonds—the shalls and shall-nots—that must exist as real moral encouragements and restraints *between* all human beings; which is to say, he dismisses entirely the reality of the complex human moral relation or "language" as described previously. As such, his principle is steadily undermining the Western world by teaching that we should ignore the possibilities of the indirect present and future harm we may do at any time to the moral fabric of our own selves, our families, our communities, and our nations.

A word about Hume's philosophy of "common life," as he called it. Hume is widely considered the first modern conservative thinker because, like the ancients, he gave foundational importance to what is naturally good: to instinct, emotion, taste, experience, greatness of mind, and to all long-lived tradition, social custom, and moral practices. These things he considered "sacred," central to the wholeness and felicity of common life, and far superior to merely rational theories or narrow rules of moral conduct. Hume himself, though among the most rational of thinkers, was wary of rationalization when used to import what he suspected were in fact hidden agendas of personal advantage. He was the first modern philosopher to put philosophy itself in the docket, and to show how, under the guise of reason, every philosophical system is at bottom an attempt to dominate public discourse by disqualifying all other systems of thought. Hume, a philosopher, wanted to rise above philosophy. So against the rising liberal view on personally reasoned morality (personal choice and will ought to determine morality), he insisted on the fundamental conservative belief that the practice of virtue (trying to be good) ought to determine will, not the other way around.

Another way to put this, which clearly signals a deep liberal-versus-conservative divide, is that in moral matters, when faced with what we *ought* to do over what we *want* to do, we should give precedence to the former. A further insight from Hume was that it is civilization that makes the act of reasoning itself possible, not the other way around. In other words (and surely Locke's contract theory was the target here), it is civilization that enables modes of reasoning, not the reverse. For acting reasonably presupposes the peaceful authority of custom, and so to use reason as a tool to attack the authority of custom (including the custom of accepting or rejecting various kinds of reasoning) is to undermine the reasonableness of reason itself. As mentioned, Hume believed that the trouble with modern thinkers is they invent moral and philosophical systems that operate as "concealed theology" (which he enjoyed exposing as such), on which they rely to form conclusions they then pass off as systematic products of superior reasoning. They argue in rational circles to defend their own feelings and biases. These systems they present as the *ultimate* last word, and as *autonomous* (supposedly independent) systems of thought that have a right to *dominion* over all other systems and ideals. All philosophical systems are really just sophisticated expressions of the will to dominate.

But Hume insisted this is the wrong direction. Instead, we should always place *affection* before *reflection*. Rather than relying egotistically on our own naked reason as the dominant truth, we should look to the long-held and well-loved customs and traditions that illuminate our common life, and these should always be assumed true unless shown to be otherwise. Not for him the alienation of the malcontent who seeks with the barbs of logic to turn common life upside down, camouflaging personal passions and prejudices as theorems of reason. Hume's conservative cure for such "philosophical barbarism" was to counsel the return of the thinker from his alienating role as *spectator* dictating theoretical solutions to the more natural human role of *participant* in common life, which he considered the sacred ground of the human world. As he put it: Be a philosopher if you wish, but be a man first! What are the six main aspects of this participation? They are the eternal human practices (not theories!) of *humility* (we should consider common life a dwelling place), *piety* (we must honor tried and true customs), *folly* (we should enjoy and celebrate life to the full as it is, and recognize the folly of false philosophy), *eloquence* (we should learn the high arts and give voice to high ideals), *greatness of mind* (we should always seek to elevate our own character and judgment), and *benevolence* (we should look after those in need).

So to summarize, the modern liberal generally accepts two of the defining notions of modernity: *cultural relativism* and personal *moral relativism*. The first arises from the belief that right and wrong change according to the cultural, social, or historical situation, and this proves there are no universal moral or cultural absolutes. The second is rooted in the liberal conviction that because morality is relative, freedom means doing whatever you want as long as you do not directly harm (aggress against) another. This belief has in turn produced the further conviction that choice is the main determinant of morality; expressions such as "it's true for you, but it's not true for me" will often be heard in response even to factual statements. This strong penchant for believing that *to choose an action is to make it moral* underlies the frequently heard liberal complaint that someone else is "imposing" a moral view. The modern liberal tends to think of moral truth as authorized by the will or the self, rather than by any objective moral truth or standard outside the self, or beyond the reach or influence of will.

The conservative, in contrast, will tend to support the belief that regardless of the cultural, social, or historical context, or changing customs and manners, there are certain permanent and universal moral truths and dispositions that, however imperfectly obeyed or followed, operate in all human societies and at all times as universal standards of conduct. Murder is murder, lying is lying; "do good and avoid evil," "justice must be done," "might does not make right," and so on are universal guides for human conduct; and the fact they are so often imperfectly observed does not make them less true. Commercial chattel slavery, to take just one example, is always wrong. It was not right in the past because everyone thought so, and wrong today because everyone thinks so. It is wrong in itself. For the conservative, cultural relativism may be true for a lot of the ordinary beliefs, ceremonies, rituals, customs, and manners of the people of the world. But when it comes to important moral matters, there are demonstrable human universals of morality and culture that are never relative and that have been true for all time. "Choice" cannot make something good that is inherently evil. As for personal moral relativism? The conservative rejects strongly the belief that morality originates in the self, or that personal choice (human will) can make something good that is inherently bad. Whether or not a religious person, the conservative will insist that morality is rooted in such universal standards of human conduct as mentioned here, however modulated by local customs. He will likely also support the existence of a God-given realm of natural law from which all human beings receive moral guidance by following its most basic precept: namely, that natural law is a command of right reason that follows nature for the common good. For the conservative, to displace this truth with a "morality" of individual will is to break the moral bonds of human society, past, present, and future.

A Little Test of Your Moral Profile

One of the most interesting recent efforts to understand human moral psychology (as proponents call this field of study) is by Jonathan Haidt and his colleagues, and can be found in Haidt's book *The Righteous Mind: Why Good People Are Divided by Politics and Religion*. He presents some fascinating insights on political/moral psychology, and illustrates the differences between liberals and conservatives. Haidt began his research as a typical well-educated left-leaning liberal, but after many years of studying how morality works in the real world, he became convinced that the traditional conservative notion of morality is closest to how almost all human communities understand morality—with one major exception. The exception is found among the only WEIRD people he found in the whole world. That acronym stands for individuals from Western, educated, industrialized, rich, and democratic societies. The WEIRDest of all people, he found, are located in the higher realms of the graduate schools of the Western world. They are the moral outliers of the human family, and in my own terminology, I would say they would all profile as the amoral grandchildren of Mill.

Haidt's moral foundations theory rests on five foundations: harm, fairness, loyalty, authority, and purity. He found that liberals score very high on (rely mostly on) the first two foundations, and much lower on the other three; whereas conservatives rely about equally on all five, but not especially high on any. You can create your own profile at YourMorals.org.

WHERE DO YOU STAND?		
On Morality and the Self		
	MODERN LIBERAL VIEW　　vs.	CONSERVATIVE VIEW
Morality	*Morality is relative*	*Morality is rooted in universal principles*
	Morality changes according to cultures and situations	Minor moral habits may change. But basic moral principles are constant and universal
Basis of Morality	*Individual choice and personal values*	*Transcendent standards and community mores*
		Morality is rooted in universal principles, religious commands, and natural moral law
Morality Known by	*Rational deliberation*	*Human nature, tradition, instinct, right reason*
	With a basis in individual liberty and equality	Not reason alone, but right reason following nature for the common good
Image of Self	*Metaphor of the onion*	*Metaphor of the glass house*
	The authentic self is internal and is found by peeling away false teachings from the past so that the self can emerge. Think of peeling an onion to get to the authentic self as the core of one's being	The self is not an object or a thing. It is a construct of soul, and is created via the second nature we acquire in the moral and social life of civil society, and through personal moral effort. Think of breaking through panes of opaque glass that obscure the truth, so that with each insight we see more clearly the truth of existence outside ourselves, and can then incorporate it into self

WHERE DO YOU STAND?		
On Morality and the Self		
	MODERN LIBERAL VIEW VS.	CONSERVATIVE VIEW
Moral Priority	*Individual freedom and rights*	*The common good*
	Individual rights and freedoms in the present have priority	Social freedom—society's rights, past, present, and future—have priority
Is Morality Private or Public?	*It should be decided privately* Rational people can make their own moral decisions	*All moral systems are necessarily public, and operate like a common language of conduct*
The Moral Flow	*Morality flows upward to society*	*Morality flows from society downward*
	Moral values are generated by free individual choices, and the sum of these make up society's morality	Moral direction arises from tried-and-true principles safeguarded by society and promoted as the common good. These are then inculcated in individuals as they mature
My Good vs. the Public Good	*Personal good is public good*	*Personal good may not be public good*
	What is good for me, if it harms no one else, is okay	We must beware that what seems good to ourselves may harm society as a whole, now or in future, directly or indirectly
Society: Abstraction, or Real Entity?	*Society is an abstraction*	*Society is a real corporate entity*
	Society is just a name for a collection, or aggregate, of individuals. So society can have no moral being in itself	Society is a real corporate entity with a real moral being comprised of an order of human relations that is more than the sum of its parts, and which supplies members of the community with shalls and shall-nots
Morality as a Simple Rule	*Morality must be rule-based*	*Moral complexity is falsified by reductive rules*
	We need a simple rule of logic and ethics that can decide tough moral issues	The search for a single moral rule ignores and can destroy the real moral complexity and the depth of meaning in a moral tradition. Rules and maxims are handy guides to morality, but not if they purge moral complexity through simplicity

WHERE DO YOU STAND?		
On Morality and the Self		
	MODERN LIBERAL VIEW vs.	CONSERVATIVE VIEW
Choice, the Good & Will	*Choice must guide morality*	*Choice does not make what is chosen good*
	Personal will and the right to choose must determine the good	Knowledge of the good must determine personal will and action, not the other way around
What We Want or What We Ought?	*Doing what we want has priority*	*Doing what we ought has priority*
	Self-flourishing, doing what we want without harming others, has priority	Doing what we ought should have priority in general over what we want, because this alone creates a human moral and social community

CHAPTER 12

On the Triumph of Will

In the process of writing any book, certain themes begin to emerge as if by themselves, and take center stage. For this book that theme is the rise and triumph of the Will over nature.[15]

The word *Will* is capitalized because, whether exercised by the state in reorganizing the natural lives of citizens, or by individuals in attempting to reorganize or avoid or foil their own biological nature, it has been a political and moral force in the formation of Western civilization, for better or worse. By *nature* I mean everything that is indelibly natural to human existence and flourishing, whether with respect to individuals (such as love of family) or to human societies (such as love and care of local ways of life and community) or to nations (such as patriotism and culture). Earlier I mentioned the old French saying (which is from an old Roman saying) to the effect that if you try to banish nature, it will always come galloping back. Much of our history has been a record of this banishing and galloping.

A key point of pride in what we still call our "liberal democracies" is the illusion that they rest on secular rather than religious values. At first glance this seems true. But if we look a little deeper it becomes

---

15 Much of this discussion on nature and the will is adapted from my October 2011 article "Getting Used to Fascism," in *The New Criterion*.

apparent, as discussed at a few points already, that almost all the political buzzwords of modernity with respect to progress, equality, democracy, and the establishment of the Great Societies, Just Societies, and so on is at bottom a secular echo—especially loud in all the totalitarian regimes of the twentieth century—of an enduring quest for the kingdom of heaven on earth. I argue that all the modern unnatural, and therefore antihuman, political and policy efforts to bend the nature of all to the will of some—of social engineers, utopians, progressives—have been expressed in two basic forms, one collective, or *macro*; the other individualist, or *micro*.

The macro forms of recent history, whether French totalitarian democracy (the French Revolution), Italian Fascism, German Nazism, or Soviet Communism, have had something in common: they were all collectivist, secular, populist, and militant, striving through the fearsome top-down powers of the state to draw all things into the ambit of a single pattern of national—or in the case of Communism, international—will, or centralized choosing. This will has in all cases been expressed through the subjugation and assimilation by force of things spontaneous, free, private, and natural to forced, artificial, rational, and unnatural designs of political and moral life.

For private religious belief? An ostensibly secular and wholly materialistic public belief system. For concepts of transcendent natural law? Man-made law only. For the private family? An array of public programs and services, from national day care to national health care to subsidized housing to government old-age homes. For private enterprise and free markets? Intensive regulation, ever higher taxation, and the direction of the forces of production to state ends (via collectivization of land and industry, regulatory control, state corporations, and so on). For countless voluntary community organizations? The substitution of equivalent tax-subsidized public administration. In short, the nanny state, cradle to grave. I have already introduced the favored word of the German National Socialists—*Gleichschaltung*, or "bringing into line"—which describes this willful forced transformation of the private and natural into the public and artificial.

On this general theme of regulation, however, our modern regimes cannot afford to be smug, for although we have never had to pack machine guns to enforce our softer but nonetheless pervasive brand of statism, it remains true that many of the policy specifics that were common to the macro form are hauntingly recognizable today in our progressive regimes. No matter where we look, we see the ever-increasing reach of government, taxation, debt, and overregulation; and in all Western democracies the trend is for the larger national and/or federal political units to absorb politically, and legally to subjugate (or bring into line), the smaller states, provinces, regions, and municipalities. It is now a plain fact of Western life that wherever we see more "democracy," we see less freedom (with the exception of the realm of the private body and sex). The European Union is an especially vivid example of this process of *imperium in imperio*: many formerly natural, ethnic, and territorial entities submitting to the unnatural force of a bureaucratic will to rationalize and centralize, right before our eyes.

What might be the reason for this mutation from hypo- to hyper-regulatory polities? In our profoundly secular age, most democracies have become unofficially atheistic, and have concluded that because there is no God to make earthly existence perfect, well then, we'll just have to do it by our own means, powered by the belief that human beings (at least of the planning type) are actually godlets (humans are "made in the image of God" is the theological template) who have a moral obligation to impose a uniform design of perfection (whether national or international) on all natural (nonrational) expressions of human life.

By the close of World War II, the macro forms of will-on-the-march that threatened to throw the entire Western world under the jackboot were either defeated (German Nazism and Italian Fascism), or stalled (Soviet Communism, until it fell in 1989). But perhaps the chief lesson of it all was that nature cannot be altered or extinguished by force from above for very long. In his bleak review of the various utopian carnages of the twentieth century, Rudolph Rummel, in *Death by Government*, verified about fifty million combatant deaths. In addition, an appalling 150 million legitimate citizens were slaughtered, not by any external enemies, but *by their own governments*. The macro form of the war against the natural, which started with a respectable reputation—recall that Hitler was *Time* magazine's Man of the Year in 1938, and Mussolini was the hero of Western intellectual chatter—ended with a very bad name and a deeply sobering lesson: government can be very bad for your health. Despite the dark failures of these macro forms, the will to triumph over nature has continued in a newer, more subtle micro form. No machine guns required (all you need is democracy).

At an astonishingly rapid pace since World War II, the many instruments of the micro form have become pervasive in all democracies. Perhaps the most insidious novelties are the worldwide computerization of data, myriad encrypted identity cards, state statistical bureaus, modes of instant satellite communication, precise cadastral (tax) maps, intensive tax harvesting (by installments) on an unprecedented scale, pervasive state and corporate invasions of privacy, regulatory takings in every private realm, sophisticated spying and security measures, and much more. Suffice it to say that none of the modern tools of control now common to our putatively free nations could have been imagined for a moment in even the most frenzied dreams of any absolutist king or despot in all prior human history. It is indisputable that we were much freer (less regulated, spied upon, and taxed) before the onset of modern democracy.

Personal examples of the loss of freedom to the statist will to control nature are close to many of us, because one of the purposes of modern property-codification and taxation regimes has been to incorporate into the state all of what one writer called the "free gifts of nature," such as forests, game, wastelands, prairies, surface minerals, water, and air rights.[16] Not so long ago, if you owned property, these things on your own land were yours, "from heaven to hell," as the expression went. No longer. Most once-private natural property is now under the surveillance of and regulated by the land, resources, water, marshlands, and animal police, and all modern democracies, in what amounts to a systemic regulatory taking without compensation, have gradually legislated away most of the historic private-property rights of owners over the free gifts of nature on, below, and above their own land.

Recently, after two years of caring for a pair of swans on my pond that might otherwise have become a meal for coyotes, I was shocked to see two smartly uniformed wildlife enforcement officers from Environment Canada pull up in a brand-new Jeep Cherokee. They served me with a $240 fine for "keeping swans without a license" (a $10 fee I had failed to renew). Protestations that it was costing me plenty in food, and in

---

16 For a striking example of the effects of the failures of the rationalist triumph over nature, see James C. Scott's *Seeing Like a State: How Certain Schemes to Improve the Human Condition Have Failed.*

electricity to run ice bubblers to keep my pond open for the swans in winter, were for naught.

Then, in the spring of 2010, in an attempt to purchase a piece of vacant land for a new home and to put in a driveway, I was informed by several layers of bureaucracy that work could not begin until July, "after the birds have left their nests," and that the one thing that would "absolutely stop the driveway" would be the discovery by a government inspector of a butternut tree in its path. My question, asked (I am ashamed to admit) in a somewhat tremulous voice: "Why are my birds to be more protected than my snakes, beetles, turtles, and groundhogs?" produced a kind of "just wait and see" look from a bureaucrat.

My main point is that, in what seems like a pragmatic response (that didn't work, so let's try it another way) of the West's progressive social engineers to the failed macro form, a softer micro form of the will over nature, also rooted in a much earlier intellectual tradition, has emerged gradually from the second half of the twentieth century, and is now in full bloom as our most pervasive, and therefore most invisible, political religion. It has produced a historically unprecedented type of polity I have been describing as libertarian socialism, characterized by a radically individualist and relativist ethic that, by way of an inventory of public orthodoxies, seeks to organize itself not as a triumph of collective will over the free nature of all citizens (nationally or internationally) as in the past, but instead as the triumph of the will of each and every citizen over his or her own individual biological nature.

What can this mean, what can this be, but a mutated, narrowed, and impoverished secular form of our old theological insistence on the moral freedom of each individual human being, now visible mostly in our tortured skewings of law and policy to grant legal priority to private will, or "choice"? This is doubly ironic, because whereas our more conservative spiritual progenitors exercised their free will to escape the dreaded slavery to their own natural bodily appetites and temptations, our more liberal polities now cite the sanctity of choice as their unassailable authority for indulgence in those same appetites. This new war of the will against social, moral, and legal constraints on natural appetite and biology has taken many forms, and what follows is a kind of fugue on that theme.

A clear indicator of the micro form at work—and this is a long-term complaint of the conservative—is the *atomization* or *individuation* of the natural social molecule: the tendency to think about the rights and needs of autonomous individuals and of our social, moral, and civil institutions as serving their needs, rather than of the value and sanctity of the institutions that individuals ought to be serving. Accordingly, our libertarian-socialist regimes have produced millions of "administered" individuals, each an entry in bits and bytes on the lockstep computers of the all-seeing state, as well as in the electronic files of any corporation that can afford such information gathering (often purchased from or provided by the state). When I was young, we had a family health card; we each now have an individual one, a process of individuation repeated in all areas of life, public and private, and now considered a normal and rational information requirement of human organization. Ironically, although we have never believed ourselves to be more free, we are individually under near-total surveillance. Video surveillance cameras are now in all public and private spaces, most phone calls are monitored "for your security"—and far from incidentally, your cell phone can be tracked to follow your every movement. Added to this pervasive monitoring is the RFID or "spy chip," which tracks your every purchase, and more. A tiny radio-frequency identification device so small it can easily be located surreptitiously almost anywhere, the spy chip is activated by a radio scanner, such that when you walk into a government building or your favorite department store, the spy chip inserted in your shirt, tie, bra, eyeglasses, or blue jeans during manufacture will reveal lots of details on your whereabouts and the pattern of your behavior. Wary credit card companies are now marketing RFID-protected cards.

The real theater for the modern microwar against the natural is personal biology—everything from the skin inward, especially sexual desires and all reproductive matters; and, for serious ideological reasons, this necessarily leads to the ultimate question of when a human being exists. This question is of utmost importance, because in a regime rooted in the freedom of personal bodily will for all, it is possible for an ideologically inconvenient "other" to throw into jeopardy the elaborate moral and legal justifications of an entire political regime. For example, if your freedom depends on your ability to manipulate or control a certain class of others who have been defined as *things* to enable your freedom, you will not easily tolerate anyone redefining them as human beings with the same rights as you have. In order to avoid a contradiction in foundational principles, many regimes in history have made entire classes of human beings disappear legally in order to sustain their ideological purity. Most Greeks and Romans, for example, simply took for granted that their empires—especially their democracies—were impossible to sustain without chattel slaves whose labors freed male citizens to participate in political life. But it is hard for a free human being in good conscience to enslave another free human being. So a special category of laws had to be invented to transform slave-humans into slave-things, or nonpersons. The most urgent question in any regime where the official political ideology is threatened by the existence of a specific class of human beings is always: How do we make the threatening other disappear legally?

What I am getting at is that the clearest ancient (as well as modern) example of the triumph of the will over nature is human slavery. It is a perverse triumph because it cannot be sustained without making an ideological target class of natural human beings disappear by law in the manner described. Although the transatlantic slave trade was the most recent commercial employment of this dark art, to "disappear" another, so to speak, is an ideological weapon employed today by almost every major democracy. That is a shocking thing to say, which I support as follows.

The slave-making operation of contemporary egalitarian democracy began the moment liberal egalitarians were forced by their own ideology to negate what any conservative would describe as the natural and eternal biological differences between the genders. They argued passionately that in order to be citizens equal to men, women must have the right to triumph over the natural consequences of their own sexual behavior by removing the natural burden of their unwanted children. This could *only* be achieved on a conscience-free basis by first converting an entire class of human beings—the unborn (or the unborn up to a specified age, depending on jurisdiction)—into material things, for which the legal weaponry of the ancients—category law—was required. In other words, *in order to sustain ideological purity*, modern libertarian-socialist regimes (this was distinctly not the case for democracy in its classical liberal, pre-egalitarian form) have had to legally transform their unborn children into womb slaves whom they declare to be nonhuman beings, or nonpersons, until born alive. This unflattering reality will be examined more closely in part 4.

Another looming reality in our aging democracies is the growing clamor—already achieved in some jurisdictions—for the right to control natural death (also examined more closely in part 4). Suicide means making yourself die. But other than the fact that to rest the ethos of a human society on a right of suicide would be to opt for something very dark indeed, we cannot object to, nor very easily prevent, this use of will. Euthanasia means someone else has to make you die; someone living must be an instrument in the killing of another, regardless of how remotely. So here too, the will, ever strident, rises for mastery over nature. Some say the rising clamor for a right to die is a sign of the victory of a culture of death. But I respond that it only looks that way. Ours is not a culture of death. It is a culture of will. Death is simply the last modern frontier to be conquered by will. In the Netherlands there is now a group called Out of Free Will campaigning for the right of people over 70 who are "tired of life" to be euthanized. Clearly, this right implies a corresponding obligation upon someone (usually a physician agent of the state) to do or arrange the killing required by such a law. The underlying logic is that, just as we can create life or make it disappear in the womb by will alone, we should have the right by will alone to order our own life ended. The legal right to "will a kill," so to speak, is shaping up as the ultimate triumph over nature, because it means openly playing God. We do not want to play the God of love and reason with whom we grew up, however, because we have switched allegiance to a God of pure will, in whose image we seek to shape the world as we please.

As for other biological aspects of nature over which we now seek a mastery of will? There are too many to count. But one of them, no-fault divorce ("two to make it, one to break it"), considered purely as an occasion for the expression of radical will, has clean removed the natural contractual basis of marriage, thus returning us to the radicalism typical during the French Revolution, when Jacobins argued that if the two spousal wills are not in accord, then no marriage exists anyway. This has had the effect of subjecting both the union of marriage and the honest contractual intentions of observant spouses to the unilateral choices of disaffected or philandering spouses. More of the determination to triumph over nature is apparent in our gender-constructing, gender-bending, and gender-merging discourse, not to mention our choose conception, choose time of birth, and choose a womb, a sperm, and an egg options. The underlying theme here is that *there is no binding natural order*, because nature can be altered by human will (of which a lot of modern reproductive technology is an expression).

Perhaps the most tiresome inebriations of anti-biology logic are produced in liberalizing campaigns calling for laws and public funding to impose androgyny upon us, the most devout exponents of which insist, as mentioned earlier, on forcing boys to play with dolls, and girls with trucks. On this score, my feminist neighbor finally surrendered in good humor when, after six months of attitude-correction of her children … nature came galloping back: she caught her daughter putting her little red fire engine to bed with a bottle.

For the conservative, another disturbing aspect of the war against nature is modern multicultural policy. In the early twentieth century Julien Freund opined that only three things matter in politics: command and obedience, the public and the private, and the insider-outsider distinction. Deep culture is a product of this last, frankly illiberal, but deeply natural, human tendency to bond socially according to widely shared values as insiders, creating outsiders (explained as the natural, and naturally exclusionist, social-bonding process in part 2). The social-bonding reality means that wherever a deep culture exists and is upheld, people will naturally tend to assimilate, and the modern nation state is—or at least was—a natural expression of this tendency. Rather ironically, then, multicultural policy, which began as an earnest attempt to denaturalize this naturally illiberal fact of human life, engages in *cultural erasure* by imagining all cultures as equal members of a single universal, diverse, and rootless "multicult." But as the French critic Pascal Bruckner observed, in so doing, it has condemned hundreds of ethnicities within these multicultural nations to "house arrest in their own skins," thus unintentionally engendering an isolating *identity politics*. In short, multiculturalism has created territorial mini-nations within nations, many of which, as in France, Belgium, England, and Holland, are now dangerous no-go zones for citizens of the host ethnicities, and for police. Nature has come galloping back once again.

Just how far does this microfascist trend of extending will over nature go? As far as the entire cosmos, it seems. I grew up with the terrible warning from Shakespeare's *King Lear* ringing in my ears: "As flies to wanton boys are we to the gods. They kill us for their sport." We are feeble beings in an immense universe. So in 1971, when the American astronaut Alan Shepard drove a golf ball a mile on the moon, it seemed a shockingly irreverent and smug thing to do. He was daring the gods by way of a gestural transfiguration of the solar system into his own personal playground. But the extension of human will over nature has extended farther still. In the notorious 1992 *Planned Parenthood v. Casey* decision of the US Supreme Court, we heard for the first time that "at the heart of liberty is the right to define one's own concept of existence, of meaning, of the universe, and of the mystery of human life." My liberal acquaintances say "of course, what's wrong with that?" But to me this oft-quoted declaration, which sounds at first like a description of God's freedom, betrays an utterly unselfconscious confidence and conceit, for it suggests that even cosmic meaning is subject to, is a creation of, personal human liberty; that there is a human right not simply to search for ultimate truth outside ourselves (recall the conservative metaphor for self as a glass house), but, in a kind of cosmic inversion, to create it *within* ourselves (recall the liberal metaphor for self as an onion). It was a pro-godlet ruling declaring that all of nature and the entire universe have no meaning except as defined by individual human will.

Our views of freedom and therefore of God have changed a lot. We used to say that because God is the ultimate good, and therefore can only do good things, we ought to follow suit. Freedom was obedience to the good (and was what the founders of the modern democracies believed before libertarian socialism took hold). But we have switched gods along with our ideal of the good to make our lives more convenient. We had to, because to sustain democracies resting on a belief in the sovereignty of each individual will, we needed a God of pure will in whose image we could fashion ourselves with every personal choice. But at such a point, with no external truth to direct or shame us, the good vanishes, is absorbed into whatever is willed; and then will is identified with truth. This switching of gods constitutes a theological revolution in Western life with profound and as yet unforeseeable implications.

WHERE DO YOU STAND?		
On the Triumph of Will		
	MODERN LIBERAL VIEW vs.	CONSERVATIVE VIEW
	~ PUBLIC WILL ~	
Law & Will	*Only human law recognized*	*Higher natural law is the standard*
	This removes all legal impediments to progressive state action	Human law that does not conform to natural law may be legal, but is not morally binding
Society & Will	*State services widely provided*	*Voluntary associations are primary*
	Grants, subsidies, government staff, facilities, etc. as a substitute for formerly voluntary associations and cultural, hobby, and sporting activities	Flourishing community events and spirit encourage citizen self-reliance and independence and block the bending of civil society to the will of the state through grant-seeking behavior
Power & Will	*Standardization and centralization*	*Division of powers and subsidiarity*
	These make equality possible. Whether in a unitary or a federal system, this entails a necessary replacement of unequal local powers and rights by a central power, either through negation of local or regional laws, by central command, or by unitary state provision of goods and services	Checks and balances of power are the best tools to prevent the rise of arbitrary government. Federal systems with enumerated state or provincial rights have been created with the specific objective of blocking excess central power of the larger will over the smaller will (the problem of *imperium in imperio*)
Culture & Will	*Universality and a unity of cultures*	*Full expression of culture under a rule of law*
	This is possible with a multicultural policy that integrates all world cultures into a single, multicultural "one world" family	Nationalism works best when each culture is allowed private self-expression, with the expectation of public assimilation to the host culture. A multicultural policy within a nation will always dissolve the host culture, just as it will dissolve the cultures of separate nations in a larger union such as the EU

WHERE DO YOU STAND?

On the Triumph of Will

MODERN LIBERAL VIEW	vs.	CONSERVATIVE VIEW

~ PRIVATE WILL ~

	MODERN LIBERAL VIEW	CONSERVATIVE VIEW
Religion & Will	*Separation of church and state* Religion should be banned from the public square. Secularism and a rational, scientific materialism and progressive public ideology must form the public belief system	*Separation doctrine is misunderstood* This was meant to prevent governments from establishing state religions, not to drive all presence of God from the public square. All moral systems sit on religion, and all philosophical systems sit on morality. Rather than achieving a separation, the West has a new religion: secular materialism is the new cosmology, evolution theory the new creation story, liberal progressivism the new teleology
Unborn Life & Will	*The will of the mother must prevail* Female biology must not block the career path or free choices of a woman, because gender is largely a social construct, and not a biological determinant, which is why androgyny is best as a social policy	*The unborn need protection from the will* … even from their own mothers and fathers. Human life is sacred from the moment of conception to natural death. Natural male and female biological differences are complements of each other, and have little to do with personal will or social constructs
Death & Will	*Death must be controlled by the will* All have a right to death with dignity. Euthanasia, which is the last frontier of freedom, must be legalized. A life that is not worth living should be ended. Individual will must prevail	*Death is part of the natural life cycle* The dying must be cared for in the best way possible, and not trapped in medical equipment. But neither should they be killed by licensed exterminators of the state, who are so often encouraged by selfish relatives waiting for the will to be read (to satisfy their own will). The default position of any society or medical practice must be the preservation of life, not a readiness to kill

WHERE DO YOU STAND?		
On the Triumph of Will		
MODERN LIBERAL VIEW	vs.	CONSERVATIVE VIEW
~ PRIVATE WILL ~		
Marriage, Will & Divorce	*Marriage is a private contract* It is a private contract between two individuals who make a vow to each other alone. Marriage is for the enjoyment of the adult couple. Divorce should be freely available at the will of either party ("two to make it, one to break it"), because no one should be trapped in a bad marriage against their will	*Marriage is a public contract* It is a public contract between the partners and society (to whom the vow of union is made). Marriage as an institution exists for the encouragement of procreation and the protection of the children of marriage. Divorce permitted for cause only ("two to make it, two to break it"). Divorce policy must aim to protect children, not parents
Biology & Will	*Biology and gender to be shaped by will* In an egalitarian democracy, human biology must be shaped by technology to provide equality for all. Gender differences must be eliminated, as well as the social and economic differences due to biology	*Life should conform to biology* What is natural and good should be the guide to social policy and gender roles, and natural differences honored, nurtured, and protected. Egalitarian efforts to alter nature always produce unintended consequences, now or in future
Universe & Will	*The universe is a site for freedom* The universe has no intrinsic meaning. Humans must shape life according to their will, and each has the right to confer a private meaning upon the universe	*The universe is a natural home* The universe must have a meaning or it would not be here. It is fine-tuned as a home for human and other forms of life. But it is mysterious, miraculous, and complex beyond the capacity of the human mind and will to fully grasp

CHAPTER 13

On God and Religion

I have always wanted to write about God, but never dared. For if God exists and has infinite qualities—all-powerful, all-knowing, and all-loving—the idea of a mere finite human being attempting to say anything definitive conjures up a storm of feelings about inadequacy, blind pride, blasphemy, and more. If God exists and *really* has those attributes, then better kneel quickly, is my instinctive reaction.

So I will speak only of liberal and conservative *ideas* about God, for a book such as this would not be complete without giving some sense of how the two sides in this debate differ in their attitudes, assumptions, and beliefs about God, religion, political life, and the nature of the universe. If I am correct that morality sits on top of religion, and philosophy sits on top of morality, then sharply opposed faith positions on God must inevitably affect everything else. The answers that different faith positions give to questions about the true nature of reality—*what* it is, *how* it is, *why* it is—determines everything else.

"Faith, you say? I just told you: I don't have a faith," insists my atheist liberal friend.

"Oh, yes you do!" I reply. "You believe *there is no God*, but can't prove it. And I believe *there is a God*, but can't prove that. So we both have a faith that neither of us can prove." That stops him in his tracks. But it certainly gets our debate going.

Not all modern liberals are atheists, of course; nor do all conservatives believe in God. But survey after survey suggests that most educated modern liberals—by far the majority of those working in schools and universities, the sciences, in media, the arts, journalism, and hundreds of related fields—self-describe as agnostic, and a surprising number are aggressively atheistic. In contrast, most, if not all, conservatives believe, either on the basis of unquestioned faith or as a result of personal experience and reasoning, that there *has* to be a creator God. This person probably attends church fairly often, and says God plays a significant role in personal and family life. These are the kind of people who feel awkward beginning dinner until someone has said grace, while a card-carrying liberal feels just fine saying "bon appétit." In this section, the stark divide between the atheistic liberal and the believing conservative will be contrasted, and it should be revealing; because as faith goes, civilization goes.

Why Is There Something?

For a long time—since Aristotle at least—the belief of most Western cosmologists was that the universe has always existed and never changes. That belief persisted until well into the twentieth century. And even then all astronomers thought that our own galaxy, the Milky Way, which is a hundred thousand light-years or so in diameter, was the whole universe. Then it was discovered that there are billions of galaxies like our own, and in 1929 Edwin Hubble proved that the whole universe has been expanding from the start. This gave support to the discomfiting idea that the universe had a beginning, and exploded in a Big Bang—which sounds an awful lot like a Genesis event. There was a conflict of opinion for a couple of decades, with half of all cosmologists still supporting the steady-state theory, and half the Big Bang. I remember reading a report of a meeting of the International Astronomical Union at Princeton in 1985, when a conflict of opinion on the nature of the universe—is it inflationary, or not?—could not be resolved. So … *they decided to take a vote!* I was flabbergasted: the nature of the universe was to be determined by … democracy? (For the record, 59 voted in support of an expanding universe, 2 voted for a steady-state universe, and 71 voted "don't know.")

But in the mid-1960s, cosmic microwave background radiation was discovered, and almost every scientist now believes this must be leftover radiation from the Big Bang event. This meant that after such a long time spent dismissing the idea of a *theological* creation event, scientists who had faith in a purely materialistic universe would now have to embark on a hunt for a purely *physical* creation event. That pretty much sums up the efforts of all cosmology for the last half century. But how it is possible for a solely physical universe to create itself?

When conservatives think about the Big Bang problem, they usually respond either with an outright "we told you so"—the Big Bang is exactly what religion describes, an instantaneous creation event—or they throw up a number of serious philosophical objections. The first is in the form of the most fundamental question of all: Why is there something in existence, rather than nothing? This question usually produces a blank stare from anyone of the materialist faith, who will shrug and say that's just the way things are, while from the person who is agnostic, it will produce a feeling of profound awe, because the "something" we call the universe did not have to exist at all. But it does. The second objection seems unanswerable: namely, that the universe could not have created itself, because in order for anything to create itself, it would have to precede itself in existence, which is impossible; for how can you precede yourself, if you don't yet exist? The third objection begins with the ancient truth *ex nihilo nihil fit*, or "out of nothing comes nothing." And I have a little story about that.

Two years ago my wife and I were on vacation in Italy, and one evening found ourselves seated in a charming restaurant in Venice beside the only other non-Italian in the place. He was the American astrophysicist Robert O'Dell, the man behind NASA's Hubble Space Telescope project. I got quite excited, because for many years I owned a sizable backyard telescope, and even this modest level of astronomy awe had been putting distance between me and the purely materialistic explanations of reality I used to support. Now I was sitting beside one of the big players in astronomy, who was affable and receptive to questions from an amateur. But I'm not sure he answered the *ex nihilo* question. I told him I thought that, although a surprising number of astronomers are spiritual people, it seems like the whole course of modern cosmology and astrophysics is at bottom a quest to find a purely materialistic explanation for the Big Bang origin of the universe. But if there was no universe before that moment, how could something be created out of nothing—meaning *nothing whatsoever?* He waxed poetic and described how physicists in fact "often see matter coming into and going out of existence from nothing." I objected, gingerly, that I thought preexisting force fields, gravity, and the laws of physics make this possible, and that those things are not "nothing." We moved on to other topics, but the unanswered question lingered.

Another niggling complaint about all cosmology talk is that scientists casually speak of the universe as an entity, a noun, a discrete object. But how is it possible to speak of a thing, an object, unless there is something other than, or outside of, that thing, from which it is distinct? We have all seen those diagrams of the universe in the shape of a football. The moment I see that shape I think there must be some kind of space or reality outside the football. In other words, how can we speak of the universe as a discrete thing unless there is something outside the universe—in which case "the universe" cannot be the whole universe?

Now let's contrast the pure liberal materialistic view of existence with the two main conservative views. First, there is the standard Christian view (paralleled in many faiths) that the universe and everything in it was created by a loving God who made his purposes known in two books— the Bible, and the Book of Nature (the laws of nature)—and that all of human history is unfolding accordingly. Then there is the less religious, everyday spiritual conservative view that arises from experiential awe, from logic, and yes, from the study of physics and philosophy, to wit: that because logically the universe could not have created itself, it must have been created by a superior being. Sometimes a conservative-minded cosmologist will argue that although the *geocentric* view (that Earth is the center of the universe) was rejected a long time ago, it has come back again in the form of the *anthropic* principle (or similar arguments), to the effect that the whole universe and all the laws of physics—down to the minute atomic structure of matter—have been fine-tuned from the very beginning to produce human consciousness—otherwise, consciousness would not be here now. The American professor of logic and philosophy Thomas Nagel makes this point in his short and refreshingly disruptive book *Mind and Cosmos*. He was preceded by another, notorious professor of philosophy who defected from the ranks of unbelievers, the Englishman Anthony Flew, who after fifty years spent as the hero of materialists and atheists published *There Is a God*, in which he concluded that it is impossible for a purely material universe to create concepts and consciousness. Both men present the entire cosmos not only as purposeful, but also as consciousness-centered.

Matter and Consciousness, Brain and Mind

The question of consciousness brings up another deep divide between liberals and conservatives on the question of whether reality is all matter, or some combination of matter and nonmatter. This difference is captured in the distinction between *brain* and *mind*. Liberals, conservatives, and neuroscientists agree that the brain is made entirely of matter. But they disagree deeply about the mind—about the indubitable existence of intangible feelings, thoughts, concepts, ideas, consciousness—which are not in the least material (have no mass, shape, measurable size, and so on). Despite the obvious existence of this nonmaterial realm, most, if not all, neuroscientists (and most secular liberals) will persist in saying that because all reality is material, mind *has to be material*, and they are confident this will be proven some day (that consciousness is "just like a computer"). Most conservatives will disagree and will argue (a bit like Descartes did) for a dualistic reality: brain, body, and all physical things in nature are material; but thoughts, concepts, feelings, and so on are nonmaterial.

When I am out for an evening with my very secular, God-ridiculing liberal friend who happens to be very interested in the sciences, we debate a lot about this. So I ask him to participate in a simple experiment, as follows: Put your hand on a tabletop and lift one finger up and down. He does. Then I ask him how it was possible to do this. He says that it's an electrical signal sent from the brain along the nerve to the muscles of the finger. I agree. But then I ask: What triggered the decision to send the electrical signal? His answer: A neuron. I reply that although a lot of what we do as physical beings, such as breathing without thought, digesting food, and so on, is automatic and happens without thought or intention, a neuron in the brain is made of pure matter, and while a brain neuron does react to chemical or electrical signals, it cannot *consciously initiate* a physical activity like lifting a finger all by itself. Therefore, what triggered the thought must be something nonmaterial. You can say it's "me," it's my "soul," it's my "self"—whatever you want—but you cannot say it is a material thing, because a thing cannot make a conscious decision.

Neurons cannot think, any more than a rock or a fingernail can think. If they could, your whole body would be entirely (instead of only half) out of your control. It would be as if inside your body there was another little human being calling the shots for you. It is impossible to imagine a purely material "thinking thing."

So we can see how, on one side of the divide over the question of the meaning of reality and human existence, we arrive at the typical secular liberal view that, because everything is material "all the way down," the universe must have created itself. And that conclusion in turn has to mean that we live in a universe with no teleology—no special origin, meaning, or purpose to the universe. Here is a concise statement emblematic of that view from William Provine, a professor of biology at Cornell University, who says this view is held by almost all evolutionary biologists: "Let me summarize my views on what modern evolutionary biology tells us loud and clear—and these are basically Darwin's views. There are no gods, no purposes, and no goal-directed forces of any kind. There is no life after death. When I die, I am absolutely certain that I am going to be dead. That's the end of me. There is no ultimate foundation for ethics, no ultimate meaning in life, and no free will for humans, either."[17]

Provine is obviously acutely aware of the consequences of his faith, because he spells out the embedded consequences of this belief in a logical chain:

no God > pure materialism > no free will >
no purpose to existence > no foundation for ethics >
no meaning to anything >

to the silent finality of his own death.

Why and How Is There Life?

Such firm assertions about the materiality and meaninglessness of the universe necessarily point us to another Great Divide concerning the origin and existence of life. The liberal materialist view flows necessarily from the arguments previously recited: as there is no God and all reality

17 This quote is from one of four debates between Provine and University of California law professor Phillip Johnson, and can be read here: http://www.arn.org/docs/orpages/or161/161main.htm.

is solely material, life *had* to have a purely material origin. That is the ideological imperative of all forms of reductive materialism. But the conservative responds that there is a huge distinction to be made between the existence of a material thing, like a rock, and something that is alive. It is fairly easy to say how a rock began, but no one knows how life began. Even simple things like the cell or the gene are not simple things at all. To this complaint the pure materialists simply throw up their hands and say that life must have begun in some primeval ooze, and after that, all of life unfolded according to Darwinian evolution to produce what we have on earth today: extraordinary, and extraordinarily complex, designs of life—but no designer.

The Darwinian theory was from the start an attempt to explain life by removing God and all other teleological theories from the picture altogether. In its modern synthesis, which is a combination of Darwin's theory and modern genetics, the theory says that evolution occurs through a process of random (accidental, mindless, purposeless) genetic mutation, and natural selection. In other words, there is a genetic coding mistake that produces a mutation in some aspect of an organism—a longer neck, say—and the mistake is either favorable or unfavorable to the organism's survival. In the case of the giraffe, it was favorable; the long-necked ones survived because they could reach and eat higher leaves, but the ones with the short necks lost out in the struggle for food, and died out.

Darwinism is called metaphysical naturalism (rather than physical naturalism) by its critics, because they are certain it is a belief system without sufficiently convincing physical proof, and therefore it is a theory in crisis. A lot of distinguished scientists from a large variety of professional fields agree, and you can see a very long list of them, organized by nation, at DissentFromDarwin.org, where they are calling for a reappraisal of the evidence. For it seems pretty clear that, after studying the controversies in this field, almost anyone except an evangelical Darwinian would conclude that the theory survives on faith. Because it is like a faith, anyone holding it is obligated to cobble together a chain of materialistic reasoning to prove that, just as the physical universe came about via the laws of physics alone, life came about by purely material means, and evolved by random genetic mutation and natural selection.

The conservative responds that evolution theory explains a lot of things having to do with biological *variation*, the sort of microevolution or *adaptation* within a species, of the kind that animal and plant breeders have relied upon for a long time to produce new "breeds" within a species. But it does not convincingly explain macroevolution, or how one species became another—like how a fish became a bird.

The weaknesses of the theory usually cited are: the fact that almost all genetic mistakes/mutations are unfavorable, rather than advantageous to a species; the paucity of transitional species in the fossil record; the fact that there is no explanation of why the human brain is vastly more sophisticated than simple hunter-gatherer survival ever required; the fact that all major species appear fully developed in the Cambrian explosion of more than half a billion years ago, and have little altered since; the accusation of tautology—a species survives because of its fitness, and we know it is fit because it survived; and finally, the fact of irreducible complexity. Complex organisms would have had to evolve all their inter-dependent parts at once in order to function and survive; and it is hard to imagine how this could take place without some kind of advance design (which yields ID, or the theory of intelligent design).[18]

The classic illustration is the mousetrap. It doesn't work at all unless all its parts are in place at the same time and working as intended (as designed). Due to these and many more failures of theory and evidence, conservative critics argue that while valid at the micro level, evolutionism has been illegitimately expanded into a total creation story, despite the absence of essential supporting facts. That is surely because for a pure materialist, recourse to any sort of nonmaterial principle, in an academic field in which all theoretical work is justified by a dogmatic faith in materialism, is simply an unthinkable heresy (and also a quick way to

---

18 One of the best summaries of ID theory is a peer-reviewed article by Stephen C. Meyer, "The Origin of Biological Information and the Higher Taxonomic Categories," published in 2004 in *Proceedings of the Biological Society of Washington*, a journal of the Council of the Biological Society of Washington. The Discovery Institute, which is dedicated to ID theory, reports on its website that "because the article was the first peer-review publication in a technical journal arguing for ID, the journal's editor, evolutionary biologist Richard Sternberg, was punished by his Smithsonian supervisors [where he was a research associate] for allowing Meyer's pro-ID case into print." This led to an investigation of top Smithsonian scientists by the US Office of Special Counsel, which was widely covered in the media, including the *Wall Street Journal* and *Washington Post*. The federal investigation concluded that Sternberg had been wrongly disciplined and intimidated. The case led to widespread public indignation at the pressures placed on Darwin-doubting scientists, not only at the Smithsonian but at universities across the United States and elsewhere.

get drummed out of your profession if your institution is a card-carrying member of the Church of Latter-day Evolution).

The moral and political conclusions drawn by the modern liberal from these shaky assumptions point to the conviction that we humans are forever alone in the universe, and so must look after ourselves and improve our world without the help of a god or a religion. However, if (as seems true) human beings at all times have expressed a deep hunger for God, and if, as Nietzsche notoriously insisted, God is dead, then there is a need for some kind of inspiring replacement for God.

From ancient times to the present, there have been many attempts to redirect the focus of this hunger for an otherworldly realm to this world. During the Renaissance, various brands of humanism were promoted by devout thinkers such as Erasmus, who argued for a *Christian humanism*. But by the more secular nineteenth century, such efforts were simply labeled *humanism*. They promoted the study of classical pagan literature, the arts, and philosophy, and highlighted what seemed like the quasi-divine capacities, dignity, and freedom of human beings. By the time modern liberalism got a stranglehold on the twentieth century, the idea was that the worship of human beings should replace the worship of a nonexistent God, and this should be called *secular humanism*. Three manifestos were published, the first in 1933. Philosopher John Dewey, a signatory of the first *Humanist Manifesto*, described it as "our common faith." Signatory Julian Huxley described it as "a religion without revelation," and in a moment of euphoria, secular humanism was referenced as "a religion" by the US Supreme Court in *Torcaso v. Watkins* in 1961. The 1973 second edition of *A Humanist Manifesto* states: "No deity will save us; we must save ourselves." In a 1983 article in *The Humanist*, writer John Dunphy created a minor furor when he summed up this "religion" as he imagined it:

> I am convinced that the battle for humankind's future must be waged and won in the public school classroom by teachers who correctly perceive their role as proselytizers of a new faith: a religion of humanity that recognizes and respects the spark of what theologians call divinity in every human being.... The classroom must and will become an arena of conflict between the old and new—the rotting corpse of Christianity, together with all its adjacent evils and misery, and the new faith of

humanism, resplendent with its promise of a world in which the never-realized Christian ideal of "love thy neighbor" will finally be achieved.

The first article of *A Humanist Manifesto* states that "religious humanists regard the universe as self-existing, and not created," and the seventh, that "the distinction between the sacred and the secular can no longer be maintained." And this, despite the fact that the manifesto is described by many as "the bible of secularism," and what Dunphy called "a new faith."

Conservative Reaction

Secular humanism triggered an immediate reaction from conservatives and religious people to the effect that this brand of humanism is a prideful, warped attempt to deify ordinary mortals, a ridiculous fantasy, vanguard of a larger attack on the entire Judeo-Christian ethos of the West, and the prelude to an atheistic and materialistic modernity that must end in rampant hedonism, moral skepticism, and decline. The modern liberal disagrees, arguing that with God finally dead (whatever that illogical statement might mean, as by definition God cannot die), we are finally free to reject religious and metaphysical superstitions and dogmas about spiritual good and evil and make our own worldly good—a more perfect world—along rational principles. This is a modern spin on the old Enlightenment ideals discussed in part 1.

In Dostoevsky's majestic novel *The Brothers Karamazov*, the darkly nihilistic character Ivan notoriously declares that if God does not exist, then everything is permitted. To illustrate the consequences of this, Dostoevsky provides a disturbing story line showing how indirect evil flows and grows from one character, comfortable in his fashionably humanistic atheism, to the angry and coldly rationalistic atheism of Ivan himself, to the deadly nihilism of the idiot Smerdyakov, who, so impressed with Ivan's philosophy of nonmeaning, murders Ivan's father—for no reason.

When we transpose that amoral sequence to the political level, we see the parallel. What begins with atheism as a fashionably clever public worldview becomes an infection of amorality that leads, as through a glass darkly, to a culture of nihilism and death. This illuminates the conservative anxiety over the fact that virtually all the defiantly humanistic political systems of the twentieth century (all exercises in what I have called the triumph of the will over nature) have conclusively demonstrated that, when love and compassion are severed from their deepest moral and spiritual sources, the humanistic systems builders have to resort to the only motive for compassion that remains: a rationalized utopianism, the basis for which is the utilitarian conviction that the end justifies the means. This slide into utopian amoralism produces the counterintuitive scenario of the true modern radical so caught up in a delirium of affection for a solely humanist perfection that he convinces himself he is morally justified in killing all who stand in the way of his dream. That is the psychology that underlies all political religions.

God and the Law

Another serious consequence of the God-divide between materialists and spiritualists has to do with their necessarily contrasting conceptions of law. For the secular humanist there is no God, nor any transcendent realm, and so the only kind of law that is real and that matters is *human law* in the form of statutes, decrees, government policy, executive orders, and so on. This is usually called *positive law* by legal theorists. Their argument is that laws are made by a duly constituted sovereign for the government of an organized, law-based society, and only these are law. The interest of the modern liberal in this exclusively human law is clearly linked to the persistent liberal interest in maximum freedom of personal will, as well as in egalitarian democracy (the progressive will of the state). In other words, the defense of human law rests on—requires—both atheism and humanism to support its foundational claim that, because there is no teleology, no higher purpose to existence, nothing must block the duly constituted will of the sovereign people.

But a long time ago, Jesus threw the cat among the secular pigeons when he announced that citizens should "render to Caesar the things that are Caesar's, and to God the things that are God's"—there is human law, and there is God's law. From that point on in the West, the former would be judged by the latter. Rousseau complained that this produced a legal dualism—two wills, or "two heads of the eagle" of power in the Christian world, and he spent all his own theoretical powers trying to unify them into a single head and will (which he called "the general will"). And that is what all the totalitarian and secular liberal powers of the West have been trying to achieve ever since. And that is why the great enemy of all human law has been the other head of the eagle: what from ancient times until today has been called *natural law.*

Natural law is a collection of transcendent moral laws that philosophers such as Aristotle and Cicero and many of the pagan, Christian, and Jewish religions, ancient and modern, have believed are knowable by right reason, insight, and instinct, and that Saint Paul said are written in the heart. In our present age of secular humanism, natural law has almost gotten buried by defenders of human law. But as the French philosopher Étienne Gilson once observed, natural law always buries its undertakers. And indeed, after the unconscionable secular totalitarian slaughters of the twentieth century, all carried out under the sole authority of human law, the natural law has indeed been making a comeback.

For religious people, natural law is knowable through the revealed laws given by God (such as the Ten Commandments). But the key point for all conservatives is that natural law is superior because it is *not* man-made. It is eternal, transcendent, and universal, and so *stands forever in judgment on all human law.* As known by common people everywhere, natural law places moral handcuffs far stronger than metal ones on all tyrants, who know they cannot lead for very long if they are held in open moral contempt under a higher law.

Nations that have evolved under the moral heritage of Christianity have always managed, in their darkest hours, to reject the idea of living under human law alone. Instead, they say what the judges of the Nazi killers at the Nuremberg trials said when German officers attempted to exonerate their heinous crimes by insisting they were only following the duly constituted human laws of Germany. The judges condemned them by declaring that *natural justice* (another term for natural law) automatically converts an unjust law into *a lawless law.* When sentencing them, the judges appealed to what they called *supra-positive principles,* including the natural equality of all human beings before the law.

So what is a simple definition of natural law? It is: a command of right reason that follows nature for the common good. In short, it is a command (not a suggestion) of conscience and of right reason (not demonstrably wrong reason) that follows nature (does not follow the humanly unnatural) for the common good (not just for personal good).

I have cited a few examples of universal natural law in other parts of this book: "Do good and avoid evil"; "might does not make right"; "do not cheat or tell lies"; "honor contracts and vows"; and so forth.[19]

But the conversion of an unjust law to "a lawless law" is an intriguing concept that captures the entirety of the conservative view of the proper workings of law. To wit: that just as we must guide ourselves by the cultivation of a higher standard of self within, all ordinary human law and all governments must be measured against a higher standard of universal natural law outside and above the state. That's what Aristotle, Cicero, and, most persuasively of them all, what Saint Thomas Aquinas argued, seven centuries before Nuremberg. He said, "*Lex iniusta non est lex*" ("an unjust law is not a law"). Today Aquinas might say, okay, I grant to you that because a law is duly constituted, it may correctly be *called* a law. But because it is unjust, it has *no moral binding power on the people*, and is therefore a law in name only. That was a very conservative thing to argue, and it amounts to a profoundly conservative principle—one that Jesus implicitly announced, too—that all civilizations need a natural-law standard above human law by which *to judge the law itself*, and therefore, by which *to judge the state*. Dictators and totalitarians hate this principle—and so do modern liberal humanists.

God and the Moral Realm

The principle—that a legitimate law may itself be judged immoral, and therefore nonbinding—cannot be found in most non-Christian cultures. In Islamic nations, for example, the religious, political, and legal authorities are one and the same, and have sole power to interpret and implement the laws of the Koran. From the twelfth century forward, especially as formulated by the influential thinker Al-Ghazali in his book *The Incoherence of the Philosophers*—a book that ridiculed philosophical attacks on religion—Muslims have accepted the view that God is an

---

19 In a move to restore public trust in the financial sector in 2014, all 90,000 Dutch bank employees were required to swear this "oath to God" (or a similar "nonreligious affirmation"): "I swear that I will do my utmost to preserve and enhance confidence in the financial-services industry. So help me God." What? A secular financial organization requires a vow of sincerity before God? But what else could it be? No one has much confidence in the sincerity of a vow sworn on the honor of "myself" or "my best friends" or "my community." Even a vow sworn as a pledge of allegiance to one's country is generally backed up by reference to God as a suprahuman witness.

impersonal God of pure and absolute will who, for that very reason alone, can do anything he wishes, at any moment—even irrational or morally contradictory things that mere humans might consider deeply evil. Ghazali rejected entirely the idea of natural causality. When we put a match to a ball of cotton, it burns. All is contingent on God's will, and he decrees that certain things should happen in a specific order. Match > cotton > fire. But God can always make things behave otherwise. An observation of the match > cotton > fire sequence proves simultaneity, but not causation. The idea is that an absolute God of infinite power cannot be limited by anything whatsoever, and certainly not by puny human opinion; it is plain blasphemy for a human being to judge God, who is wholly beyond the reach of human comprehension. Learn the law of God and obey it is the humbling theme.

Christianity came to the same fork in the road in the Middle Ages— the choice between believing in a God of Pure Will and a God of Reason—and took the latter path. And that is why there can be no meeting of the minds between these two religions. Christians have long argued that God is not only a personal god, but also a god of reason, rather than of pure will only. So there are many things such a god cannot (or at least would never) do. For example, although God may indeed have an absolute will, he could never do something evil, because part of the very nature and definition of the Christian God is absolute goodness and love. In short, God could never use divine will for evil purposes, for otherwise that would contradict his own essence, or nature. Nor can he invert the goodness of his own creation. Which is to say, he cannot make what is evil good, nor what is good evil. This is an important distinction because it means some things like charity or murder are good or evil *in themselves*, and not just because God says they are good or evil. Neither can God make 2 + 2 = 5, nor what is false true, nor true, false. God cannot die, either. Nor can he make square circles, or circular squares. He cannot tire himself, corrupt himself, or change in any way that makes him less than a perfect God. And, so Christians believe, he would never decree an unjust, or irrational, or unnatural moral law for mankind.

I have elaborated here because this view of God has had a powerful effect on the conservative notion of a higher morality, and therefore on what constitutes legitimate political power and the proper checks to be placed on democracy and the constitutional rights of states. Throughout the modern era, however, the secular liberal reaction in most Western democracies has been both to eliminate the concept of higher law and, with legal legerdemain, to sidestep the constitutional limitations on state power rooted in that concept.

On Religion and the State

Of this large and complex topic only a little can be said here of the radical difference between the liberal and conservative sides with respect to the proper relation between religion and government. But as a general observation, we can say that ever since the eighteenth century Age of Reason there has been a surprisingly successful drive by secularists in many, but not all, Western nations to privatize a once public religiosity by removing much of its influence from the public square, and above all to ensure that the state does not establish a national religion. Sweden had a state Lutheran church until 2000, and England still has a national religious establishment, the Anglican Church of England, of which the British monarch is the supreme head. If we think of no state support for nor restrictions on religion, the only modern nation with such a complete separation of church and state is the United States. Barely half a century ago the Christian cross and the Ten Commandments could be found displayed somewhere in almost every public school, and citizens stood proudly to sing their national anthem ("in God is our trust" in America and "God keep our land, glorious and free" in Canada). Although religion has been successfully purged as an active influence from public schools, many private schools still have a strong religious foundation, and almost all older universities in the United States and Canada were founded under religious auspices, obvious from a glance at their gothic arches, cloisters, chapels, and stained glass windows. But in terms of public life as a whole, religion is increasingly a fossil remnant in most Western nations, and this has been a deliberate undertaking of the modern secular liberal project.

The Founders of America and Canada never questioned that religion is the bedrock of public morality. But as the histories of many colonists had included religious persecution, they fought for religious tolerance for all, and were adamant that government must be prevented from establishing a national church and persecuting nonconformists in its name. Their most passionate religious interest, in other words, was *to ban the state from running a national religion, not to ban religion from the state.* Certainly not to privatize religious feeling. They fully expected religion to have a strong presence in public life and in all the institutions of society, and never imagined that the icons of their belief, such as the cross and the Ten Commandments, would be ripped from the walls of schools and public buildings by modern secularists. They were religious almost to a man, and were especially wary of radical secular regimes (such as were mounted during the French Revolution) that substituted the worship of man (in the form of the Goddess of Reason) and fickle and changeable human law for the worship of a transcendent God and the permanent truth of a higher moral law.

This brings us back to our main theme, which is that, while it may be true that many liberals are religious and many conservatives are not, the secular liberal narrative that all transcendent reality, morality, and law is to be dismissed as myth and banished from the public square remains dominant. Accordingly, the subtext is that secular humanist worship will continue to mean the worship of human progress and will. The conservative view has always been that human beings do better, and do less damage to others, by worshipping a transcendent God and living under a higher moral law they cannot change, than by worshipping themselves and living under a changeable human law that is vulnerable to the will of those who would manipulate them.

WHERE DO YOU STAND?		
On God and Religion		
	MODERN LIBERAL VIEW vs.	CONSERVATIVE VIEW
Which Comes First?	*Philosophy, morality, religion*	*Religion, morality, philosophy*
	Philosophy is reason, and so must dictate morality. Religion is to be tolerated privately, but banished from the public square	Morality sits on religion, and philosophy and politics sit on morality. If the moral system of a culture is to be conserved, its source in religion must be preserved
Theism & Atheism	*Atheism rejects faith*	*Atheism is a faith*
	The foundation of atheism is a rejection of the idea of God	Atheism is a faith in a godless universe. But the absence of God cannot be proven, any more than the existence of God can be proven
The Universe	*The universe is self-created*	*The universe had to be created*
	The Big Bang proves that the universe had a material beginning	Nothing comes from nothing, and not even a universe could create itself, because to do so it would have to precede itself in existence, which is impossible
The Role of Consciousness	*Consciousness is material*	*Consciousness is nonmaterial*
	Everything in the universe is material, and so consciousness also is material, and has a material cause. Brain and mind are the same substance	Ideas, concepts, and feelings are clearly nonmaterial realities common to all human beings. A material thing cannot do anything conscious. Brain, which is material, is not the same as mind, which is nonmaterial
Purpose	*The universe has no purpose*	*The universe must have a purpose*
	The universe is purely material and self-created. Neither it nor life has any purpose	The universe must be here for a reason, because neither it nor life can self-create *ex nihilo*. Human consciousness was in the cards from the beginning, or it would not be here now. The universe appears to be fine-tuned to produce life and consciousness

WHERE DO YOU STAND?		
On God and Religion		
	MODERN LIBERAL VIEW vs.	CONSERVATIVE VIEW
Evolution Theory	*All life is produced by evolution*	*Evolution theory is a creation story*
	The modern Darwinian synthesis, combining evolution via random mutation and natural selection with genetics, explains all life, and is incompatible with religion	Darwinian evolution theory explains microvariation within species, but fails to explain the evolution of new species from existing species by macroevolution. It also fails to explain the irreducible complexity of complex biological organisms
Humanism	*Humanism must replace religion*	*Humanism is the worship of man*
	Humanism is the only rational way to end religious strife and create a better world through human values	Humanism is a bogus religion of man that exposes us to manipulation by others who invent their morality as they go. All humanisms lead from a war of merely human values to relativism, to nihilism, and on to totalitarianism. Communism, nazism, and fascism are all humanistic systems
God & Law	*Only human law counts*	*Natural law guides human law*
	As there is no God, we only have human law, which is any law made by a duly constituted sovereign of a law-abiding people	An unjust law maybe called a law, but it is not morally binding if it offends the higher natural law. Individuals must measure themselves as well as nations according to the standard of natural law
God & State	*Banish religion from the public square*	*Ensure religion stays alive in public*
	There must be complete separation of church and state and all traces of religion removed from public spaces	No state control of religion is wanted, but God must be kept alive in public life. The heritage of the West is Judeo-Christianity, the foundation of public and private morality

PART IV

CHAPTER 14

Issues That Divide

The widest divide between liberals and conservatives opens up whenever hot social and moral issues such as gay marriage, abortion, and euthanasia come to the table. These have become so incendiary they cannot be discussed with any expectation of a rational exchange of views such as was possible only a few decades ago. The modern liberal view on virtually all these topics has been in the ascendant for almost a century, however; its dominant feature is the relaxation of legal, social, and moral prohibitions and controls in favor of expressive individualism and self-determination. The conservative view is identifiable as a rearguard struggle to conserve the underlying principles, affections, and sanctity associated with the topic under attack.

In part 2 of this book, the argument was made that the trend to hyper-individualism and the privatization of morality has been a key factor in the mutation of democratic regimes from their original basis in liberty through an egalitarian stage, to their present and perhaps final stage of libertarian socialism. This is a trade-off that has resulted in systematic attacks on social freedom in the name of equality from above by governments and courts, and in the name of individual privacy, security, freedom, and rights by individuals from below—both of which, I have argued, are eroding the once formidable buffering force against statism provided by a flourishing civil society.

In addition to the three issues to be discussed in this section, there are many others within which this same process can be observed. What is common to them all is an *inversion of priority* from the traditional understanding that individuals are to serve and strengthen the larger purposes, values, expectations, and principles of their own civil society, as expressed in traditional institutions and in life events such as marriage; childbearing; and care of the disabled, sick, and dying; to the expectation that these things must serve individual expectations and will, and are to be reshaped for that purpose. The relaxation of moral controls or checks on formerly shamed personal behaviors and appetites, and of legal controls by way of the elimination of prohibitive laws against many of those behaviors, is sharply evident in the table on libertarian socialism in part 1. A neutral sociologist of the future will surely look back at this trend and say that what underlaid this inversion was the moral lassitude of an entire culture, a loss of will on the part of the people as a whole to safeguard the boundaries of their collective *social freedom*—that ancient right of any flourishing civil society to determine and defend its core shalls and shall-nots—against attacks mounted in the name of freedom, equality, and democracy by individuals, and by the state itself.

This trend explains why, whenever attempting to resist this moral relaxation, conservatives find themselves villainized as dinosaurs and the targets of liberal outrage (that tiresome word), and why rational discussion between liberals and conservatives can no longer settle fundamental differences of opinion. Although each side may use the same words—freedom, human nature, democracy, equality, and so on—they have radically different meanings in mind. What follows in this section is one man's no-holds-barred effort to expose this baleful trend by way of some frank discussion, comparative analysis, and direct questions for readers having to do with what are arguably the three main issues that most clearly reveal the liberal-versus-conservative divide.

Human beings will always be able to *think* whatever they want about each other. That cannot be controlled. And until very recently, those living in the free world, at least, have always been able to *say* whatever they wanted, as long as they did not defame someone's character in writing (libel), or with speech (slander). Even then, you could be charged with such offenses only if the things you said or wrote about someone were not true. If they were true, they were not judged unpleasant or hateful statements, but rather true statements about unpleasant or hateful facts.

Today, in contrast, you can be charged with the crime of hate speech in many Western nations for stating a bald truth, and if you are tried for that crime, truth is no defense. In other words, citizens of the free world are now directed by law to express moral approval of certain kinds of conduct or opinion that millions of them in fact find morally unacceptable, and are cowed into silence about conduct and opinion they would much rather praise and promote. As a result, citizens of the West now live in morally supine, dishonest societies, and most surprising of all, seem to have lost what was once considered the simple moral courage to articulate and rationally defend their personal views in public. The basis of the moral language spoken in any civil society, like it or not, is discernment and judgment, distinguishing the good from the bad, and defending the former against the latter. But if by law we must praise things we in fact consider bad, or fall silent about things we consider good, moral speech is impossible, a charade, and a lie. When it comes to what everyone today thinks of as social issues, much of the tension comes down to which side of the Great Divide they are on, and why. The frank discussion in this part of the book is put forward in the hope that these ongoing debates will eventually migrate from their current, mostly emotional stage to a focus on the underlying principles and ideological positions on which they rest. Let's see what both sides have to say on our first divisive topic.

CHAPTER 15

On Homosexuality and Gay Marriage

Despite significant conservative resistance, homosexuality, as the psy-choanalyst Charles Socarides put it, has shifted in little more than twenty-five years from the love that dare not speak its name to the love that can't shut up. So it needs to be discussed. I don't much like the word *shift*, because it acknowledges what looks to everyone like an irreversible social and moral change, but says nothing about the cause. This section presents the underlying cause of the modern embrace of homosexuality and gay marriage as an ideological byproduct of our prior embrace of libertarian socialism. The conservative arguments displayed in this book against the homosexual lifestyle can get pretty tough at times. But they are not aimed at particular individuals; they are aimed at exposing the flimsiness of the liberal case for homosexuality. A liberal friend objects that many conservatives are homosexuals, too. I reply that in raising this objection he has unwittingly emphasized my main thesis: like modern liberals, many political conservatives (who are not true philosophical or moral conservatives) have embraced the libertarian-socialist solution to modern democracy's contradictions. Like the liberal, they have split the public from the private realm, and have quarantined their sexual behavior as something off-limits to public moral judgment. Now to the arguments from both sides.

The opening liberal position is that LGBT (etc., etc.) citizens have the same individual rights and freedoms as everyone else, and so discrimination against them must stop. The state has no place in the bedrooms of the nation, and as long as no one is harmed, what homosexuals do privately is no one else's business. People who condemn homosexuality are just closed-minded, homophobic, anti-freedom rednecks who make liberals justifiably angry. The gay man who loves another man may want to enter a marital union, just like anyone else, and so demands equality and the same social respect for his sexual and marital choices, as would a heterosexual person. He observes that the most progressive nations now have equal rights laws, and that almost everywhere in the developed world homosexuals are winning the battle for gay rights. He has his sexual orientation, just as others have theirs, and so no one has the right to deny him equal legal and tax benefits, adding that what he calls *heteronormativity* is oppressive and hateful. As for children? If two lesbians or two gay men want to adopt and raise a child together, or use artificial means, surrogates, or whatever to have their own child, they should legally be allowed to do so, and should have the usual state support for that choice. Liberals observe that open-minded courts in almost all democratic jurisdictions have eliminated—or will soon eliminate—the heterosexual qualification for marriage, and have passed laws allowing "any two persons" to marry, justified on the same legal basis of conjugality that heterosexuals enjoy.

The conservative responds that homosexual citizens already have all the same rights, freedoms, privileges, and protections as do other citizens, as *individuals,* but that when conservatives talk about marriage, *they are not talking about individuals.* They are talking about a special, venerable institution that is *social* in nature, and that in the Western tradition *has never been concerned primarily with individuals,* nor with individual sexual appetites. Rather, it has been specifically concerned with the legal formation of heterosexual conjugal *unions*, and the protection of the children of those unions. For Western nations there have always been three marriage partners, not just two: the man, the woman, and also civil society—the citizens, to whom the marital promises are made. The proof of this is in the pudding: divorce proceedings for couples with children are still much more complex and difficult because in most societies, the interests of the children are considered far more important than those of the divorcing parents—an emphasis that began to reverse in favor of the priority of adult choice and freedom only in the last half century.

The conservative complains that until modern liberals began attacking the exclusively heterosexual terms of marriage, this supra-individual union always had a unique social and moral meaning, structure, and purpose, namely, *the perpetuation of civilization through the production and protection of children*. If the term *civilization* has a meaning, surely creating, raising, and protecting new citizens and educating them by passing on as much as possible of the best humanity has achieved is a big part of it. This is an enormous challenge and duty in which almost all citizens (and their governments, in defending, subsidizing, and privileging marital unions) share, and want to share. Accordingly, the historical, moral, and legal justifications for marriage are deeply rooted in the concept of marriage as *necessarily* a heterosexual, as well as a *child-centered*, union, and not at all as a homosexual or *adult-centered* one. Adult individuals are just a means to this crucial supra-individual social, moral, and civilizational end. So once again: for the conservative, this debate is *not* about *individual* rights. It is about *society's* rights. For until very recently, marriage has only ever been about the formation of heterosexual unions, the social and political significance of which has always been greater than the social or political individual needs or demands of any two people wanting to marry. Practically speaking, unless the marital model upheld by society celebrates the potential of this model to produce children, then whether two individuals marry or do not marry carries no particular interest with respect to the civilizing process, nor to the state—nor should it.

From this perspective, the conservative position may be the most liberal one (in the classical sense of that term), because other than to prevent crimes, governments have no business regulating or interfering with the private lives of citizens except for the commanding public motive just mentioned, namely, *the survival of the state itself.* States have always been aware that with the right laws and economic incentives they can persuade (lure? entice?) a lot of men and women to live together, and that if this works there are going to be lots of babies—future citizens (and taxpayers). Another way to say this is that traditional, exclusively heterosexual marriage policy has served as a kind of survival insurance for civilization, and a protective legal haven for children. Just so, in the Western world at least, even though we say anyone can live freely with whomever and however many others they wish, we have invented various privileges and protections in the form of special laws and tax benefits that are *offered to all individual adults equally* as a lure to get them to form the only type of human union that has survival potential for the state. Traditionally, those who chose not to opt in to this unique natural arrangement were left alone, and expected nothing from society or the state for declining to accept and abide by the qualifying conditions of marriage. They left the state alone, and the state left them alone.

A typical liberal complaint about this argument is: But what about heterosexual couples who don't have or want children? Why should they have the benefits of the institution? To which the conservative replies: Either such couples reject the whole idea, they are too old, or they badly want children but have sadly been unable to conceive together. But no state can predict such choices or outcomes in advance, and a policy that is effective in general cannot be disqualified for particular exceptions. All public policy operates like a very large net, rather than a one-by-one hook, in an attempt to encourage the behavior model most likely to produce the desired result. In this light, states have always insisted that any *individual* who wants the privileges and benefits of marriage can easily *qualify* for them by entering the only kind of human union of legitimate interest to the state, and until recently, the only one for which it has been willing to pay.

Liberals observe that medical advances and technology have made the need for childbearing heterosexual unions obsolete, because today anyone can have a baby to further the procreational purposes of civilization without needing to be heterosexual. But this seems a weak argument. In 2012, only about 1.5 percent of all births in the United States were conceived by means of expensive assisted reproductive technology, mostly by heterosexual couples unable to conceive naturally. A very small number of these conceptions were for the benefit of a gay person or couple.

But the main conservative point is that all states engage, and must engage, in a myriad of *positive policy discriminations* that require some form of qualification in order to achieve their policy objectives and the benefits they authorize. This intentional discrimination, and this alone, is what makes a policy a policy, in contrast to a general handout offered to everyone for no particular reason (other than to garner more votes). In other words, if a policy has any chance of being effective—of changing public behavior one way or the other—that chance will come by means of a goal-directed *positive discrimination*. Here are a few examples. If you want welfare support, you have to qualify by being poor. If you want senior citizen benefits, you qualify by reaching age sixty-five. For child benefits, you qualify by having children. For military awards, you qualify by serving with distinction in the armed forces. For national honors or any other high recognition, you qualify by way of skill or merit. No one in their right mind would allow a citizen to enjoy any of those benefits without qualifying for them, for that would be considered cheating the policy as well as the taxpayer.

The Equality Argument

The liberal response to a withheld positive policy discrimination is usually the "equality" demand—all citizens must be treated the same. But the conservative replies that welfare for everyone would not be a targeted policy; it would become a general handout. Seniors' benefits for people of any age would be a ludicrous contradiction. And why would we give child tax benefits to people who do not have, or may not want, children? And just imagine how it would corrupt the real and symbolic sanctity of courage and self-sacrifice to hand out the nation's highest military award for bravery to all citizens equally, even to cowards. That would be a very upside-down world indeed. So in strict *policy* terms (rather than in general handout terms), to offer exactly the same benefits to all those who qualify for them is indeed an exact equality of policy. Because all legitimate policies are *intended* to discriminate in a precise and positive way against all who do not qualify under the terms that were the sole condition for receipt of benefits, the conservative says the charge of inequality is the weakest of arguments.

The same qualification argument applies in defense of the institution of marriage. Traditionally, individuals in the Western world wishing to marry and to receive state benefits and legal protections had to qualify by conforming to four simple conditions with respect to *gender, number, age,* and *incest.* These were intended to keep the institution of marriage stable, like a four-legged chair, and above all to ensure it was a procreative model: you had to marry someone of the opposite gender, you could marry only one person at a time, you could not marry anyone beneath a certain age, and you could not marry a close blood relative. You want the benefits and legal protections of marriage? Just abide by those qualifications, and line up!

It seems illogical to a conservative that anyone should be allowed to reject the most foundational of these four policy qualifications, and yet still believe they have a right to marital benefits. For why should a government hand out benefits to someone who refuses the only convincing reason for allowing the state to regulate the institution of marriage in the first place? By now, if they have given up on the failed equality argument, the next most common and passionate justification offered by the liberal is usually "love." I love my partner, and that is a sufficient qualification for equal treatment, is the reasoning.

The Love Argument

The conservative as passionately objects, and responds that love is the flimsiest of motives for inviting the state into the regulation of private life. The reasoning is as follows. First, if, as the liberal maintains, the presence of love between two persons of the same gender is the only qualification needed to force government to provide full marital benefits, then when the love fades, or disappears, or turns to bitter anger, shouldn't the government have a right to withdraw those benefits? The liberal will reply that lots of heterosexual couples fall out of love, too, and nevertheless continue to receive benefits. But that is precisely the conservative point: *governments have never justified or denied marital benefits by the presence or absence of love.* They have been justified by the fact that *whether or not* two people love each other, they have qualified for benefits in abiding by the four conditions of gender, number, age, and incest, the most important of which is the gender qualification: choosing to marry someone of the opposite sex, thereby opting in to society's larger procreational project.

A further conservative objection to relying on love as the qualifier for marital benefits is the plain fact that much of the civilizing project of the Western world, whether by way of parental guidance, religion, literature, music, or philosophy, has had to do with the difficult business of teaching citizens the difference between good love and bad love. This distinction comes as a shock to anyone of romantic sensibility who thinks that all love is good love, and to homosexuals in particular, who understandably dread the possible demolition of their love argument. But the conservative insists this point needs to be argued. The grounds of the case are that one of the most treacherous realities of all human existence, at all times, has been the addictive appeal of powerful forms of love that not only are demonstrably bad for those who love and the people they love, but also—and this is the key conservative point—*bad for society as a whole.*

Philia is one of the many Greek words for love, and psychiatric manuals list hundreds of terms ending in *philia* that describe many different kinds of bad love. Some of the more common self-crippling (and society-crippling) forms of love are a warped and blinding love of self, of food, of money, of alcohol or drugs, of violence, of stealing, and also—the conservative is convinced—of homosexuality. Other well-known kinds of bad love often in the news are adulterous love, which is deceitful, and so bad love on the face of it; and pedophilia, the sexual love of children, which is morally reprehensible for obvious reasons. Polygamy is another one, because it is a blatant repudiation of the Western ideal of the indivisibility of unitive love between one man and one woman (despite this, there are a lot of Muslims in the West living this way). Many forms of bad love are very kinky, and some disgusting. *Kleptophilia*, the love of stealing, sometimes for sexual arousal, is pretty odd. *Scopophilia*, otherwise known as voyeurism, is sexual arousal from watching others naked or involved in sex. Addictions to pornography fit here. And then there are some really bizarre ones, such as *nosophilia*, the love of sex with terminally ill people; *zoophilia*, a sexual interest in animals; *coprophilia* and *urophilia* (both made notorious by the Marquis de Sade), which are, respectively, the sexual love of the taste or smell of feces and urine; or arousal from someone defecating or urinating on you, or from doing these things to them. And ... I can't go on. An hour on the web will reveal many hundreds of *philias and paraphilias.* The conservative position is that some vigorous counterargument is called for whenever anyone proposes love as the main defining qualification for tax and social benefits and state support of homosexual marriage.

The Sex Argument

Once the love argument is dropped, the liberal will often move on to protest that he nevertheless has the same sexual freedom and right to "have sex" as anyone else. To this there is a conservative reply that again comes as a shock—even to many conservatives who have never really thought deeply about this before—as follows. Anyone who has spent a little time in the life sciences will soon see that the term *sex*, whether used by biologists, zoologists, or any other life scientist, is universally a *reproductive* term. But homosexuals cannot reproduce with each other. So strictly speaking—that is, scientifically and logically speaking—a homosexual person can have sex with someone of the opposite gender, but never with someone of the same gender. So to say homosexuals "have sex" with each other is a practical, logical, and scientific contradiction. When we say gay people are having sex, we are confusing *sexuality* with *sensuality*, and on this line of reasoning we should be speaking of *homosensuals* rather than of *homosexuals*. No one is denying that such behavior is sensual, they are just saying it is not sexual. To repeat: no serious scientist uses the word *sex* or its variants to describe anything but biological or botanical activity that at least has reproductive *potential*. That is the essence of planetary *sexual* activity. Accordingly, any human or animal behavior that *looks* like sex but lacks procreative *potential* or design can only be mock sex, or self-pleasuring sensual behavior. Masturbation, for example, which most people in the world have enjoyed from time to time, is not sex for the simple reason that you cannot have sex with yourself. Logically speaking, it is, and can only be, erotic auto-stimulation. A wet dream is not having sex, either. And when your male dog mistakes another male dog for a female (or tries this on your leg), he is just instinctively enjoying the sexual motion in the mistaken hope he has landed on the right target. By the same token, two men who put their penises in each other's anus are clearly not having sex. In fact, if we were trying to define the most mock-sexual human activity possible, this would pretty much fit the bill. I can hear the shrieks already: "But some heterosexual women like anal sex, too!" To this there is only one rebuttal. Heterosexuals in love or in sex with each other will do many things of which others may approve or disapprove. But we are silent on that score, because the chances they will eventually get it right are high, and then society will have more babies. But the chances of two homosexuals getting it right are nil.

The Conjugality Argument

In many countries such as Canada, the justifying legal ground courts have cited to permit "any two persons" to marry and qualify for marital benefits is *conjugality*. That is because the legitimate worry of governments is that, without this notion attached to the definition of marriage, any two same-gender heterosexual persons—say, two retirees, two soldiers, two spinsters, two cousins, or simply two aging friends—could qualify as "any two persons," and then receive the considerable tax and legal benefits of marriage, even though they have no intention whatsoever of living as homosexuals. In other words, by presenting as "any two persons," it is easy to cheat the system.

So what is the legal basis of conjugality? The word is formed from the Latin root *conjungere*, which means "to join." It has always implied the joining of spouses in marital union, and the courts of the Western world have always understood the primary sense of this joining to be the sexual union of opposite genders. But to speak bluntly again: it is impossible to join two penises or two vaginas. So if, as argued earlier, there can be no sexual (nor any legal) basis for joining two people of the same gender in the most truthful sense of the words sex and conjugal; if, as used to justify homosexuality, these two words are entirely empty and dishonest—then what, exactly, is the policy purpose for calling such a liaison a marriage?

The Homophobia Argument

At this point in the argument, the angry liberal usually calls the frustrated conservative "homophobic." But for the typical conservative this is a nonsensical term used to direct public anger and hatred at people who happen to disagree with the normalization of the homosexual program. Worse, the word itself is inaccurate, and misrepresents what most conservatives actually feel. *Phobia* means "fear," a term that is doubly nonsensical in this context, because whether conservative or not, it is hard to find anyone who fears homosexuality. It is more likely they deeply disapprove of it and are alarmed by its social, health, and moral consequences for society. Indeed, when a conservative is called homophobic, especially if he has heard the tiresome and unproven claim that homosexuality is genetically caused (and so can't be helped), he will often think, if not reply, as follows: the mere sight of homosexual behavior—two men deep-kissing each other, for example—causes a natural repugnance in almost all people, probably because human beings (with the apparent exception of homosexuals) have been genetically programmed via Darwinian natural selection to shame and shun anti-procreative behavior in order to ensure the survival of the species. Repugnance is natural. In short, if liberals can argue that gayness is genetic and natural in some people, conservatives can argue that repugnance for homosexuality is genetic and natural in everyone else. Game, draw, match. And speaking of survival, the conservative worries that the daily bombardment by gay-normalization propaganda in the West has led the public to ignore the fact that homosexuality is bad for your health, which no one denies: governments report that about three-quarters of all AIDS deaths in North America have been of gay males—another good reason to shun this behavior. So the conservative gets confused, and wonders why homosexuality has instead been accepted and promoted, unlike other unhealthy and dangerous behaviors. Examples? Alcoholism and drug addictions are bad for kids. So we teach them to avoid both. We do not hand out six-packs of beer or bags of cocaine in schools. Homosexual behavior and AIDS are also bad for kids. But instead of discouraging this behavior, we teach them it is normal, and hand out condoms in the schools. In 1995 I interviewed Dr. C. Michael Roland of the US Naval Research Laboratory in Washington. He was then editor of the journal *Rubber Chemistry and Technology*, and had done a lot of research on the "intrinsic flaws" in the latex used for condom manufacture. He said the AIDS virus is very small—about 0.1 percent of a micron in size—and that because "the natural holes in latex rubber range from 5 to 70 microns," the HIV virus can pass through your average condom quite easily—as another critic put it, "like a bullet through a tennis net."[20]

The Case for Causes: Genes, Choices, Families

Now we come to arguments about the possible causes of homosexuality, and there are three main ones. The first is favored by liberals, the second by both liberals and conservatives (if for very different reasons), and the third mostly by conservatives.

---

20 Readers who want to know the full story can read it at http://www.williamgairdner.com/ condomania/.

The first is the sexual orientation argument—surely one of the most successful terminology-replacement campaigns ever conducted. Just about everyone now accepts the idea that all human beings have a sexual orientation, a phrase suggesting there is within us all some kind of deep inner force rather like a magnetic field that orients us like a compass needle in a specific sexual direction, and that this force is very likely itself generated by an as yet undiscovered gay gene. This conviction has got into the public mind, liberal as well as conservative, like a harpoon, and it will not be gotten out any time soon. With most liberals it is automatically assumed as true.

But the conservative replies that no one knows why some people prefer to love and attach to someone of the same gender. There is weak evidence for a possible genetic (or epigenetic) factor, but those on the hunt for a gay gene admit that even if a genetic component is found, it will likely only be one of many biological, social, and psychological factors. Studies of twins, for example, show that, although in a set of identical twins there is a higher likelihood that if one twin is gay the other will also be gay, the concordance can range anywhere from a 7 to 50 percent likelihood that both will be gay—a ratio that is a far cry from a 100 percent genetic determination. Another conservative reply is that, even if gayness were found to have a genetic cause, it would not mean that homosexuality is within the range of normal behavior—there are a lot of human disabilities and mental and physical diseases that have a genetic component (such as Huntington's, type 1 diabetes, MS, schizophrenia, and more). Furthermore, evolution theory suggests in no uncertain terms that if it had a genetic cause, homosexuality would have died out through natural selection long ago, as only a vanishingly small number of homosexuals procreate. Liberal evolutionists attempt to rescue the genetic causality idea by invoking the "helper at the nest" argument. This is the idea that, just as some types of birds who lose out in the battle for a female's favors will hang around the nest helping her raise the other guy's babies, homosexual humans somehow contribute to the survival of the babies of their relatives. No need to comment further on this feeble notion.

A caring conservative will agree that if, as so many liberals argue, there really is a gene that somehow produces homosexual appetites and behaviors, then homosexuals ought to be sheltered under laws against discrimination, just like minority ethnic groups. But even then, the conservative reply is often that gayness is an unnatural *behavior*, it is not like having a genetically caused physical disability like blindness, or being born black or Chinese. To feel an urge to drink alcohol or to use hard drugs may one day be found to have some genetic component. But that is not to *be* an alcoholic or a drug addict. Nor, if such a genetic cause were discovered, would we hand out supplies of booze and drugs to kids to satisfy their cravings. We would counsel them to stop. Which is to say that if gays didn't do what they do, nobody would care. Stop the behavior, and you stop the problem. At this point the notion of choice arises.

The last time I was at Stanford University I saw a large liberal banner that read "Born Queer, or Queer by Choice, There's No Difference!" The conservative warns that actually, there is, for in the unlikely event that a gene is ever isolated, pregnant women all over the world will hasten to abort their babies because they don't want a gay child. There would be a silent holocaust by *homocide*—a discriminatory killing of gays in the womb—just as there has been massive gendercide in many parts of the world to eliminate millions of baby girls, mostly in countries where boys have a higher future-income potential for their families. Some gay-gene researchers are aware of this eventuality, and argue that if a gay gene is ever discovered it would be ethical to inform the parents, but that abortions of children with the gay gene should not be allowed. This is a clear example of a researcher linking one liberal ethic (homosexual rights) with another (a duty to inform the parents), and countering it with a conservative ethic (do not abort the child) for a liberal purpose (protect homosexuality). The next section deals with liberal-versus-conservative arguments on abortion, and there we will see that once a liberal abortion regime is permitted, there can be no ethical ground whatsoever for forbidding abortion for any reason, gay or otherwise. The liberal in this case wants to rescue the unborn child from abortion because he knows it is gay. The conservative wants to rescue it because he knows it is human. This is ideological warfare on the ground.

When the gay gene argument fails due to lack of proof, the second cause, the gay by choice argument, becomes the bail-out position, usually linked to passionate calls for individual freedom and equality. On that note, we have seen that the main liberal emphasis in the homosexual debate is on fairness and equality, while the main conservative emphasis is a defense of the sanctity of marriage and a protest against unnatural sexual behavior. The liberal thrust identifies with what is called gay liberation, which is a variation on the various pansexual movements that have popped up over the centuries promoting the idea that *all sex is good sex*, no matter with whom, or how many, as long as there is consent, and no violence or harm to others. This is a variant of the *all love is good love* argument that was previously critiqued. Its most recent ideological roots can be found in eighteenth-century romantic naturalism, a movement promoting the goodness of nature, natural feeling, and *the free and open expression of one's authentic self*. And the liberal self is conceived as trapped deep within an inauthentic and suffocating shell of social and moral artificiality that must be peeled away to allow for the full expression of the true self. This sort of wave of sexual liberation feeling came surging to the fore once again after the unconscionable slaughters of World War II, when a widespread condemnation of the West by the young over the moral failures of the European states sparked the political protests of the 1960s. A certain element of that flower-child, free-love disposition has continued ever since (which some describe as *neoromantic*).

It was inevitable that such protests against the moral and political failures of elders would blend with protests against sexual restraint, and when mixed with the new availability of the Pill, weed, and drugs, that the result would be demands for sexual freedom as a potent symbol for political and personal freedom. There were soon widespread efforts to liberalize and normalize sexual and social behaviors that the "uptight" conservative society of that period considered either morally undesirable or abnormal. Male-style sexual freedom was soon made possible for women by the birth control pill, and freedom of women from their own unwanted children was made possible by abortion on demand (by 1973 in the United States, and 1988 in Canada). Traditional marriage and marital fidelity too came under attack through efforts to normalize alternative group marriage, plain old group sex, polyamory, no-fault divorce, "swinging," and the like—all newly elevated symbols of freedom and freethinking. But surely the most radical of these protests was the idea that homosexuality and bisexuality are natural, healthy, and desirable alternative lifestyles—especially so when conceived as free lifestyle *choices* rather than as a result of some genetic inheritance or abnormality.

For radically liberal intellectuals, the vanguard of this conflation of free choice with free love and sex was especially visible in direct attacks on normal society that appeared in such as the now-defunct Dutch journal *Paidika,* which published from 1987 to 1995. In it, sophisticated academics promoted sex with children (especially homosexuality with young boys) as the highest form of social and moral freedom (freedom from all moral restraint, that is). Here is their mission statement, which illustrates a reliance on a general antiauthoritarian, pro-freedom language to justify the normalization of the abnormal: "... to speak today of pedophilia, which we understand to be consensual intergenerational sexual relationships, is to speak of *the politics of oppression* ... we intend to demonstrate that pedophilia has been, and remains, a legitimate and productive part of the totality of human experience." And here is a snippet of an interview by the editors of *Paidika* in June of 1991 with a Dr. Ralph Underwager, a minister and a pedophilia supporter, who said, "Pedophiles can boldly and courageously affirm what they choose. They can say that what they want is to find the best way to love.... With boldness they can say, 'I believe this is in fact part of God's will.'" Here, to the typical liberal justifications of love, freedom, and choice, we get the bizarre notion that mature men having their way with little boys is God's will. I do not want to suggest for a moment that most liberals support this kind of thing—far from it. But I do suggest that what is easily visible in the tendency of all liberalizing democracies is the identification of liberalized sexual mores with open-mindedness, freedom, and love, as if a conscience-free acceptance of what so many others (including many ordinary liberals) consider forbidden is a sign of high intelligence.

A little time spent on the web will reveal many similar initiatives calling for liberation through sexual freedom. An active American version is NAMBLA, the North American Man-Boy Love Association, an organization that promotes homosexuality as "consensual intergenerational sex" with young boys. One of the four listed goals of this organization is "supporting the liberation of persons of all ages from sexual prejudice and oppression." This website has more quasi-pathological cries for "freedom" than there are prickles on a porcupine, all implying that a sufficiently strong desire for freedom and democracy justifies almost any nonviolent behavior ("through our web site and publications, NAMBLA provides a public forum for a diverse range of viewpoints supporting sexual liberation and youth liberation"). Here is the same cry from the influential American homosexual activist David Thorstad, from a speech he gave in Mexico City in 1998: "Our movement today stresses the liberation and empowerment of young people ... a vision of sexual, economic, and political liberation for all. Freedom is indivisible." The conservative argument, presented in our discussion *On Freedom*, however, is that freedom is in fact divided into many kinds, of which the personal and sexual liberation implied here is just one. Most important of all is the realization that freedom and morality have no necessary connection except insofar as we need to be free agents to choose good or evil. So the conservative rejects the liberal tendency to equate freedom with the good, and so also the notion that to be liberal, or open-minded in the sense of relaxing sound traditional moral standards, is a sign of intelligence. The conservative question is rather: Why is intelligence associated with rebellion against moral standards that have stood humanity in good stead for so long, rather than with protection of them? Accordingly, to the liberal argument that homosexuality is a freedom that harms no one else, the conservative replies, not so. Human beings are capable of justifying and normalizing all sorts of unnatural behaviors in the name of freedom, and what many pansexualists so energetically attack as a restraint on their individual freedom is in fact part of a thoroughgoing attack on the entire conservative sexual and family order of the Western world—an order that has evolved over many centuries with the special objective of protecting women, children, and the institutions of marriage and family from the freedom of selfish, pleasure-seeking males in particular, and especially to protect the young from the freedom of homosexual predators. The English conservative writer Roger Scruton refers to people who attack what is good in their own national home as *oikophobes* (from the Greek *Oikos*, home). On this note, the Gay Rights Platform of 1972 in the United States, fully supported by its Canadian equivalent, laid out the gay agenda pretty clearly. It called for the abolition of all laws governing sexual age of consent, the abolition of all laws against sodomy and adult or child prostitution, the right of homosexuals to adopt and have legal custody of children, and the abolition of all laws that restrict the sex or number of persons entering into a marriage unit. The liberal war against the family and traditional society in the name of individual freedom could not have been more clearly spelled out, and so the march continues. I am myself a witness to the speed of this liberalization: when I said publicly in 1993 that one day homosexual marriage would be legalized, I was roundly criticized by liberals as an extremist. More recent warnings about the deep desire of the homosexual community to revolutionize traditional society abound. In Canada's *Xtra Vancouver* newspaper, managing editor Robin Perelle wrote in 2011 that "the gay rights movement is shifting norms in Canada. And with that comes a message to those who won't evolve: Your outdated morals are no longer acceptable, and we will teach your kids the new norm." Abraham Lincoln himself observed that "the philosophy of the school room in one generation will be the philosophy of government in the next," and this truth has not been lost on the radical homosexual movement. In 2011, Daniel Villarreal wrote in the online magazine Queerty, "We want educators to teach future generations of children to accept queer sexuality. In fact, our very future depends on it…. Recruiting children? You bet we are." Readers, take heed.

I should mention possible cause number three, which is psychosocial in nature. Conservatives tend to support this type of explanation because, of the three causal possibilities, this is the only one that holds hope for a return to what is biologically and psychologically natural. Liberals who consider homosexuality to have a physical or genetic cause, or who support the notion that it is a freely chosen way of life (and because it is chosen, is as morally dignified and normal as any other), dislike psychosocial explanations precisely because they are necessarily rooted in a therapeutic notion of what is normal.

The most persuasive work in this vein is a variation on psychoanalytic *attachment* theory, which holds that in the very early years of life, a child will complete a normal process of strong emotional attachment to both father and mother; and if this essential attachment process is interrupted or fails for any reason, an unmet need is created in the child. The most frequent family pattern in the lives of homosexuals seems to be the presence of an emotionally remote, detached, or simply absent same-sex parent, and an overly indulgent, too intimate, and controlling opposite-sex parent. A distant father and a smothering and controlling mother, in the case of boys; and the reverse in the case of girls. The result is that the child seeking the love that comes with normal same-sex parental attachment feels spurned, and fails to attach to his or her same-sex parent. The love deficit that results causes the child to live as what some therapists describe as "a hidden orphan." This condition results in an inner approach-avoidance conflict: the child has been hurt by the offending same-sex parent (who may be wholly unaware of the situation), and becomes less able to form trusting relationships with a same-sex person. This results in a push-pull situation because the wounded child also feels a strong reparative urge to mend the love deficit caused by the failed attachment, and is, so to speak, condemned to keep trying. This is apparently the psychosocial profile found in the majority of families with a homosexual child. In sum, the psychologically orphaned child strives to heal the felt deficit by attaching to people of the same gender in a search for *replacement love*. Attachment therapists insist that the real underlying need is the reparative love, not the sexual behavior that accompanies adult homosexuality. Therapy in such cases focuses not on trying to get homosexual males to date girls, or lesbians boys, but in showing homosexuals how to deal with their inner conflict in such a way that they can eventually develop healthy, nonsexual same-sex attachments, and thereby they will be freed to respond to, rather than reject, opposite-sex love. If the underlying thesis is true, it suggests that the gay pride parades inflicted on Western publics are in fact the marches of poorly attached adult children suffering from arrested development, who, although they appear to be shouting about gay rights, are really deeply crying, "mommy, mommy, daddy, daddy."

The Parenting Divide

Finally, a word on the liberal/conservative divide over gay parenting. The liberal is no doubt correct that homosexuals can be as loving and caring as any other parent. Nevertheless, the core conservative objection is that no one has the right to redefine marriage *so as intentionally to impose a fatherless or motherless home on a child as a matter of state policy*, for we have as yet no clear idea what the permanent long-term negative consequences of such adult-centered homosexual arrangements are for children (though attachment theory suggest they cannot be good, because the absence of one of the parents in the child's life is intentionally created in this scenario). On that score, the conservative says that gays and their liberal sympathizers in the media, government, and the courts stand guilty as charged: they have intentionally set up a parenting model that is against nature. The conservative admits that ordinary divorce fractures the unity of a child's world, and usually means rotational living with a mom and a dad, which is fracture enough. But to make a motherless or fatherless home a child's norm by law, for the sake of adult satisfactions, cannot improve that situation. This is especially so if attachment theory proves to be a strong explanatory cause of homosexuality, for then it is likely that the policy normalization of fatherless and motherless homes, with their built-in absence of one parent, combined with the growing use of full-time daycare and live-in nannies, earlier entry into schools, and the never-ending stress of both parents working in a commercial society, may serve to generate more attachment deficits, and so more homosexuality.

WHERE DO YOU STAND?		
On Homosexuality		
	MODERN LIBERAL VIEW　vs.	CONSERVATIVE VIEW
Sexual Privacy	*Sex is private activity*	*Public morality protects the vulnerable*
	The state has no place in the bedrooms of the nation	Western law reaches into bedrooms to buttress sexual mores and protect women and children by prohibiting rape, violence, incest, polygamy, prostitution, and dangerous sex practices
Love	*Love justifies a claim to public benefits*	*Love is unrelated to qualification for benefits*
	Love between any two persons is sufficient to claim a right to marry, and to state benefits	Love is a boon in marriage, but is far too variable to serve as a sole foundation for marital policies. Even then, states have a vested interest in the *kinds* of love they are asked to support. Homosexual love has never been one of these until recently, because it is unnatural and procreatively sterile

WHERE DO YOU STAND?		
On Homosexuality		
	MODERN LIBERAL VIEW vs.	CONSERVATIVE VIEW
Fairness & Rights	*Means equal benefits for all who ask*	*Means benefits only for those who qualify*
	Denial of equal marital benefits to gays is discrimination. Gays demand their right to marry and be honored by society and the law. To disallow marriage to gays is to treat them as second-class citizens. Marriage and its benefits are a right	All policies require qualification: welfare for the poor, not the rich; medals for heroes, not cowards; pensions for seniors only; etc. Marital benefits have been denied to gays because they cannot procreate with each other. To grant the same rights to gay couples is to attack and weaken the natural basis of marriage, which is a civil and legal privilege, not a right
Harm	*No harm to individuals is the moral basis*	*No harm to society is the moral standard*
	What gays do privately harms no one. Other citizens have no right to regulate or judge the gay lifestyle	Marriage converts private relationships into public ones. Public institutions like marriage have profound survival value to civilization. To demand equal benefits of marriage while not qualifying for them is to cheat the public purse and cheapen the sanctity of the institution as a whole, both of which harm society
Homophobia	*Fear is the root of antigay feelings*	*Natural moral upset is the root of disapproval*
	To speak against gay rights is to be homophobic. Gays have a right to defend and promote gay rights, and straight people should face up to the root of their irrational fear of homosexuality and deal with it	*Homophobia* is a slur term aimed at people who disapprove of homosexual behavior. Conservatives do not have a fear (phobia) of homosexuality. They are more than likely deeply upset by it, and have a right to say so, just as gays have a right to celebrate it. It is quite common to like a homosexual person while disapproving of their homosexual behavior (and wanting them to stop it), just as it is possible to like an alcoholic while wanting them to stop drinking

WHERE DO YOU STAND?		
On Homosexuality		
MODERN LIBERAL VIEW	VS.	CONSERVATIVE VIEW
Homosexuality & Innateness	*Homosexuality is natural*	*Homosexuality is unnatural behavior*
	Gay sexual orientation is innate, maybe genetic, like being born black or white. Natural sexual orientation should be encouraged in all people	*Orientation* is a wiggle word aimed at normalizing unnatural behavior by making the public think it can't be helped. Notwithstanding extremely rare mistakes of nature, all human beings are born male or female, and they naturally complement each other. Even if a gay gene were found, we should not promote homosexual behavior any more than we should promote alcoholism or cocaine addiction were a gene for alcoholism or cocaine found
Homosexuality & Choice	*What is freely chosen is good*	*Choice has no necessary relation to the good*
	All human beings are free to choose their own sexual preferences. No one has a right to deny others free choice. The gay-rights movement all over the world is a campaign to liberate individuals from the restricting judgments, laws, and social prejudice of others	The conservative denies that something is good for society just because someone has chosen it. We can all freely choose things that may be good or evil in themselves, and the job of civilization is to teach us the difference. Even a choice we defend as good for ourselves alone may be bad for others, bring shame on all, or weaken the integrity of society and the sanctity of cherished ways of life

WHERE DO YOU STAND?		
On Homosexuality		
	MODERN LIBERAL VIEW vs.	CONSERVATIVE VIEW
Procreation	*Procreation and marriage are unrelated*	*Procreative model is the basis for benefits*
	Whether or not two people have children is not a condition of marriage. Many straight couples do not have kids, and this fact invalidates the case for procreation as a qualifying condition for state benefits	The only credible reason for states to provide marital benefits is the procreative potential of heterosexual couplings. This means the institution itself must be privileged (even for sterile couples or older people who marry) and thereby uphold the procreative model as an ideal for the young
Good Parents	*Two fathers or mothers is okay*	*All children need their fathers and mothers*
	Gays are good parents, and two fathers or two mothers for a child instead of one of each is a positive experience for the home. There have been many kinds of marriage and child-rearing in history, and the traditional Western model is just one	Good fathering or mothering is more than parenting, and is a virtue, whether we are gay or straight. The conservative complaint is simply that *no one has a right to impose a fatherless or motherless home on a child as a matter of state policy*, nor to normalize such a condition. A father and mother in every child's home should be the social standard and goal

WHERE DO YOU STAND?		
On Homosexuality		
	MODERN LIBERAL VIEW vs.	CONSERVATIVE VIEW
Effect on Children	*Gay homes provide stability*	*Gay homes encourage homosexuality*
	Children raised in gay homes do as well as those raised in mother/father homes	A mother/father home is the natural and optimal situation for all children and should be the objective of all policy and law. Children raised in a homoerotic environment are very likely to see it as normal, and are more likely to imitate this behavior
Defense of Marriage Act	*No to DOMA: Legalize gay marriage*	*Yes to DOMA: Ban gay marriage*
	To ban gay marriage constitutionally is to institutionalize hatred of gay citizens	Traditional marriage as the union of one man and one woman only must be protected in the law of the land as the foundation of a procreative society. To force legalization is to offend the moral and religious beliefs of millions of citizens, whose tax dollars should not be used to subsidize what they believe is morally wrong
Religion & Gay Rights	*Religion is a separate issue*	*To legalize gay rights is to offend religion*
	Religious rights are a private matter and not connected to anyone's sexuality. Many gay people are religious	Hundreds of millions of religious people believe that homosexuality offends God and religion, as is clear in all religious teaching. The legalization of gay rights is an attack on the Judeo-Christian foundations of Western civilization and a grievous blow to the sanctity and dignity of marriage
The Polls	*53% support gay marriage*	*Popular support does not make something right*
	[Gallup poll, May 2013]	Principles and standards of what is natural and good for society should always trump polls. Gay marriage, which seeks the legalization of intrinsically sterile unions, cannot meet that standard

CHAPTER 16

On Abortion

About twenty years ago, during a lunch meeting, the political writer David Frum asked me what I thought the single most defining moral issue of the future would be. "Abortion," I replied, and gave as my reason that the architects of our formerly liberal but now egalitarian democracies had not yet come to confession; they have not yet fessed up that the mass killing of millions of unborn children in the free world is the price they were willing to pay for ideological purity. Which is to say that the abortion right is the final political outcome, solution, and nexus of a centuries-long encounter between liberal democracy in its present mutated form and conservatism—or to put it another way, the encounter between the demands of political equality and the unavoidable lifestyle inequalities experienced by women as dictated by natural biology. Pure classical liberal democracy could have continued for a long time without an abortion right. But once it mutated into an egalitarian form it required a method for erasing the glaring natural differences between the freedom naturally available to one half of the citizenry, and the other. In a liberty-based regime, biology is accepted as a natural difference between the genders; but in an egalitarian regime, biology threatens equality of liberty. Hence the modern war against biology emphasized throughout this book. The solution to this otherwise natural state of human affairs was to create an abortion right permitting the voluntary purgation of biologically based lifestyle inequalities.

In my apolitical, knee-jerk liberal youth I supported abortion under the usual reasoning that whatever the girl was carrying, it was just a bit of inert tissue; that it was great to have a backup plan available; and that because having a baby would ruin a young girl's life, the abortion option was a no-brainer. But over time, and due to extraordinary medical and scientific revelations showing *what is really in there*, and because I eventually had children of my own and witnessed the whole miraculous creation of human life, I began to change.

In previous sections I have alluded to this topic because it is so intimately connected to the opposing beliefs liberals and conservatives tend to hold about the dominion of will over nature, or the reverse; about God or the absence of God; about religion, materialism, and so much more. I will lay out some disturbing facts on abortion, and then ask a handful of pertinent questions which I invite readers to answer as honestly as possible. Then I ask them to reflect on the linkage explored here between the abortion right, democratic ideology, and the standard legal technique for converting human beings into things or property that alone has made human slavery possible throughout history, whether outside or inside the womb.

Again, not all liberals support abortion, not all conservatives are against it, and many are in the middle, or on the fence. But in broad-brush terms, most liberals are proabortion, and most true conservatives are antiabortion. (I specify "true" conservatives again, because so-called fiscal conservatives are seldom true conservatives; they are libertarians who usually support choice in all things, including abortion.) Note also that I did not use the favored liberal freedom term, *pro-choice*. And that is simply because everything we do, or decline to do, requires a choice. We choose to abort, or not to abort. So *choice* must be rejected as a meaningful term. Instead, let's cut to the chase. Today there is such angry polarization between most liberals and conservatives on the question of abortion that consensus is considered impossible, and if the citizens of the modern democracies share anything, it is a sense of relief that this, and many other morally difficult matters, are routinely decided by the edicts of courts, the activities of which seem aimed at efficiently deflecting genuine public debate. It's another topic, but I believe that the tendency for elected representatives in democratic legislatures to avoid lacerating debate over difficult moral issues by pushing them upstairs for decision by judges is a form of moral and political cowardice that has contributed to the infantilization of ostensibly democratic populations, and is directly linked to the decline of (liberal) democracy in our time.

And that is why we need to ask: What happened? Why, in less than a half century, did the citizens of almost every modern democracy change in character from a people who once valued human life so highly that they criminalized all abortion with a profound moral certainty (with only a few exceptions having to do with rape, or a real threat to the life of the mother) to a people so liberalized that, in a country like Canada (which since 1988 has had no law whatsoever against abortion), they publicly subsidize the right to terminate human life in the womb at any stage of pregnancy, even up to the moment of natural birth?

Some will immediately object to the phrase *human life* on the ground that almost all courts of the free world typically take the liberal view that a fetus is not legally a person or a human being until it is born alive. Such legal and verbal legerdemain is now a fact of Western life. But there are other facts forming a chain of logic that should expose what the conservative considers the bogus use of such terms. Even if we all were to agree that what a pregnant woman is carrying is not a fully developed person or human being, we nevertheless cannot deny that in every case what she is carrying *is alive*. Were this not so, there would be no need for anyone to claim a right to "terminate" a pregnancy. In other words, whether proabortion or antiabortion, those taking shelter under any of these euphemisms nevertheless are in fact talking about *actual* life, and not what some judges describe as "potential life." So step one is that both liberals and conservatives are obliged by the evidence to agree that what a pregnant woman is carrying is alive.

Step two, the conservative insists, is then to admit the plain truth that in every case, absolutely, the life a pregnant woman is carrying is *a human life*, for no one believes she is carrying a live puppy, or a swan. Having come this far, and only once we decide to face this singular truth as honestly as possible, the conservative then wants to ask a crucial question. Namely, *how can it be morally acceptable for one person in full possession of his or her own human life to terminate the human life of another?* The saying I once heard, "All who support slavery are free, and all who support abortion are alive," drove home to me like a stake in the heart the naked injustice in the act of one human being who was not aborted deciding to end the life of another human being.

By any measure, most people, whether liberal or conservative, who adamantly support abortion are grievously uninformed. They simply don't know how we have arrived at the new *moral* ground we suddenly seem to be standing on, what changes in the *law* have enabled such a strange about-face, and finally, what the current *practices* of abortion are that this shift in morality and law have made possible. The answers, explored here, are each followed by a plain question.

How We Got This Way—the Change in Our Moral Thinking

Until about the middle of the nineteenth century, most philosophers and religious and political leaders in the Western world accepted as obvious the idea that we live—and ought to live—under common moral under-standings. Which is to say, as explained elsewhere in this book, moral standards until very recently were considered communal and *public* by their very nature. The mere idea that morality should serve the private interests or circumstances of solitary individuals had heretofore always been considered absurd, if not a sign of moral incapacity.

But with the growing emphasis on individual freedom and equality and the retreat from religion and community authority came the increas-ingly shrill demand for private individual rights divorced from duties, and with this an entirely new idea: that each human makes up his or her own private moral system with every individual *choice*. This in turn shined a light on private individual will as the key determinant of moral authen-ticity, as it slowly became a substitute for public moral understandings. Elsewhere in this book I have pointed to John Stuart Mill's harm prin-ciple as the most notorious formulation of that process of substitution whereby community moral standards in so many Western nations have been elbowed aside in favor of individual rights and freedoms.

The Flimsy Legal Right

Canada has had the most liberalized abortion regime in the history of the world since 1988, when unfettered abortion at any stage of pregnancy, up

to the moment of natural birth, became possible. In that year, a law placing certain strict conditions on abortion was struck down as unconstitu-
tional because abortion services were not equally available everywhere. In
other words, a law made by the people that declared unlimited abortion
a crime was struck down because the crime was not equally available to
all women. The result is that Canadian law to this day does not say that
abortion is right or wrong. It says nothing at all, even though no poll in
that putative democracy has ever shown that a majority of Canadians
accept unlimited abortion on demand.

As in so many other democracies, however, the conjuring began
the moment liberal intellectuals and judges decided, mostly for radical feminist reasons having to do with the growing demand for gender
equality and moral autonomy, that a woman ought to have a right to
choose abortion. However, this was a right that could only be exercised
by first invoking a well-known and frequently used legal technique for
reducing a specific class of human beings—in this case the unborn—to
the status of property, of an offensive animal, or of a disease. This political, legal, and psychological technique has been widely used in human
history—especially in totalitarian regimes and dictatorships—whenever
states, politicians, or courts seek to justify the incarceration, enslavement,
or slaughter of an enemy.

It is important to make the conservative case that this subversive legal
technique has been exactly duplicated by all Western liberal democracies,
in a sinister parallel that is far more than an analogy, and that can be
summed up in the following statement: There is no difference between a
declaration of nonpersonhood that creates, objectifies, and makes invisible to its perpetrators a class of born-alive slaves such as have existed in
all regimes of chattel slavery, and a declaration of nonpersonhood that
creates, objectifies, and makes invisible to its perpetrators a class of alive
but unborn slaves such as exist in the wombs of pregnant women in
almost all liberal democratic regimes. If this logical and factual parallel
holds, as I think it does, it points to the shocking conclusion that *almost
all the major democracies of the Western world have become slave regimes of a
new kind*, and this has been made possible only by the sanctification of
individual will as their primary moral foundation.

A physician friend throws this technique of pure will into stark relief
by asking why, on one side of a one-inch-thick hospital wall, physicians

are spending millions on high-tech machinery and surgical skill to save and preserve the life of a three-pound premature baby, while on the other side of the wall, other physicians are about to throw an aborted baby of exactly the same weight and gestation into the garbage? Clearly, if at the same moment the two mothers decided (willed) to make opposing choices, the first child would become legal garbage and disappear as a human being, while the second child would suddenly and miraculously arise from the deadness of its thinghood and be declared fully and legally human. The source of such an existential transformation is only the naked will of the mothers (fathers have no legal say), whereby human life is created *ex nihilo*, or extinguished, not by God or biology, but by human will alone. Which is why I say we fancy ourselves godlets now.

I am not at the moment focusing on the moral question. I am simply trying to present the bald truth that, as a political extension of the will to triumph over nature, the Western democracies, by ideological imperative, have adopted a legal technique for converting millions of human beings into objects, or subhuman beings, and thereby have converted themselves into slave regimes of a new kind. This is especially odd because, if we use the word *disappear* as a verb, it is clearly possible to disappear a man as a human being and make him reappear as a chattel slave, just as it is possible to disappear an unborn child and make it reappear as a womb slave. The essence of all human slavery is the transformation of a human life into an object that is owned and controlled as the property of another. And yet the same liberal who insists that chattel slavery is simply abhorrent and unconscionable will very likely support womb slavery and abortion as an important expression of a woman's democratic freedom. Conservatives who reveal this parallel to their liberal friends will be astonished at the unwillingness of abortion sympathizers to see and condemn this form of slavery. It has been rendered invisible to them by their own will. ("I once was blind, but now I see.")

The reasoning produced for striking down Canada's abortion law and granting a pregnant woman, and her alone, a right to decide the life or death of her unborn child was that if any woman who did not want her child did not have equal access to abortion, then the *security* of the mother's person (which now means her psychological health as a freely choosing individual) has been put at risk (note the irony: put at risk by her own will). She was then said to be justified in protecting herself from this insecurity threat by demanding the (almost always tax-funded) professional removal of the offending object, or enemy, from her womb.

The same sort of legal and verbal legerdemain was used in the United States, where the justifying ground for this practice was not security, but the mother's right to privacy. If the life within the womb is unwanted by its own mother, it is considered a kind of enemy object, occupying the property of the mother's womb without consent, an illegal trespasser that (*that* and not *who*) has invaded her privacy. Here again we have an echo of the originating narrative of modern democracy: citizens should not be controlled by laws that do not have their consent, just as their bodies should not be controlled or occupied by another without their consent.

Surely the most arch, self-centered, and bizarrely twisted argument in this vein was made by Murray Rothbard, a hero of sorts to modern libertarians and liberals. In his seminal book *For a New Liberty: The Libertarian Manifesto*, Rothbard relied on all three of the most common ploys. He first described the unborn child as a fetus, to imply a valueless thing or nonhuman object, and then moved right along to the themes of the fetus both as occupying enemy and as a disease by insisting that whenever a fetus occupies a womb "unbidden," it is like "a parasite," an unwanted aggressor on its mother, who in demanding her right to abort is only acting in self-defense; and so the fetus-aggressor must forfeit its own life. This same sequence of arguments has been used throughout history by all those who seek to dehumanize their enemies before killing them.

The Nazis described the Jews as parasites. Gloria Steinem, the poster woman for radical feminism in the 1970s, argued that a woman should have the right to remove any parasitic growth from her body. In 1989, Canadian artist Rick Gibson and the owner of a London gallery that had exhibited his work were fined a few hundred dollars for outraging public decency: Gibson's artwork was a sculpture entitled *Human Earrings*—a female mannequin head with earrings made of freeze-dried human fetuses. But to the conservative, the argument that the unborn child is an unbidden enemy in its mother's womb cannot be dignified by the name of reasoning; the most telling retort is that we might as well give a starving man money, then call him an aggressor against our property and murder him to get it back. So the second crucial question is: *Can it be right and good for any civilization that the decision regarding whether another human life has intrinsic value—and so, whether he or she is to be protected by society, or killed—should be made according to the changeable will of a single individual?*

The Practice of Abortion

Now let us ask what is actually being done to unwanted human life. How many unborn lives are ended? How large are they? What are the methods? Once those who are proabortion learn a little of the bald truth many are horrified, backpedal a lot, and start to suggest ways to restrict abortion, if not to end it. This grisly aspect will only be touched upon here. But suffice it to say that of the approximately 1.1 million or so abortions performed annually in the United States (down from a peak of 1.4 million in 1990) and the more than 120,000 performed in Canada, most are done in the first trimester of pregnancy. The vast majority of these aborted souls would have been perfectly healthy citizens. The routine methods of abortion at this stage involve vacuum aspiration, or, if later than twelve weeks, injection with a saline solution that burns and kills these babies; scraping the womb; and so on. Many people who support abortion don't know much about the details of this horrendous subject, believe all abortions take place very early in the pregnancy, and believe this only involves getting rid of a microscopic cluster of meaningless human cells. That is what I used to believe.

But many people, and even many countries and American states, are changing their minds, because the debate surrounding abortion has been altering rapidly, not, as we often think, due to the religious or moral objections of conservatives, but because of neonatal science, neurology, DNA studies, cell biology, CAT scanning, surgery on infants in the womb, and so on.[21]

We know now that a human heart starts beating at around twenty-one days, because we can now see it and hear it; that a human life in the womb has a distinct and unique personal genetic endowment (and thus

---

21 On the 41st anniversary of the *Roe v. Wade* decision of 1973 that opened the floodgates to abortion on demand in the United States, NARAL Pro-Choice America announced that, to its dismay, the tide seems to be turning: by 2013, some twenty-four American states had enacted fifty-two pro-life measures (such as shutting down abortion clinics or banning abortions after twenty, twelve, or even as early as six weeks). There is a Great Divide in America on this issue: about 51 percent of Americans describe themselves as pro-life, and 42 percent as pro-choice.

is in every strictly biological sense a genetically complete and unique, if undeveloped, human life); and that studies with tiny digital cameras clearly show terrified second- and third-trimester babies trying desperately to escape the vacuum tube (or other device) inserted into their mothers' wombs to suck away their lives or tear off their limbs. By now, millions have seen the moving photo of the tiny hand of Baby Samuel reaching out of a small incision in his mother's womb to grasp the surgeon's finger during an operation to mend his spina bifida. The ex-utero surgery scenario is legally bizarre, because once taken outside the womb for treatment, though still attached via the umbilical cord to its mother, a child becomes a full person with normal human and civil rights (because he or she is "born alive"). But when put back in the womb to finish gestation, he or she disappears again as a human being or person, deemed to be without value and to have no legal defence or rights until and unless he or she is eventually born alive once again.

These are simply facts. The distressing reality is that of the total of all abortions in the United States and Canada, about 10 percent, or well over one hundred thousand every year, take place in the second trimester. At this point, many unborn babies are about twelve inches long, and weigh up to a couple of pounds. At this five- or six-month stage of development (when the human life to be terminated looks in every way like a small human being), there are often "evacuation" problems, and so the most efficient and "safe" way to get a sizable baby out of an unripe womb is in pieces—by ripping off its arms and legs and crushing its head with forceps for easy extraction, after which extracted body parts are counted and thrown into a garbage pail. Those who want to read a viscerally upsetting description by an American physician of his real-life accidental encounter with recently aborted babies and their body parts, which fell out of a hospital garbage bag from a truck onto the street in front of him, should read the essay "The Street of the Dead Fetuses" on my website.[22] Those who don't believe these grisly facts can search online for "abortion photos" to see shocking pictures of babies acid-burned to death or torn apart in this way.

There is more. Some thirty-two US states have banned third-trimester abortions because unborn children at this stage are very large—about

---

22 Be prepared: http://www.williamgairdner.com/the-street-of-the-dead-fetuses/.

twenty inches, and between six and eight pounds. As mentioned, Canada has no law whatsoever against late-term abortions, and it is true that, even where they are allowed (or more precisely, not prohibited), most abortionists will refuse to perform them. But not all. When women who want to get rid of their large second- or third-trimester babies do find a willing abortionist, there is an especially gruesome practice called partial-birth abortion (formally called intact dilation and extraction) that I am obliged to describe briefly here, because although it was successfully banned in 2003 by conservative President George W. Bush, liberal President Bill Clinton before him refused to ban it outright, because he wanted to preserve the technique for mothers whose lives were endangered. Ultraliberal President Barack Obama, when a senator, refused to vote against it on several occasions, and one of his first acts as president was to reverse Bush's ban on US funding of abortion in other countries. What was this conflict of presidential authority but an embodied instance of the moral war in the Great Divide?

It is impossible to verify if, where, or when this method may now be in use in Canada. But there is no law to stop it, and no one is telling. In the last year for which I have seen numbers for the United States, the National Coalition of Abortion Providers estimated that four to five thousand partial-birth procedures took place in the United States. Ron Fitzsimmons, then executive director of this organization, told the *New York Times* in 1997 that in the vast majority of cases, the procedure was being performed on a healthy mother with a healthy fetus of twenty weeks or more along, confessing that "he had lied through his teeth" about its employment, and that watching this procedure had made him "physically ill." He nevertheless continued to support a right to abortion, and was honest enough to add that one of the facts of abortion is that women enter abortion clinics to kill their fetuses. "It is a form of killing," he said. "You're ending a life." For the conservative, this refreshing frankness cannot repair the moral error, but it is an improvement on liberal lying.

For this method, in almost all cases, the unborn child's position is manipulated until it can be pulled out of the womb feet first. When the abortionist sees the back of the baby's head he stops pulling, takes a sharp instrument, and jams it into the back of the baby's skull. Observers have said that at that precise moment the child startles, as if falling. The abortionist then inserts a vacuum hose into the hole made and sucks out the brain to collapse the skull; this makes extraction easier. An alternative method is by cutting or "disarticulating" the neck, which means the abortionist manually slices through or breaks the baby's neck prior to extraction. The legal reason for the partial-birth technique is to kill the baby before its entire body leaves the birth canal, when by law it would transform from a thing into a human being, and would expose the medical staff to charges of murder. Thirty-two US states as well as the Supreme Court have banned this procedure, though all include exceptions in the event the life of the mother needs to be saved. In such cases, the Supreme Court specified that there must be "an injection that kills the fetus" first.

So a natural and ultimate moral question that rears its head for the conservative is this: When not forbidden by the laws of the people, and especially when subsidized through the tax system, these acts necessarily implicate the entire nation morally; accordingly, *is it possible for any reasonable person to say that these killings are right and good, or that a country that sanctions them is right and good? And if they are evil, as they seem to be, is not a country that refuses to forbid them also evil?*

WHERE DO YOU STAND?		
On Abortion		
	MODERN LIBERAL VIEW vs.	CONSERVATIVE VIEW
A Fetus or a Human Baby?	*The fetus is not yet human*	*The fetus is human from conception*
	A pregnant woman is carrying a fetus, not a human being. It is just a collection of cells, a material thing without any value	Every pregnant woman is carrying a developing human life, a human baby with a unique genetic endowment
The 'Born Alive' Rule	*A fetus becomes human when born alive*	*This rule is just a legal salve to conscience*
		A human baby is the same person and of the same value, from conception until natural death

WHERE DO YOU STAND?		
On Abortion		
	MODERN LIBERAL VIEW vs.	CONSERVATIVE VIEW
Abortion and Slavery	*What is in the womb is property*	*Human beings are never the property of others*
	In the womb the fetus is a thing, and may be treated as a wanted or unwanted thing as the mother wishes because she owns her own body, and no one has the right to tell her what to do or not do with her body	All slave regimes in history have used legal tricks to define human beings as things—which is what is done with slaves, so as to work them or kill them without conscience. Modern democracies have a class of unborn humans in the womb whom they have defined as nonhuman, just as they once defined blacks as nonpersons and property, in order to enslave them without conscience
Obligation to Protect	*No obligation prior to birth*	*Obligation begins at conception*
	There is no moral obligation to protect a fetus until it is born alive	All human life is created by a mother and a father; once created, there is no right to end another's life. All parents have a duty to protect the lives of their own children from danger from the moment they create them. The most liberal duty of all is to protect the weakest members of society
The Right to Choose	*Choice is a fundamental right*	*It's what is chosen that matters*
	Personal morality is decided by individual freedom of choice alone. No one has the right to impose their own moral views on others	All human actions, good or bad, are chosen. The mere fact of choosing a thing does not make it good or bad. Choosing to end the life of another cannot make that act good
Sex & Pregnancy	*Sex and pregnancy are separate acts*	*They are linked physically and morally*
	Sex is a private choice and separate from the choice to become pregnant. Both acts are free choices of individuals and can be denied or negated at will	The sex act is a private choice that entails the possibility of pregnancy. To choose sex is to choose the possibility of pregnancy, with all its moral obligations

WHERE DO YOU STAND?		
On Abortion		
	MODERN LIBERAL VIEW vs.	CONSERVATIVE VIEW
Morality: Private or Public?	*Morality is private and individual*	*Morality is public by nature*
	Abortion is a private moral matter, to be decided by each woman, and society has no right to interfere or to limit or dictate individual freedom in moral matters	All morality is a shared public language. No moral community can survive for long if each member invents morality anew to suit themselves. Society as a whole has the ultimate legal right to determine the value of human life. To leave this to the random choice of individuals is to opt for a vigilante society in which the sacredness of life is not safe at any stage
The Role of Will	*Mother's will decides life or death*	*No human should have this right over another*
	Only the mother—not the father, and not society or the state—has the right to decide whether her unborn child shall live or die	No society or state should ever surrender the right to determine the value, or the life or death, of another human being to an individual. Society has a duty to protect all citizens, even from their own parents

CHAPTER 17

On Euthanasia

We live in a technologically advanced society in which the lives of the dying can be unnaturally prolonged for a very long time, and the question of whether or not we should be doing this is controversial. Although we all know with absolute certainty that we will die, it is a fact of life shrouded in uncertainty: we don't know if we will die naturally, or may want to end our own lives for some reason, or will be kept alive by machines against our will, or will ask to have our life ended by a physician, or without our consent may be killed by such a person.

These possibilities have made euthanasia yet another watershed dividing liberals and conservatives, and the direction in which things seem to be moving (like so much else discussed in this book) is toward increased liberalization, a gradual relaxation of traditional moral attitudes, prohibitions, and laws against compassionate killing. Hence the high emotion surrounding yet another Great Divide. Let us begin by looking at how we end.

How We Die

The focus of this section is euthanasia, rather than suicide. However, most people who support euthanasia do not really know the difference between these two things in practice.

As it happens, there are only three ways to die, with variations. You can let nature take its course (natural death). You can kill yourself without help (suicide), or with someone's help (assisted suicide), as when someone buys you the pills but you take them yourself, or they help you to the edge of the cliff but you jump off yourself. Or you can be killed by someone else with your consent (voluntary euthanasia), or without your consent (murder, in essence). When consent is not given, a distinction is made between involuntary and nonvoluntary euthanasia. *Involuntary* refers to a situation where the person to be killed has the capacity to give consent, but has not done so. *Nonvoluntary* refers to a situation where the person is unable to give consent due to coma or dementia. But whatever the case, euthanasia of any kind, to put this bluntly, always means *someone else is going to kill you.* In the case where euthanasia is legalized and performed by a licensed physician, it is professional, state-sanctioned killing. One further clarification: the person who is going to kill you can do so by an act of *commission* (called *active* euthanasia), such as by administering a drug overdose; by sedating you, then giving a lethal injection; or by taping a garbage bag over your head to suffocate you, and so on; or by an act of *omission* (called *passive* euthanasia), such as when you cannot feed yourself, and someone decides to stop giving you food and water.

All religions and most moral systems of the world ban euthanasia, and most societies in history (with a few exceptions such as the honor-suicide cultures of ancient Rome and of Japan—and now, the Islamist suicide bombers with whom we are all too familiar) have banned suicide, and assisted suicide as well, although banning suicide is mostly for the purpose of imbuing society with a respect for life, as it is impossible to punish a suicide.

The Ideological Divide

The standard liberal approach to this topic (as for so many others discussed in this book) is grounded in what is said to be the nonnegotiable demand for self-sovereignty and freedom of choice: the inalienable right of an individual to control his or her own body, life, and death. No one wants to spend their dying days trapped in a tangle of medical machinery, wires, and tubing, controlled and kept alive by others against their will. With this feeling there is a great deal of sympathy from all sides.

So the words *freedom*, *autonomy*, *choice*, and *dignity* spring immediately to mind on this side of the debate. But at bottom, the main justification for legalizing active euthanasia (by consent) of an adult patient is the notion of human autonomy, and this is today the central and acutely liberal principle of modern bioethics. When linked to political ideology, this ethic can take on a global connotation, as in the following arresting statement from a 1996 legal brief in support of euthanasia filed by the American Civil Liberties Union in *Vacco v. Quill*:

> The right of a competent, terminally ill person to avoid excruciating pain and embrace a timely and dignified death bears the sanction of history and is *implicit in the concept of ordered liberty*. The exercise of this right is ... central to *personal autonomy* and bodily integrity ... a mentally competent, terminally ill person has *a protected liberty* interest in *choosing* to end intolerable suffering by bringing about his or her own death.
>
> A state's categorical ban on physician assistance to suicide—as applied to competent, terminally ill patients who wish to avoid unendurable pain and hasten inevitable death—substantially interferes with this protected liberty interest and cannot be sustained.

Individual Will or Society's Will?

It is not quite clear why this principle has been granted dominion over what many in our tradition have always considered the higher societal, philosophical, and theological principles of fundamental importance to the common life of civil society. Somehow, the idea of individual free choice has had a kind of talismanic power conferred upon it to transform acts formerly judged illegal and immoral by society as a whole into moral and legal acts, if and when they are freely chosen by individuals. This shift bespeaks a move away from a societal concept of *common conduct*, of ordering one's life according to the commonly accepted will of all (what many thought democracy used to entail), to the concept of *individual right*, of ordering one's life according to personal will alone—a shift we have seen at work under the rubric of hyper-individualism elsewhere in this book. No doubt this emphasis on the dominion of individual choice over societal choice has been shaped by corollary commitments to materialism (the idea that the universe is solely physical, self-generated, and without any end purpose) and secularism (there is no higher being to offend by choosing suicide or euthanasia). And we saw in the previous section on abortion (which is often called *pediatric euthanasia*) that these same words and feelings came to the fore because the liberal view is that every woman has an inalienable right of free choice to control her own body (conceived, on Locke's principles, as her own property), and so also has a right to get rid of the body in her womb without moral, physical, or legal interference from others; and so ... also has a right to get rid of her own body, if and how she so chooses. The key words that point to the liberal imperatives are the *right* of the *individual* to unrestrained *freedom* as to *choice* in handling one's own body, and anything in it; and therefore, *choice* of death.

The general conservative response to the demand for a euthanasia right is opposed on all counts, as follows. Life must be considered a richly complex and unfathomable process from beginning to end, in which we are conceived in a human body, will be nurtured in our parents' arms, and expect to die in our children's; and we are wholly vulnerable at both ends. A little reflection reveals that in society at large, nothing protects a vulnerable human soul such as a dying person from the ambition of others to harm or to kill them, except for the obedience of all to an inviolable higher standard, as expressed in belief enshrined in law that every human being is of equal value regardless of physical condition. This protection is encapsulated for all human beings in the most basic of all commands of natural law, which is that we should pursue the good and avoid evil, a command that is considerably strengthened if it is deemed to flow as a directive from a higher being. But when faith in a higher moral law is aggressively challenged by secular public opinion, the motive for all human action becomes increasingly utilitarian. Human value is then no longer judged according to intrinsic value, but by someone's preconception of the degree of its usefulness (or uselessness). History shows that many civilizations, each in its own way, have experienced this process of despiritualization, in which a transcendent value system is slowly abandoned for a secular, materialist, and utilitarian one. This signals the onset of a barbarism identifiable in the willingness of a people to benefit by sacrificing their own kind to the purity of their belief system, or ideology. This may take a straightforward consumption form, as it does in cannibalism and the sacrificing of human victims to pagan idols; or a political form, as found in all genocidal movements aimed at cleansing the body politic of people devalued as ethnic parasites; or a camouflaged ideological form, as when we kill the unborn to appease the gods of individual freedom and equality; or an economic form, as when we justify euthanasia as a savings in health-care costs that will benefit others more in need.

The Opposing Words

So the outlines of this divide become clear. A secular, self-oriented, materialistic (man is a machine), and utilitarian cost ethic (money can be saved) is opposed by a more spiritual/religious, socially oriented, transcendent (man is more than a machine) value ethic (human beings have no price). So opposing liberal words like *right*, *individual*, and *freedom* are key conservative words such as *obligation*, *civil society*, and *law* (as in liberty under law, and protection for the inviolable value of life).

On one side of the divide we find a belief in the individual political and moral right to control one's own life and body, conceived as personally owned property (usually asserted as higher than any social or ethical right or obligation), such that all laws forbidding euthanasia are considered "suffering laws" that condemn citizens to unnecessary pain and suffering. Suffering laws are seen as offending international prohibitions against cruelty, such as we find in the European Convention on Human Rights (adopted in 1950), article 3 of which says, "No one shall be subjected to torture or to inhuman or degrading treatment or punishment." This prohibition is frequently cited in defense of a euthanasia right, though it was originally inserted as a ban of torture.

On the opposing side is the conservative conviction that all civil societies have a *social right* and a *social freedom* to override individual desires by collectively *forbidding all killing directed at their own members*, a right that is superior to and trumps any individual claim of a liberty right to be killed by another. In this vein, to the surprise of many of the liberal persuasion, and perhaps explained as a response to the memory of the European horrors of World War II, the Parliamentary Assembly of the Council of Europe adopted a nonbinding resolution in 2012 stating that "Euthanasia, in the sense of the intentional killing by act or omission of a dependent human being for his or her alleged benefit, must always be prohibited." This was the first time that euthanasia had been so clearly rejected (albeit in a form that is nonbinding on member nations) by an important European political institution, and despite the fact that a number of European nations, including Holland, Belgium, and Switzerland, have been practicing active euthanasia for a long time.

And what have medical doctors themselves been saying? The World Medical Association, which numbers more than nine million members, adopted a resolution in 2005 asserting that "physician-assisted suicide [PAS], like euthanasia, is *unethical* and must be condemned by the medical profession. Where the assistance of the physician is intentionally and deliberately directed at enabling an individual to end his or her own life, the physician acts unethically.... The World Medical Association reaffirms its strong belief that euthanasia *is in conflict* with basic ethical principles of medical practice, and ... strongly encourages all National Medical Associations and physicians *to refrain from participating* in euthanasia, even if national law allows it." This last is quite an interesting case of a worldwide professional association urging its members to actively engage in national repudiation of law. Meanwhile, the American Medical Association, although failing to make the essential distinction here between PAS and euthanasia, states that "physician-assisted suicide is fundamentally incompatible with the physician's role as healer, would be difficult or impossible to control, and would pose serious societal risks. Instead of participating in assisted suicide, physicians must aggressively respond to the needs of patients at the end of life." The Canadian Medical Association has also condemned euthanasia, stating that "Canadian physicians should not participate in euthanasia or assisted suicide." And in a country with a terrible history of killing millions of its own citizen (about twenty million, during the twelve years of the Nazi Third Reich), the German Medical Association issued a *strong rejection* of active euthanasia or any "killing of the patient," stating that "the physicians' involvement in suicide contradicts medical ethics." (In 2011 this phrase was rewritten as "the physicians' involvement in suicide is not a medical task," which strikes this author, at least, as an attempt to avoid the ethical questions.)

Although no mention is made in such statements of any theological principle or God, they nevertheless rest upon the standard Judeo-Christian ethic, to the effect that all human life is to be valued equally and protected, and that neither the individual will of another human being nor of any state has the right to trump this principle. So what the liberal describes as suffering laws that make individuals suffer, the conservative describes as "protection laws," because they aim to protect the most vulnerable members of society from the nefarious intentions of others—whether relatives, professionals, or states—to eliminate unwanted or costly citizens in the name of freedom or budgets.

The Life Principle or the Death Principle?

In general, the conservative will argue that all societies must choose between the principles of *eros* and *thanatos*—the life principle or the death principle—because any society that chooses to operate with both of these principles immediately introduces a profoundly disturbing ethic of suspicion, under which any citizen or class of citizens may become the object of an official judgment of nonvalue, without recourse. In effect, the death principle necessitates a rank ordering of human beings: death is best for some; life for others. But to inject the arbitrariness of will into the valuation of life is to create social and moral paranoia such as is found in all totalitarian states, and as exists in the Netherlands today, where for reasons soon to be explained, aging and ill citizens live in fear of the new death powers of their own government.

The life principle generates a very different kind of society in which the foundational assumption is that all human beings have an intrinsic and equal value solely *by virtue of their human nature* or existence, which has nothing to do with their physical condition of the moment. This assumption appeals from the particular (individual) to the general (all humanity), and in doing so seeks to invest society with an ethic of the sanctity of human life. To live in common under such a principle is to be irrevocably bound by a common interest: all for one, and one for all. Accordingly, no one's (particular) living body could suddenly lose its (general) sanctity just because at a certain moment that person's will to live is absent, any more than it would suddenly regain a sanctity it never lost if the will to live were revived. This belief in an *intrinsic sanctity* of human life that is *untouched by will* explains why all societies honor their dead with such respect and dignity. There is no middle ground in this debate, simply because the law, and public respect—or disrespect—for life, must head either in one direction, or the other; life and death are absolutes, and require absolute laws to defend or deny them. This is why, when we suddenly come across someone lying in a coma on the street, our default assumption is that they would want, and *ought to want*, to live, and we react accordingly. By instinct we call the ambulance and the police, not the morticians and the undertakers.

The Substitution of Utility for Value

The moment a competing death principle is introduced, however, it begins to elbow out the equal-value standard, which is soon replaced by a calculation of utility value: all citizens get stamped with a "best before" date. A Dutch medical authority, when asked recently why the Dutch do not routinely provide palliative care to the suffering, answered: "We don't need palliative medicine, we practice euthanasia." A utilitarian rank ordering of human life in the degree of flourishing or uselessness, with a view to ultimate disposal, will always be bent to serve whatever is deemed most useful to the state. Because use of a public service like health care is always a cost to others, resources must be rationed according to some system of triage, a logic that is especially compelling in socialized regimes, where the sick and suffering who are past their "useful" lives are said to be draining scarce medical resources. Accordingly, in an environment where we feel devalued, we seek to regain value by seizing control of our own death in an act conceived as a noble freedom. In a society where we have successfully submitted the natural lives of the unborn to individual will (with pediatric euthanasia), such that we now have only "wanted" children, we demand the right to submit our own death to our own individual will via adult euthanasia, so that we can have a wanted death—a clear example of forcing the submission of the naturally random, frightening, and uncontrollable to the preemptive control of individual will: "Death shall not conquer me; I will conquer death!"

For many reasons, then, wherever euthanasia is supported politically, it inevitably becomes joined to the purposes of state on the same logic. Under national socialism in Germany, international socialism in the former Soviet Union, and elsewhere, the death by extermination of various classes of people (Jews, intellectuals and artists, Christians, political dissidents, etc.) is linked to the state's yearning for and defense of ideological purity. The same mind-set is visible in a softer way in our libertarian-socialist regimes, justified as a means to equality, freedom, and fairness. In 1984 Richard Lamm, then governor of Colorado, shocked a lunch meeting of Colorado health lawyers by announced that the senior citizens of his state had "a duty to die and get out of the way." They were, he said, wasting precious resources that "the other society, our kids [need to] build a reasonable life." He likened the elderly to leaves falling from a tree, "forming humus for the other plants to grow." In 1991 in Canada, a well-known Anglican priest, Tom Harpur, justified the killing of feeble patients with lethal injections on the ground that such physicians were "fulfilling their total responsibility toward the patient's well-being." And on the world stage, Jacques Attali, then president of the European Bank for Reconstruction and Development and a former advisor to French President François Mitterrand, said that "as soon as he goes beyond 60–65 years of age, man lives longer than his capacity to produce, and he then costs society a lot of money. Indeed, from society's point of view, it is preferable that the *human machine* should stop suddenly, rather than face progressive deterioration.... Euthanasia will become one of the essential instruments of our future societies ... the fundamental freedom is suicide; therefore the right to suicide, either directly or indirectly, is an absolute value in this type of society." Well, this high official obviously did not understand the distinction between suicide and euthanasia. But we get the message. Humans are just machines; they cost the state money; they are free to kill themselves (and should). In any official climate of dogmatic secularism, structural debt, exploding health-care costs, and a creeping utilitarian ethic in which human beings are thought of as disposable machines, the liberal-versus-conservative euthanasia debate can only grow louder, along the following lines.

A War over Compassion

The most basic emotional divide on this topic has to do with conflicting claims of compassion. The liberal argues that to condemn someone who wants to die to pain and suffering, especially if they are trapped in medical machinery, is cruel and unusual punishment. All human beings have a right to die with dignity by choosing how to end their own lives. The state does not own us, our life, or our death. We own ourselves. For the liberal, to deny a freely willed death to an autonomous and competent individual is to deny their humanity, to reduce them to the status of a helpless animal. So for the liberal argument to succeed, killing, normally conceived as the ultimate objectifying cruelty, must be reconceived as compassion, and its refusal as discrimination against the suffering.

The conservative response, and that of every religion and known moral philosophy, is that under a life principle, neither euthanasia nor any form of assisted suicide should be legalized, because it is plainly the ultimate lack of compassion to kill, to murder, or to encourage the death of an innocent human being for any reason. As so many opponents of euthanasia have warned, what we must all hope for is not the death with dignity that liberals call for (and which for the conservative is a redundant expression, given that human dignity is intrinsic), but rather death with decency—to be treated well in dying, according to our intrinsic dignity.

A further objection of conservatives is the too frequent use of *substitute judgment*, which must be assumed in any euthanasia regime by the person(s) granted the killing right. Substitute judgment is normal and permissible when *allowing* someone to die naturally who has lost all capacity to give consent. I gave this permission myself in the case of a dear but familyless friend who was brain-dead and was being kept alive with machines. The machines were unplugged, and he was allowed to die. Some will say: What is the difference? Well, there is a world of difference between unplugging a machine that is keeping a near-death person alive, thus allowing nature to take its course, and using, say, a lethal injection intentionally to kill that person. Substitute judgment is a wholly illegitimate and noncompassionate procedure that offends the life principle, as well as all natural law principles, if actively used to kill someone.

Degradation of Physicians

Liberals are aware of the dangers of euthanasia, and most of them propose it only as a last resort, after all palliative-care efforts have failed to eliminate suffering. They propose to carefully regulate, train, and license selected physicians for this task. But conservatives warn of the gradual degradation of the entire medical profession in a euthanasia regime, which becomes manifest as a subtle public fear of the entire profession.

For to license *telostricians*, as they have been called—to turn healers into killers—introduces a profoundly schizoid element into social life that signals the end of all physician-patient trust, as we shall see. There are also serious "slippery slope" worries that the legalization of euthanasia always seems to bring about. The Hippocratic oath, which has been in use by the medical profession for nearly 2,500 years, asked all physicians to swear: "I will prescribe regimens for the good of my patients according to my ability and my judgment and *never do harm to anyone....* I will give *no deadly medicine* to anyone if asked, nor suggest any such counsel; and similarly I will not give a woman a pessary to cause an abortion."

But the oath was liberalized by the World Medical Association into the Declaration of Geneva of 1948 (with subsequent additions and deletions), to allow what the original oath (still in use in some places) forbids, absolutely: harm by killing. The new oath asks the doctor only to swear "I will maintain the utmost respect for human life," eliminating the original definition of life as beginning "from conception." This liberalization intentionally opened the door to pediatric euthanasia, whereby different jurisdictions could settle on their own definitions of when human life begins. And although the liberalized oath still speaks of "the health" of the patient as the physician's first consideration, the original spoke of "the health and life" of the patient. That change allowed physicians to plead an adverse effect on the health of the mother if not permitted to abort her healthy child, as well as the poor health of the dying when killing-as-caring is not permitted.

The conservative is convinced that all of this amounts to a dangerously false compassion, for once an entire society begins to believe that killing in certain circumstances is caring, then ... why even bother with consent? Let us—let the state—simply define the classes of citizens we believe need our compassion, and get on with the killing, is the progression of this attitude. When joined to revolutionary movements of political, ethnic, or eugenic cleansing, this sentiment takes on all the deadly coloration of a pious and patriotic devotion to national well-being. The chilling truth is that the original Hippocratic oath has only been suspended twice in Western society in its entire existence: totally, during the twelve years of the Nazi Third Reich; and since the 1960s, either eliminated, suspended, or modified (depending on the medical school) to permit abortion and euthanasia. This is the slippery slope in action.

The Economic Arguments

Those favoring liberalization say that the useless prolongation of life is very expensive, both for the medical system and for the families of the dying. Hospital respirators and other high-tech hookups can cost thousands per day, and the nation's families spend millions on special chairs and scooters, lifts, beds, and other devices. In a time of scarce resources, this is an illogical use of public funds, and private care at home can bankrupt a family. The conservative will generally agree that no one who is clearly terminally ill should have their life prolonged artificially at public expense, or against their expressed will. But complaints about private costs in a free society are groundless, because private medical spending contributes to the medical-care industry and is not a cost, but a revenue and an economic boon. The main conservative concern is that, under a utilitarian ethic in a socialistic regime, public health authorities will use the saving of money as a reason to hasten the death of those they define as living unworthy lives. Then those who are pressured to reduce public health costs will naturally find arguments for euthanasia compelling (at least for others, if not for themselves). A further economic concern is that, if legalized, euthanasia will end up being used to kill more ethnically and economically disadvantaged people than those who can afford higher-quality care. The difference between living in a poorly run, underfunded, unionized government hospital or eldercare facility, surrounded by the sick and dying, and getting around-the-clock care in your own home, rendered by well-paid private professionals, is considerable. In response to the cost factor, a Medicaid program in Oregon offers a "free euthanasia" service to the poor, billing it as "comfort care." In California, efforts to legalize assisted suicide failed because a Latino civil rights organization promoted a resolution saying, "We urge a 'NO' vote [on the bill] because we believe it is unconscionable to talk about legalizing physician-assisted suicide when low-income people do not have access to comprehensive medical care including pain management and hospice care." These poor people saw euthanasia as a form of ethnic and social cleansing. In the province of Quebec a euthanasia bill was passed in 2014, in violation of Canada's Criminal Code. Lisa D'Amico, who has severe cerebral palsy and fears she will end up totally incapacitated and wholly dependent on others, went to the Quebec Superior Court to try to strike the bill down, saying that inadequate health care places her "in a situation of great vulnerability," and she fears that the state might decide to euthanize her. Of the bill, she said, "As long as they can't give us the care we need, I can't agree to give them the power of euthanasia." This is class warfare over how we ought to die.

Documents to Help You Die—or Live

Not surprisingly, liberals eager to enforce the autonomy argument are vigorous supporters of the "living will," a legal document executed in advance with the intent of precisely controlling caregivers as to the treatments they may or may not administer to the dying. The main conservative objection to these documents is that they are seldom executed as intended. First, because no one can possibly foresee all the future circumstances of the one who wrote the will; and second, because there is always a serious lack of simultaneity between the execution of the will and the precise conditions of an illness or a death that may come years later, when the original wishes may have changed, but were never noted. I can only offer my own bad experience with this flaky document, which I doubt is unusual. My father's living will specified that he wanted to be "let go," and not fed or otherwise kept alive if he "could not feed himself, could not read the newspaper, could not walk or talk," and so on. I was his sole executor. Near the end, and in sound mind but progressively unable to do any of those things, even to swallow food, he almost angrily insisted, repeatedly, on having surgery to implant a feeding tube in his stomach. So I opted for the surgery. But how was I supposed to know which was his true will—the one he had written, or the one he indicated to me so vigorously?

The Harm Question

The question of the absence of harm to others has arisen often in this book as the foundation of the modern liberal moral standard, in this case claiming that if the option to be killed by another is freely chosen, and there is no harm to others, there should be no moral impediment. But the no-harm argument is repudiated by the conservative as a simplistic and impoverished standard for morality on a number of grounds. The first is that it is extremely rare to find any normal, nonsuffering person who would give a rational, informed consent to be killed. People who do this are usually in pain and suffering that has not been properly eased with good palliative care, and so they fear more pain, dependency on family and family resources, are usually deeply depressed and lonely, and have lost all hope of a good death. What we think of as a choice to be killed is, in truth, very rarely a truly free choice. But if the choice is not free, informed consent is not possible, and so any consent given is invalid. Furthermore, experience has shown that as soon as pain, depression, and loneliness are properly treated, almost all those who said they wanted to die ... change their minds. In other words, most people who ask to die do not really want to be killed; what they want is relief, caring support, and love. In this sense, the conservative argues that to present euthanasia as the first option psychologically harms the patient long before any killing is done.

Harm is also done by those who insist on a euthanasia right to those who don't want anything to do with it, because of the pall of resignation this generates—a general death mood that is profoundly unsettling to the living. So much is this true that we cannot really argue that the act of suicide concerns only the suicide. Too often self-killing mutates into a form of other-killing because the mood of profound despair it generates can infect others and ignite a rash of copycat suicides. To this we must add the very real legacy of psychological and moral pain, grievous memories, and forlornness created by the one choosing to die, which is left as a deeply felt harm in the minds and hearts of family members who may have serious moral objections to euthanasia—a harm that can never be undone. To the prevalent liberal insistence that suicide is "about me" and "my choice" to die with "dignity," the conservative reply is that your death is not just about you. It is "about us all," and how each of us dies sends a message to the entire community about the value of human life. No man is an island.

The Rights Divide

To the liberal claim that we all have an inalienable right to die, just as we all have an inalienable right to life, the conservative responds as follows: It doesn't make sense. To choose something like euthanasia cannot create a right to it, for the reason that rights do not exist in a vacuum. They always presuppose an obligation on someone. If you have a legal right to medical care or welfare, for example, someone has an obligation to supply these things to you. But can we really argue that a legal right to be killed creates an obligation upon another, or upon the state, to do the killing? Can someone legally be forced to kill? To have a right to die is meaningless if it only means suicide, because it's just a right to kill yourself, which you can do without needing a right. And anyway, you cannot exercise a right against yourself. But if it means a right to euthanasia, it has to mean a legal—and perhaps constitutional—right to *force* someone else or the state to kill you on demand. In such a situation the progression of rights would be from the legal right of a citizen to be killed if so chosen to the right of officials with power over the infirm, the sick, the dying, and the disabled to exercise substitute judgment to eliminate those whose lives they deem not worth living. Things have already proceeded this far in the Netherlands and in several other jurisdictions. And we saw it in action with disastrous results in the totalitarian regimes of the twentieth century.

The Dutch Case

The Dutch slippery-slope phenomenon, in which procedures legally and morally forbidden eventually become tolerated, has, for conservative opponents at least, unintentionally provided the most compelling example of liberal good intentions gone bad. A substantial report in *Current Oncology* in 2011 summarized euthanasia in the Netherlands (and elsewhere) by stating that in 30 years

> the Netherlands has moved from euthanasia of people who are terminally ill, to euthanasia of those who are chronically ill; from euthanasia for physical illness, to euthanasia for mental illness; from euthanasia for mental illness, to euthanasia for psychological distress of mental suffering—and now to euthanasia simply if a person is over the age of 70 and "tired of living." Dutch euthanasia protocols have also moved from conscious patients providing explicit consent, to unconscious patients unable to provide consent. *Denying euthanasia or PAS in the Netherlands is now considered a form of discrimination against people with chronic illness, whether the illness be physical or psychological, because those people will*

be forced to "suffer" longer than those who are terminally ill. Non-voluntary euthanasia is now being justified by appealing to the social duty of citizens and the ethical pillar of beneficence. In the Netherlands, euthanasia has moved from being a measure of last resort to being one of early intervention. Belgium has followed suit, and troubling evidence is emerging from Oregon specifically with respect to the protection of people with depression and the objectivity of the process.[23]

The idea that a physician could face a charge of discrimination for refusing to kill is morally bizarre, to say the least—a world upside down that will surely lead to lawsuits charging wrongful survival, in the same way there have already been some successful multimillion-dollar suits for wrongful birth when physicians have refused to abort, or when a test for fetal abnormality gave a false negative and the parents subsequently sued the lab on the grounds they would have chosen abortion had they known the truth.

The Dutch have practiced both euthanasia and assisted suicide since 1973, and both of these became legal in 2002, even though by September of 1991 the Dutch government itself had released a surprisingly candid

---

23 This thorough overview can be read here: http://www.current-oncology.com/index.php/oncology/article/view/883/645. In an effort to summarize the legalization trend, the author, a Canadian physician who specializes in palliative-care technology, wrote: "To date, the Netherlands, Belgium, and Luxembourg have legalized euthanasia. The laws in the Netherlands and Luxembourg also allow PAS. In the United States, the states of Oregon and Washington legalized PAS in 1997 and 1999 respectively, but euthanasia remains illegal. The situation in the state of Montana is currently unclear; a bill legalizing PAS was passed by the state legislature in 2010, but was recently defeated by the state's Senate Judiciary Committee."
"In the Netherlands, euthanasia and PAS were formally legalized in 2001 after about 30 years of public debate. Since the 1980s, guidelines and procedures for performing and controlling euthanasia have been developed and adapted several times by the Royal Dutch Medical Association in collaboration with that country's judicial system. Despite opposition, including that from the Belgian Medical Association, Belgium legalized euthanasia in 2002 after about 3 years of public discourse that included government commissions. The law was guided by the Netherlands and Oregon experiences, and the public was assured that any defects in the Dutch law would be addressed in the Belgian law. Luxembourg legalized euthanasia and PAS in 2009. Switzerland is an exception, in that assisted suicide, although not formally legalized, is tolerated as a result of a loophole in a law dating back to the early 1900s that decriminalizes suicide. Euthanasia, however, is illegal. A person committing suicide may do so with assistance as long as the assistant has no selfish motives and does not stand to gain personally from the death. Unlike other jurisdictions that require euthanasia or assisted suicide to be performed only by physicians, Switzerland allows non-physicians to assist suicide."

report prepared by Jan Remmelink, attorney general of the High Council of the Netherlands.[24]

The Remmelink Report (and many corroborating reports since) was the first to signal that the worst slippery-slope fears of critics had all come true, revealing a simply appalling situation in which many thousands of Dutch citizens had been euthanized by their own government, including large numbers of dying but competent patients who had not given consent, and who had no idea their own medical team was about to kill them. The slope has become even slipperier since, and based on the real-life experience of the Dutch, we may over time expect to see the same reality unfold elsewhere. The Euthanasia.com website offers ghastly reports too numerous to mention on the cold-blooded medical killings of nonconsenting citizens that take place every day, and the suspicion is there are many more unreported cases. The latest official reports are that about 3 percent of all deaths in Holland annually are by euthanasia, and about 7 percent of those are of people who had no knowledge and gave no consent. The same percentages, applied to the United States, would mean about 75,000 people euthanized every year, of whom about five thousand would be put down without their knowledge or consent.

The latest sophistication in euthanasia services in Holland is *mobile death squads,* or "euthanasia on wheels." If your own physician refuses to kill you, the state will oblige. One call, and a doctor-and-nurse team will appear at your door. If you qualify under the government's physical, mental, or emotional definition of pain and suffering, they will put you down, free of charge (rather, prepaid—it's tax funded).

How poignant and morally distressing it is, then, to hear that in order to protect themselves from their own licensed medical killers, many ill and elderly Dutch citizens have arranged to carry an anti-euthanasia card in their wallet, called a protective medical decisions document, or PMDD. This is a declaration prepared by anxious citizens that they hope will prevent the government from killing them. You can read up on this instrument and how to design one to protect yourself at PatientsRightsCouncil.org.

---

24 Readers can find this report at https://archive.org/details/RemmelinkReport, and can find a large collection of more recent reports and articles on the euthanasia situation in the world at large at http://www.euthanasia.com/index.html, and specifically for the Dutch situation by clicking "Netherlands articles" on that site.

What an irony it is, and what a distance this suggests we have traveled in the name of freedom and autonomy from our former comfort in a common human conduct and a mutually felt security of the life of all. In the existence of these two documents—the living will, the ultimate liberal document that is supposed to ensure you will die or be killed in the way you wish, and the PMDD, the ultimate conservative document that is supposed to ensure you are not killed at all—lies a profound caricature of the modern democratic state, and for the conservative at least, a testament to its moral evisceration.

WHERE DO YOU STAND?		
On Euthanasia		
	MODERN LIBERAL VIEW VS.	CONSERVATIVE VIEW
The Act	*It's an act of mercy*	*It's an act of homicide or murder*
	Euthanasia fulfills the desire to die of people not able to kill themselves	Euthanasia is making someone else die, whether with or without their consent
Value of Life	*The value of human life is relative*	*Human life has intrinsic value*
	Those to be euthanized, with or without their consent, are living lives of inferior quality beneath the dignity of a human being. States may decide that some people have lives not worth living	The value of a human life and its dignity do not ever change. Only its physical condition changes along a continuum from optimal to something less. In this sense all human beings are physically disabled, and always less than optimal in some way
Autonomy & Choice	*Choice dictates a euthanasia right*	*Choice cannot dictate morality*
	Personal autonomy, the right to choose how one lives and dies, is the highest moral good. Individual freedom to control one's own life and body is an inalienable right	A choice to do something evil cannot make it good, nor can one person's choice to die oblige another, or the state, to kill them. There is no inalienable right to die by forcing someone else to kill you

WHERE DO YOU STAND?		
On Euthanasia		
	MODERN LIBERAL VIEW vs.	CONSERVATIVE VIEW
Compassion	*Euthanasia is compassionate*	*Killing can never be compassionate*
	To end a suffering person's life for them is a gift of mercy and compassion. It is immoral to willfully prolong a person's life by refusing to help them die when they want to go	Good palliative care removes almost all pain and suffering. True love and compassion are incompatible with killing. Almost all who want death change their minds when made comfortable and surrounded by loving people
Utility or Value?	*Value of life based on utility*	*First command of natural law: Preserve life*
	When a life is so degraded that it has lost all value, a practical and utilitarian decision should be made, either by the person dying or by someone who acts in their interest	All human beings need a standard higher than utility to protect them from being abused or reduced in value by physicians or states that have surrendered the ideal of intrinsic human value, or family or relatives who prefer them to die
Life or Death Principle?	*The death principle*	*The life principle*
	Because all have a right to life, all have a right to choose their own death, and so to demand euthanasia. A right to die is an extension of the right to life	All have an obligation to treat each other decently in life, and while dying. But there is no such thing as a right to force someone else to kill you. Once introduced, a death principle permeates society with dread and suspicion
Individual or Social Freedom	*Individual freedom*	*Social freedom*
	Individual rights and freedoms, autonomy, control over one's own life and body, and one's own death are the highest goals of a free and democratic society	The common good of humanity dictates the social right and freedom of all to forbid the killing of individual citizens, and must trump all ancillary rights and freedoms

WHERE DO YOU STAND?		
On Euthanasia		
	MODERN LIBERAL VIEW vs.	CONSERVATIVE VIEW
Suffering or Protection?	*"Suffering" laws* Governments that forbid euthanasia are forcing those in pain to suffer	*"Protection" laws* Governments that forbid euthanasia are protecting citizens from becoming victims of a culture of death
Economics & Death	*Prolonging life is costly* Where medical resources are limited, it is immoral and costly to extend life needlessly when those resources could be used for the needs of citizens who are not terminal. Public medical funding must be directed to the highest and best uses, because in any public system all demands for medical care are a cost	*Love and pain relief are not costly* No one wants to be kept alive by a machine against their will. But all human beings should have decent comfort and care in dying. What must be avoided is entrapment in a publicly funded system whereby the dying are judged as undeserving and their care is considered a drain on the system. In a private or mixed medical system, all medical services purchased are revenues, and not costs
Eugenics & Social Cleansing	*Unworthy lives are a burden* Dying and mentally incompetent people are living lives not worth living, and the humane offer of euthanasia allows them to die with dignity, whether decided by themselves or by the state	*Beware rank ordering of human value* When human beings are defined as living unworthy lives they are soon considered unworthy in themselves, like damaged goods, and are then vulnerable to manipulation by the state (eugenics/ethnic cleansing), or by economic calculators (costing too much), or by "compassionate" medical experts who confuse caring with killing
Hippocratic Oath	*The oath had to be modernized* The original Hippocratic oath was too limiting and had to be adapted to the demands of modern life and medicine	*The oath was modernized to enable killing* The oath was altered to enable physicians who wish to abort children or euthanize patients to do these things without breaking the oath

WHERE DO YOU STAND?		
On Euthanasia		
	MODERN LIBERAL VIEW vs.	CONSERVATIVE VIEW
The Living Will & the PMDD	*The living will controls choice in dying*	*The PMDD protects a person from being killed*
	The PMDD is a defense against an imaginary threat. Euthanasia regulations, standards, and physician licensing can always be tightly controlled to avoid any misuse or abuse. A living will is a freedom document that controls exactly how a dying person will be treated	The living will is a flawed document at best and rarely works as planned, because it lacks simultaneity with the timing and the facts of the dying person's situation. The PMDD is essential in a climate of medical suspicion to protect patients from unwanted death
Harm	*No one is harmed by euthanasia*	*Many are harmed by euthanasia*
	To choose euthanasia for oneself harms no one else	Consent to be killed is too often biased by pain and by feelings of guilt for being a burden to family. Most in this situation do not really want to be killed, so informed consent is not possible. The practice of euthanasia causes resignation among the ill and dying, and suspicion that healers have become killers. Surviving family members who disagree morally with the idea of legal killing are left behind to suffer the consequences, and inherit a message of despair that cannot be undone
The Rights Question	*Euthanasia is a right*	*There is no right to kill or be killed*
	Just as there is a right to life (except for unborn children), there is a right to die. Any competent individual who freely chooses euthanasia should not be denied and condemned by the state to suffer	It is absurd to claim a right to die, because all rights for some entail obligations upon others to satisfy that right. But we cannot obligate anyone to kill an innocent person. Therefore the right-to-die argument fails

AFTERWORD

Each section of this book stands on its own, but also forms part of a larger story describing a divide in the fabric of Western civilization that appeared suddenly in the eighteenth century, like one of those disturbing, deep gashes in a formerly quiet road that we see in photographs of places devastated by earthquakes. The divide has continued, and widened, with modifications, ever since. The subtitle of this book—*Why Liberals and Conservatives Will Never, Ever Agree*—seems to suggest there is no hope the divide will ever close. But if, as I believe, good debate is a spur to elevated thought, that may be a good thing.

It's not the fact that we live in the tension of a divide that matters so much. It's that public discussion, the quality of thought, speech, and argument across the divide, seems more focused on a preservation of the emotional stakes than on the quality of the debates themselves—the underlying facts and philosophical and moral positions held by each side. In that spirit, my humble ambition and reason for writing this book was the hope that it will encourage readers to turn their backs on the rhetorical devices of emotion, invective, and hostile silence, and then to search out and speak up about the deeper reasons for holding the views they do. Then who knows? Some may find they want to shift, sharpen, soften, or even change a position they have held for a long time, due to some new understanding to which the book has led them. In this spirit, I hope it is not vain or overly optimistic to think that the quality of the divisive cultural climate in which we now live might one day improve and rise, instead of continuing downward; that we will once again hear really interesting television and radio debates over the foundational differences in the broader liberal and conservative conceptions of many of the topics in this book that are the real reason for policy differences at the surface, instead of so much of the unrewarding complaints that pass for serious discussion. Most of all, I hope that individual citizens will take courage, leap into the Great Divide to discover the truth or falseness of their own ideas, and resolve to speak their minds openly, and unafraid. Then the work of this book will be done.

INDEX

Page numbers followed by *n* indicate notes.